Designing and Leading a Successful SAR

This professional guidebook and training manual introduces the Sexual Attitudes Reassessment and Restructuring (SAR) training program for professionals working in the broad field of sexology. The authors, who have led over 45 SAR training programs in seven different countries, provide an overview of the history and modern day context of SARs in the first part of the book. In Part II, they provide a toolkit for creating your own SAR, using 21 photocopiable workbook pages, handy checklists, and practical tips. Part III focuses on lessons learned from past SARs and future predictions for cutting-edge SARs. This book is necessary reading for clinicians and educators who wish to offer SAR training programs or integrate "The SAR Approach" into their practice.

Patti Britton, PhD, MPH, is past-president of the American Association for Sexuality Educators, Counselors and Therapists (AASECT); clinical fellow of the American Academy of Clinical Sexologists; diplomate of the American Board of Sexology; AASECT certified sexuality educator and supervisor, on the advisory council of the American College of Sexologists; academic dean and faculty at the Institute for the Advanced Study of Human Sexuality; faculty at The Chicago School (TCS) of Professional Psychology, Saybrook, and Pacifica Institutes, and California Institute of Integral Studies. Dr. Britton is the co-founder of SexCoachU, the world's premier credentialing and training institute on sex coaching and is a sought-after author, speaker, trainer, and pioneering sexologist known around the world. She has served AASECT as the chair and member of the Ad Hoc SAR Task Force for four years. She has written over five books and hundreds of articles in sexology and was the recipient of the AASECT Sex Educator of the Year Award in 2016.

Robert E. Dunlap, PhD, is a past AASECT certified sexuality educator and is a clinical sexologist, with specialization in BDSM/kink and fetish populations. Dr. Dunlap is also academic dean and faculty at the Institute for Advanced Study of Human Sexuality and faculty at California Institute of Integral Studies. As co-founder of SexCoachU and SexologyU, he administers all programs, oversees all media development, and assists in the professional training of students and outside professionals, including as a SAR co-leader around the world. Dr. Britton and Dr. Dunlap host a popular weekly radio show at http://TheBoomDoctors.com.

Designing and Leading a Successful SAR

A Guide for Sex Therapists, Sexuality Educators, and Sexologists

Patti Britton and Robert E. Dunlap

Routledge
Taylor & Francis Group
NEW YORK AND LONDON

First published 2017
by Routledge
605 Third Avenue, New York, NY 10017

and by Routledge
2 Park Square, Milton Park, Abingdon, Oxon, OX14 4RN

Routledge is an imprint of the Taylor & Francis Group, an informa business

Library of Congress Cataloging-in-Publication Data
A catalog record for this book has been requested

ISBN: 978-1-138-23698-1 (hbk)
ISBN: 978-1-138-23699-8 (pbk)
ISBN: 978-1-315-30111-2 (ebk)

Typeset in Frutiger
by Apex CoVantage, LLC

Dedication

. . . To recognize the Woodhull Freedom Foundation for its generous and valued contributions to the recognition of sexual freedom as a fundamental human right, and to declare September 23, 2010, as "Sexual Freedom Day" . . . RESOLVED, BY THE COUNCIL OF THE DISTRICT OF COLUMBIA, That this resolution may be cited as the "Sexual Freedom Day Declaration Resolution of 2010."

September 23 (2004) is also the day that Patti's daughter, Holliday, lost her 20-year battle to HIV/AIDS. We dedicate this book to her and the many who have suffered because of sexual ignorance, social shame, and lack of access to proper sexual health care. In the name of Sexual Freedom we dedicate this book to all who read it, and we enlist our readers to join our mission to create a sexually enlightened and sexually free society worldwide.

Contents

Foreword xi
Reverend Dr. Ted McIlvenna
Acknowledgements xiii
Introduction xv

PART ONE: THE STORY OF SAR **1**

1 What Is a SAR? **3**
Read This First! 3
Adult Learning Styles 3
What Is a SAR? 4
Defining a SAR 5
SAR Significance Today: Trends and the Crying Need 6
Porn for All 7
Dearth of Professional Medical Training 8
Mental Health Care Deficit 8
Rise of Polyamory 9
The End of Binary 10
Technology Good and Bad 11
Religious Conservativism 12
Isms: Diversity, Inclusivity, Social/Racial Justice Trends 12
True Mission of SAR 13
Distinctions within SAR 13
Classical vs. Contemporary SAR 14
Specialty SAR 14
Summary 15

2 Historical Perspectives **17**
History and Evolution of SAR 17
Beyond San Francisco 21
Topic-Specific SAR Models 22
SARguide for a Better Sex Life: The Ultimate Guidebook 23
Prior Research on SAR 24
Sexological Worldview 27
Summary 28

3 Our First SARs **31**
My First SAR, by Britton (Winter of 1970s) 31
My First SAR, by Dunlap (2005) 34
Summary 38

4 Our Lived Experience: 43 SAR Programs Later **39**
2007–2009: Inaugural SAR 39
Small Group Process 40
2010–2011: Other Locations in Los Angeles 40
Composition of Participants 41
Los Angeles Speaker Selection 42
Los Angeles Field Trips 44
Structure for Los Angeles SAR 45
International SAR Events 45
2012: Amsterdam, Holland (The Netherlands) SAR 45
2013: Vancouver, British Columbia, Canada SAR 49
2013: Prague, Czech Republic SAR 51
2014: Berlin, Germany SAR 56
2013–2016: Warsaw, Poland SARs 61
Special Request: Woodhull Freedom Summit SAR 67
Society for the Scientific Study of Sexuality (SSSS) Pre-Conference Workshop 69
Living the SAR Life 70
Summary 71

PART TWO: DESIGNING YOUR SAR **73**

5 Preparation Time: What You Need to Know and Do as a SAR Leader **75**
Basic SAR 75
Advanced SAR 76
Designer SAR 77
Nude SAR 79
SAR for Grown-Ups 79
Highlights from ASPEX (Advanced Sexological Personal Exploration Xperience) 81
Taboo Topics 83
Bestiality and Zoophilia 83
Sex with Vegetables 85
Violence and Snuff Films 85
Adult-Child Sex / Child Pornography 86

Grievance Policy and Procedure 87
Liability Protection 89
SAR Online Survey 2016 89
Summary 90

6 The SAR Leader's Tool Kit: 21 Elements to Make Your SAR a Success 93
Instructions for Maximizing Your Success 93
Element 1: How SAR Works 94
Element 2: SAR Purpose 94
Element 3: Planning and Preparation / Event Management 97
Element 4: Budgets and Income Projections 104
Element 5: Logistics for Venue Selection 108
Element 6: Field Trips and Erotic Venue Options 113
Element 7: Curriculum Design: Content and Structure 116
Steps to Your Design 118
Element 8: SAR Learning Objectives 119
Element 9: Topic Selection 124
Element 10: Media: Selection, Editing, and Legalities 126
Element 11: Speaker Selection: Revealing the Soul of SAR 131
Element 12: Materials and Supplies 134
Element 13: Student Journals or Notebooks 139
Element 14: SAR Leaders 139
Element 15: Small Group Facilitators 146
Element 16: Creating "Safe Space" (and other Demands) 150
Element 17: Small Group Process and Takeaways 153
Element 18: SAR Evaluations 158
Element 19: Damage Control: Preventing SAR Fallout 163
Element 20: Your Ideal SAR 167
Element 21: SAR Readiness Checklist 169
Summary 171

PART THREE: REFLECTIONS: LOOKING BACK, LOOKING FORWARD 175

7 Looking Back: Lessons Learned 177
The Sheer Power of SAR to Transform Lives 177
Contrarian Voices 178
Using "The SAR Approach" as a Model for Teaching and Training 179
Cross-Cultural Perspectives and Trend-Spotting 180
The Luminaries Speak Out! 183
Summary 184

8 Looking Forward: Future SAR Delivery Options **185**
Self-Curated 185
SAR in a Box 186
Virtual SAR 186
Imagine This! 187
SAR Experts Reveal Their Forecasts 187
Hopeful Suggestions for a More Sexually Positive and Healthy World 191

Index 193

Foreword

First of all, I want to thank Patti and Robert for a wonderful read. Second, this book is a magnificent exploration of a process started and perpetuated by many people who now call themselves sexologists. In a way, the book is sacred history about one of the great educational movements that came out of the Sexual Revolution. It reminded me again that "would that I had learned by heart some lyric read that day, I knew not what was a giant hour that soon would pass away."

In this book, you'll find many hours of sexual discoveries and enlightenment. Let me add two personal notes. The first was the result of an evaluation of our initial educational program in the basement of the Glide Church in San Francisco. There were 30 clergy, three media helpers from Winterland and the rock bands in the park from San Francisco, Laird Sutton, and me. We put it all together and called it the first *Fuckarama*. A janitor came in to participate and reported to the head of the Glide Foundation, who contacted the local Methodist Bishop; they came to see me and asked what happened. I simply said it was sexual attitude restructuring. The Methodist Bishop said that I had better modify what I was doing otherwise I would not be preaching in any Methodist church, but he would leave me alone if I always told the truth about sex.

Laird and I decided we needed to make a film for our SAR about an older couple. We arranged for Ed Brecher, the writer-historian, to make a film with his lady friend. We decided to make the film in a Sausalito houseboat. On the morning of the afternoon shoot, a young woman came into my office and called me a dirty rotten whoremonger because of what I was doing to her mother, making a film with the lecherous Ed Brecher. I called Ed to cancel the shoot, and he said that he would replace the woman with Sally Binford, the great anthropologist studying the Sandstone phenomena in Southern California. They made the film, which has become the most popular sex education film ever made. Five years ago at the Institute, a middle-aged woman came into my office and introduced herself as the woman who stopped her mother from making the film years before. She wanted to tell me that her mother had died, and in those final moments she had said that the only real regret in her life was not having made the film with Ed.

Thank you, Patti and Robert, for this book, which has reminded me of so many giant hours for myself and has let me know about the giant hours of the many people they have touched in these new chapters of SAR.

Reverend Dr. Ted McIlvenna,
Founder of the Institute of the Advanced
Study of Human Sexuality and *SAR Original*

Acknowledgements

We want to extend our deepest appreciation first to those courageous participants of the past 43 SARs, who willingly showed up in our SAR rooms to learn, grow, heal, and expand their concepts of human sexual expression in its full potential. Thank you to our wonderful editor, Elizabeth Graber, whose patience and vision allowed us to leave our legacy for future SAR leaders to follow. Special thanks to our research assistant, Celina Criss, without whom we couldn't have managed an online survey and so easily have obtained critical data from the dedicated SAR experts who assisted us in this process. We acknowledge our esteemed peers among SAR leadership, who generously gave of their time and shared their unique insights during personal interviews: Ted McIlvenna and Laird Sutton, SAR Originals, and YiLi Lin, Hani Miletski, Stephanie Mitelman, Wayne Pawloski, Mark Schoen, Bill Stayton, Christian Thrasher, and Gerry Zientara. Special thanks to *all* of our survey respondents: Eli Coleman, PhD, Academic Chair in Sexual Health, PHS, UMinn; Christian Thrasher, MA, CSC, CSE; Bat Sheva Marcus, LCSW, MPH, PhD, Clinical Director, Maze Women's Health; Justin A. Sitron, PhD, Associate Professor, Director, Interdisciplinary Sexuality Research Collaborative, Widener University; Stephanie Mitelman, AASECT Certified Sexuality Educator and Professor; Rev. Dr. William Stayton, Professor Emeritus, Center for Human Sexuality Studies, Widener University; Wayne V. Pawlowski, MSW, LICSW, AASECT Certified Sexuality Educator; Sara Nasserzaeh, PhD, Psychosexual therapist and AASECT Approved CE Provider; Linda Wiener, MSW, LCSW, Certified Sex Therapist, Supervisor and AASECT Approved CE Provider; and Hani Miletski, PhD, MSW. Without all of you this book would not have the spice and depth that completes our story and helps to forge our template for successful SAR programs. Finally, we want to honor each other, as we have sacrificed at times to make SAR a central component of our work in the world. We are so fortunate to cherish each other as life partners and as SAR co-leaders, who share the passion and zest to continue our mission to assure that SAR is everlasting as a phenomenon around the world. As we often say to each other when the going gets rough, "It is what it is!"

Introduction

This is an explicit book, so please be aware of this lightning rod topic. It is overtly sexual and we discuss a broad display of sexual expression. This is our story, our evolution as SAR creators, leaders, and advocates. It is our passion to share this book with you, with no frills, no pretentions, baring it all to you, as we would expect of ourselves and our participants in the SAR room.

In Part One you are going to read about where SAR began and why. You'll find out the historical evolution, sometimes revolution, of SAR and learn from some of its proponents. We'll show you how we got started, our own personal first SAR experiences, and how we have conducted our SAR programs in the US and worldwide. We consider ourselves—and others often remark that we are regarded as—the "Gold Standard" of SAR.

In Part Two you will then learn the basic knowledge to prepare you for SAR. You will then be shown, in step-by-step workbook style (in the SAR Leader's Tool Kit), how to design and lead a SAR of your own. Finally, we will reflect on the journey of our experiences and take you into our projections for what a future SAR may be like.

We use terms such as he/she/they as much as we can, and we have changed the names in our stories of what goes on in the SAR room with speakers, participants, and our team. We are as honest as we can be about a topic that demands authenticity and courage to speak openly about. We hope you enjoy it as much as we have enjoyed revisiting our past nine years around the world to gather our wisdom, experience expertise and share it all with you now so that you can go out and replicate a successful and well done SAR. The world needs you!

Love & Light,
Dr. Patti Britton and Dr. Robert E. Dunlap

Part One

The Story of SAR

1

What Is a SAR?

"We are the recorders and reporters of facts . . . not the judges of the behaviors we describe"

—*Alfred Kinsey*

READ THIS FIRST!

This book is going to take you on a journey of self-exploration. We are eager to train you as a professional as you seek to carry out your own dreams to design and lead a successful SAR. Offering and leading a SAR can be a challenging path, like hiking up a steep mountain edge and reaching the top (panting all the way), to find the light at the pinnacle of a difficult climb. Maybe you are seeking information, or your own inspiration, to craft a profitable or memorable SAR experience for your tribe. Maybe you are just curious about how SAR works and feel intrigued to explore it further. Either way, this book is your guide (think *recipes*) for success. To bring you to that apex of expertise and readiness for SAR leadership, we have built this book using a variety of teaching methods.

ADULT LEARNING STYLES

Adults learn in different ways, accessing different mechanisms for gaining knowledge and acquiring skills. You may be a visual, auditory, or kinesthetic (somatic/sensory) learner. Right brain people tend to have to feel or sense their way to knowing; left brain people need a calculated, linear approach to feel competent to complete the tasks ahead (UCMAS, 2016). Since the late 1980s, research has been deconstructing what were assumed to be reliable means for determining pathways to learning, showing that learners possess what are often termed eight *multiple intelligences* (Armstrong, 2016). They include:

- Linguistic intelligence ("word smart")
- Logical-mathematical intelligence ("number/reasoning smart")
- Spatial intelligence ("picture smart")
- Bodily-kinesthetic intelligence ("body smart")
- Musical intelligence ("music smart")
- Interpersonal intelligence ("people smart")

- Intrapersonal intelligence ("self smart")
- Naturalist intelligence ("nature smart")

Social science teaches us that often we learn better from the telling or reading of a story rather than just a presentation of facts (Bair, 2016). In a fascinating study on the use of storytelling as pedagogy, Eck states, "A variety of educational researchers offer learning theories that support storytelling from a number of perspectives, including brain-based learning theories, experiential learning theories, reflective learning theories and transformational learning theories. . . . Furthermore, neuroscience research reports that the human brain is naturally wired to receive and remember every human experience within the structure of a story" (Eck & Lee, 2006, pp. 2–3). In this book, we use many stories (some humorous) to role-model for you the myriad elements of a SAR and reveal our own SAR Lived Experience. We use a variety of learning modalities to engage different types of adult learners, as you will also need to do. We bring you inside our SAR doors and let you peek behind the curtain of how our SARs got made. We recount the history of SARs and how others manage theirs. We share our tips and recommendations as we go along. Then we show you, step by step, how to make a SAR flourish for you. We hope you enjoy this book!

WHAT IS A SAR?

SAR is the essential experiential training that challenges sexual values, attitudes, and beliefs. As a real-life couple and SAR co-leaders, we have provided SAR programs for the past nine years to over 900 individuals in seven different countries. SAR, considered to be the *sensitivity training* of the field of sexology, has never failed to move us personally for its power to expand lives. Our programs have been populated over the years with diverse and passionate speakers, including some of the most famous names in sex history: Adult film star Nina Hartley is one example, as is Xaviera Hollander, the most famous madame of the world's oldest profession and author of over 25 books on sexuality. All of our speakers share from their Lived Experience as a pathway to promote greater understanding of their sexual evolution and sometimes their role in sexual revolution. We always curate a melee of mixed media from films, television shows, and downloads from the Internet. Often we delight in showing the newest of our treasured finds from our international travels to the darkest corners of sexual entertainment. Most of all we have been impressed by the presence of the most courageous, open-minded, heart-centered, and hungry SAR participants, who are eagerly seeking to explore the landscape of human sexuality, and, ultimately, themselves as emerging sexual humans.

Our speakers have ranged from trans persons of unique origins as MTF, FTM, Gender Queer, and in between, with shared visions for their proclaiming their authentic sexual selves; to black leather-clad BDSM masters wielding a cat o' nine tails or sparking electric knives; to garden-variety, plain-looking, free-love-seeking, polyamorous lifestylers. We have had the privilege of hosting SAR programs in some of the most beautiful cities of the world, such as Prague, with its world class Sex Machine Museum, as well as in some of the most historically conservative cultural venues, such as in Poland. There we have led SAR programs for the past four years to crowds of practitioners and therapists yearning for a more positive approach to viewing the human sexual experience. Our SAR programs have spanned some of the most liberal sites for optimal sexual expression (think Berlin), where even our own mental constructs of eroticism have shifted, thanks to our experience of alternative sexual-cultural norms or demonstrations of fresh formats for kink/fetish play.

Our programs have served people from all aspects of the field of sexology and other helping professions, including physicians, nurses, sex workers, therapists, counselors, shamanic healers, tantric educators, sexologists, and more. We even have had a few real-life couples join our SARs just to expand their erotic possibilities for personal exploration. Our joy has been elevated as we host these events, in setting up a safe container that promotes a personal and professional transformative experience for our participants—one that lasts a lifetime. We have never been disappointed by what SAR can bring to the lives of our participants, whether it's a first-timer consensually being flogged; a therian (more about that later, we promise) wearing her full wolf costume and prancing with furry paws, tail, and ears; or a field trip to an Amsterdam sex shop with demonstrations of rope suspension of naked women in bondage that fill the viewer with compassion, shock, and awe. You are about to enter the world of SAR, so buckle up and prepare to be a change agent as you change yourself.

DEFINING A SAR

SAR is defined as a training event for professionals seeking credentials or just learning about themselves or the field of sexology. SAR consists of material and experiences that push the adult learner to confront his or her values, attitudes, and beliefs (VABs) about a wide range of issues within the broad field of human sexuality. We like to look at this process as getting to know who you are—what you believe, feel, and think—and then enticing you to explore the vast world of human sexual expression.

SAR is a requirement for certification at the esteemed American Association of Sexuality Educators, Counselors and Therapists (AASECT, 2016), the premier credentialing organization in sexology in the United States and internationally. AASECT also serves as a model for other organizations worldwide in establishing best practice criteria. At our own online training organizations, Sex Coach University and Sexology University, SAR is also a requirement prior to earning certification after a rigorous, extensive training of over 200 hours is completed as a sex coach.

SAR is regarded as the *sensitivity training* for the broad, overarching field or discipline of sexology: the study of human sexual behavior and its impact on self, others, and the environment. Reverend Dr. Ted, founder of the Institute for the Advanced Study of Human Sexuality (IASHS), an approved graduate education provider in the state of California since 1976, offers that sexology is "What people do sexually and how they think and feel about it" (McIlvenna, 1989). As fellow Academic Deans and graduates of this institute, we believe that this notion of sexology is a theme that also informs SAR itself.

On our websites (SAR, 2016), we define SAR as follows:

Sexual Attitude Reassessment and Restructuring *or* SAR *is a highly provocative, experiential, cognitive and affective experience, which is designed to push comfort levels, elicit feelings and confront attitudes, beliefs and values about sexuality. Presentations encompass media, (including contemporary film, television and art), along with presentations and panels of live speakers/demonstrations showing the potential range of human sexual expression today. Topics will be revealed at the course itself; the element of surprise and the psychological state of non-expectation form part of the basis for this course. [No nudity or touch is ever required of participants.]*

Small group process drives the understanding and impact of the elements of the presentations in this course. SAR is not a clinical training in sex therapy nor is it traditional sex education; rather, it enables the participant to move emotionally, intellectually, spiritually, and psychologically into a zone of greater knowing, acceptance, and tolerance of human sexuality in all of its possible dimensions.

This SAR fulfills the 10-hour requirement toward AASECT Certification and earns 16 CEUs. Dr. Britton is a national AASECT-approved provider of CEU.

SAR SIGNIFICANCE TODAY: TRENDS AND THE CRYING NEED

Do you know the terms *non-vanilla*, *CNM*, *hetero-normative*, *sexually inclusive*, *erotic intelligence*, and *cross-culturally aware*? If not, then this book is for you. As we view the world and witness trends, we recognize that there are several shifts taking place. We all feel a threat from the effects of terrorism, or uncertainty in the economic markets, or a sense that things are changing all around us and we'll never keep up. The same holds true in the broad field of sexology; students and SAR participants exhibit angst about becoming competent at what they do to meet the burgeoning sexual needs of clients, students, or other audiences. A series of tidal waves affects us all: lack of ample training in sexuality among health care professionals; emerging tools of technology that could create virtual sex that replaces human skin contact; advancing brain studies and other scientific breakthroughs, like 3-D printing of human organs or functional extremities, including genitals; a wash of sexually explicit media that influences our creative minds; trends to live larger, with more sexual self-expression, in bigger, more global, online venues—juxtaposed with a movement toward tiny houses, which surely have an impact on sex. In some ways, our SAR programs reflect the escalation of extremes, with increasingly risky or intense depictions of sexual styles through images and behaviors shown on tiny glass screens in front of our eyes and seeping into our sensibilities every day. SAR is the foundational model to address the changes and expressions that exist in our world today. It also is the template for future sexual expression and a roadmap toward sexual liberation, if done well.

Porn for All

The contemporary world is filled with opportunities for viewing and consuming pornography. It is ubiquitous. In a recent Google search engine report, the term *porn* yielded 145 million results (Get the Latest Pornography Statistics, 2013). Even young children with Internet access, when proper parental filters are not in place, can view explicit sexual imagery if they have the deftness to get online and push the right keys on the family computer. Porn dependency, as we call it (rather than the more pejorative term of *porn addiction*), is a common complaint among sexless couples seeking sexual therapy or coaching. In our own clinical practice, we observe male clients who report that they simply cannot stop themselves from the solo practice of using pornography online to self-soothe, reduce anxiety, avoid intimacy, or express their erotic desires through this sexual outlet. "Various international studies have put porn consumption rates at 50 percent to 99 percent among men, and 30 percent to 86 percent among women, according to Gert Martin Hald, PhD, and colleagues" (2014).

Another source cites that 66% of young men and 16% of young women view porn online at least once a week (Weir, 2014). Those statistics are staggering when you consider that, as a counselor for these teens later in life, especially when they may find themselves sexually bankrupt in partnered relationships, you are going to need the comfort, sensitivity, and skills to direct them to more healthy, sexually affirming outlets for their libidos.

Despite the 24/7 availability of adult entertainment found in sexually explicit materials (online or in other forms, such as magazines, books, or DVDs), viewing an array of adult porn in a setting with a group of total strangers and noticing your own response is not the same as sitting at your own computer fantasizing about your erotic object of desire. SAR provides a unique experience that no other means does, as many of our SAR participants state in their SAR evaluations. One participant notes, "I had a totally different experience watching porn with my peers."

Dearth of Professional Medical Training

Another phenomenon present today is the lack of training in human sexuality among key professionals serving the physical and mental health care needs of individuals. The reality is that medical school education is perilously underserving the needs of their students. "In . . . 2003, Solursh et al reported . . . most medical schools provide only 3–10 hours of instruction. Of 101 medical schools who responded to their survey, human sexuality was taught as a course in only 31 schools and was required by 26 of them" (Brewster & Wylie, 2008, p. 385; Sexual Medicine Society of North America, 2016). In a significant journal article about sexually explicit materials used in the UK for medical education, Brewster and Wylie (2008, p. 385) discuss inhibiting factors for medical professionals, including "lack of expertise, complexity and time constraints as well as reticence to address the subject" (see also Gott, Galena, Hinchliff, & Elford, 2004).

The data applies to obstetricians, gynecologists (GYNs), and urologists in training, all specialists in the sexual body parts and functions of their patients. Disappointingly, having been a Sexual Health Educator who trained 30 to 50 such GYN residents at Stanford Medical School in the late 1990s, Britton found that even then there were few programs that taught about the sexuality-related care that patients deserve. Aspects of gynecological discussions avoided asking about the quality of a patient's sex life, sexual desire, or sexual function. Residents did not know how to administer a proper breast, pelvic, and bimanual exam of both the vagina and rectum, which Britton and others taught them by using themselves as real-life models. This type of program was crucial for learning how to address sex openly in the context of sexual health care; furthermore, in Britton's experience in Stanford's accolade-winning program, half of the GYN students were women and the majority of them had never had a pap smear test or a gynecological exam! Such is the sorry state of medical school comfort with explicit sexuality.

Mental Health Care Deficit

The late Jeanne Shaw, a luminary in sex therapy, talks about the therapist's comfort zone and the maturation of the therapist him/herself by saying "Bowen (1974), and numerous others, reminds us that the most effective therapy is practiced by therapists who have explored their own issues . . . claimed their own projections, reinforced their own integrity and self-respect, and moved forward in their own living and personal development" (2012, p. 191).

In the state of California, a leader in the preparation and density of qualified psychotherapists and especially Marriage and Family Therapists (MFTs), the California Board of Behavioral Sciences (2016), the credentialing body that regulates this industry, requires a mere 10 hours total of education in Human Sexuality. In fact, as an Adjunct Faculty leading the California State Certificate Program

(2007–2010) for what was then the California Graduate Institute (now The Chicago School of Professional Psychology), few of the graduate-level students were comfortable taking the basic 3-unit, 42-hour, required course in Human Sexuality, and fewer still took the elective 2-day SAR course. Lack of comfort in even opening a conversation with clients about their sexual issues is one of the reasons that so few mental health practitioners address sexuality at all, as evidenced by sex researcher Jane Guyn in her study on what therapists need to know to work with clients' sexual concerns (Guyn, 2015). Rather, they tend to refer out to us as sexuality specialists to fix the sex parts, while they verbally process the distressed minds or wounded childhoods, as if the sexual aspects of their clients' human experience are cut out as separate entities from the whole of self.

These are the origins of our SAR programs, in part inspired by the lack of education available to aspiring psychologists and therapists receiving their ticket to work with clients soon after their studies and internships were completed, sexuality included. Many of the MFTs, PsyDs, and other well-educated professionals in the state of California have attended other trainings that we have provided. One training, our weeklong Clinical Sexology Skills, attracted over 20 mental health professionals who felt underprepared and inadequate in addressing even the most prominent and generic sexual issues that clients present in the therapy room. How tragic! If all of them would have taken a SAR program offered during their graduate studies, more of them would have opted for a pathway that was inclusive in serving both the mental health and the sexuality needs of their clients. They would have potentially become better therapists and psychologists in the long run.

According to the research conducted by sexologist Jane Guyn (2015), numerous studies echoed the findings that therapists seldom address the sexuality aspects of their clients' lives (Harris & Hays, 2008). Furthermore, other research clearly shows that therapists tend to lack comfort with and willingness to deal with the sexual issues that their mental health clients present (Binik & Meana, 2009).

Rise of Polyamory

One of the big trends we see all over the world as we lead SAR and other training programs is the rise of interest in the consensual non-monogamy (CNM) movement, sometimes referred to as *poly lifestyle*. We don't particularly like the term *lifestyle* because it can become a term used to marginalize people; however, it seems to fit well here, as it governs how these couples and individuals structure their matrix of how they live and form relationships. Our friends and faculty, Mark Michaels and Patricia Johnson, have written a powerful and insightful book, *Designer Relationships: A Guide to Happy Monogamy, Positive Polyamory, and Optimistic Open Relationships* (2015) that sketches out not only the definitional concepts that relate to CNM but also templates for how to navigate a variety of highly nuanced relationships for optimal well-being.

Historically speaking, not until the 17th century did monogamy become the cultural norm. We have found that even though much of the population of the civilized world seems to rely on the pair-bond of long-term monogamy, sanctioned by law and church, the trend of *open* relationships is growing. We have met with poly advocates who prefer an ideal communal type of 24/7 live-in mode, while others dab their toes in and out of this option to expand the container of an otherwise secure pair-bonded relationship, such as legal marriage of same- or other-sex couples. Polyamorous relating is not a passing fad; it is a foundational shift in how couples form their intimate bonds. Poly is here to stay.

The End of Binary

If there is one theme that has gained traction in our current cultural memes, it's the concept of non-binary. This is the marching song for the transgender movement globally. Bucking the tendency to place a person in a box or label them is dramatically changing, especially as we note the public transition from male-identified image to female-identified image of celebrity Caitlyn Jenner. The transgender movement is one that has been influencing how we conceptualize male/female, man/woman, he/she/they/one, and other aspects of ditching the labels and opening to the true human person, both inside and reflected on the outside. It is significant, too, that the murder and suicide rate for trans persons is at an all-time high, despite the media buzz around the movement. For trans persons, the suicide rate is 10 times that of the overall US population. Forty-one percent of trans or gender non-conforming people surveyed have attempted suicide (Malone, 2015).

At our SAR programs, we insist on having a live transgender speaker or a panel to show the diversity among trans persons, if possible, given the location of our SAR and the availability of live speakers. We will talk more about that later in Chapter 6. The part of SAR that showcases the personal stories of persons of trans origin and all of the issues surrounding self-acceptance and coping with the myriad psychological, mental, emotional, physical, and spiritual issues that pervade the lives of trans persons is crucial. Our friend and colleague Mark Schoen has created one of the best films on trans, known as *Trans the Movie*, and it is widely used when a live speaker in not available. Trans identified men, trans women, and gender non-conforming people already populate your conferences, your clinical settings, your classrooms, and elsewhere. The fact is that sometime in your own life you will meet or already know a trans person, and that person's life is in some ways no different from your own; in other ways, it is a total 180 from yours. If you are a therapist, counselor, or educator, please be aware of how your clinical care affects a trans person. Be clear about what else you may need to know, learn, and do to better serve them as part of your clientele.

Technology Good and Bad

Today's life is governed for most of us by little electronic devices that rule our entire day and even our night as we sleep—or don't sleep. Whether it's a smart phone, a tablet, a laptop, desktop, or virtual work that never stops, it has impacted our lives in paramount ways. At our SAR programs, we have a ground rule that states, "If you have your phone turned on in the room during a SAR and we find out, you risk a hefty fine." We emphasize this notion of *being present* in the room by warning that we will fine you $10,000 if a phone is found in use (unless, of course, a participant informs us of a personal crisis or situation that demands its being on, which has almost never occurred in over nine years).

The truth is that most people in developed nations today, and in some developing ones as well, have access to the Internet by smart phone. One exception is where political forces censor that access (for example, in China, one of our students could not access our private Facebook page in preparation for her SAR). As it relates to SAR and the primary content areas for our live SAR speakers, the rampant availability of online access to almost anything has changed the global landscape. Whether you are looking for BDSM, trans, or other sub-cultures of sexual expression (sometimes viewed as alternative sexualities), having Internet sites where peers and good information can be found can produce a positive, normalizing effect. Of course, inaccuracies abound, and one of our pet peeves is the insidious presence of pseudo-experts (often marketing themselves as sex experts). Some of them purport to possess credentials that they have not earned; others have had sex with over a thousand suitors to become an expert on sex. Some, too, have gained expertise from having overcome a sexual trauma or injury, then advertise themselves as a professional expert in that topic. As our friend and noted sex therapist Marty Klein recently remarked at a national sex ed conference, "Being a victim is not the same as being an expert." Touché!

Sex is layered, complicated, and not easily dissected. We believe that qualified credentials matter. We acknowledge the prevalence of what are deemed as legitimate sources for communities, such as fetlife.com for the BDSM/kink/fetish world (think *50 Shades of Grey*) or talented bloggers who are writing about everything sexual you can conjure up today. Nonetheless, use *caveat emptor* as your guiding light when browsing the Internet for your sex education. If somehow you do not know the term BDSM, you have been hiding under a large rock for years now. The explosion of interest in and knowledge about Bondage and Discipline, Dominance and Submission, Sadism and Masochism (the primary definitions for BDSM) have infiltrated our collective psyche since the release of the best-selling trilogy by E. L. James (2012) and permeated even the array of titles on the cookbook shelves at any large bookstore! Our favorite is *50 Shades of Chicken* (Fowler, 2012), a parody with tasty fowl recipes and hilarious images of bare-boned, naked chicken in compromising bondage positions.

Religious Conservativism

If there is one consistent theme that influences values, attitudes, and beliefs about sexuality, it is the power of religious messages. Those influences are often deadly or permanently harmful: think sex abuse in the Roman Catholic church, the sin of self abuse (aka masturbation), the banning of premarital sex before marriage, stoning homosexuals in the Middle East for who they love, and more. Religious conservatives have dominated the cultural thinking in many of the venues in which we have led a SAR. Those include participants in Warsaw, Poland, where Catholicism has negatively affected sexuality for a long historical period of oppression; a male participant who hailed from the southern United States as a religious conservative leader in a fundamentalist Christian church who attended our SAR programs in stealth to learn how to better serve his sexless or sexually damaged parishioners; the imam from a Muslim faith who worked with battered teens around their rape experience; or the minister from a Baptist church who longed to come out himself as a gay man to his community and serve as an empowered role model. Those are the ravages of religious repression that are echoed by many of the voices of religious anti-sex messaging. Many of these right-wing zealots in the United States today are attempting to reverse the sexual freedoms granted thus far, such as same-sex marriage, GLBT equality, and access to abortion. The Religious Right continues to fight against keeping children from access to sane, safe, comprehensive, and sound sexuality education. The role of a SAR is to bring about greater acceptance of others, whose views and expression may differ from your own, and to expand perception of possibilities. The work of a SAR is just part of the battleground for sexual enlightenment and sexual freedom.

Isms: Diversity, Inclusivity, Social/Racial Justice Trends

Isms (such as sexism, racism, heterosexism, ageism, and more) pervade the marketplace even in this somewhat enlightened era of the second decade of the 21st century. College campuses and news stories abound regarding Political Correctness, the impact of which affects the content of comedy entertainment, the debates over the US First Amendment that guards free speech, academic freedoms, and protection of the individual. If you read any current news source, the issues of social/racial justice, diversity, and inclusivity are raging today (Strauss, 2015; Crouse, 2016). Those issues may influence how you conduct or find resources for your own SAR. Combating isms and phobias is at the very heart of what a SAR is meant to do.

We do our best to promote and display diversity and inclusivity regarding race, ethnicity, religious affiliation, sexual orientation, sexual/erotic expression, and age in our selection of speakers, media, and even the constellation of our

SAR attendees, as you will learn in Chapter 4. Perhaps the most telling aspects of getting ready to offer your SAR will be in these sensitive areas of public discourse. Media are not that easy to find that show cross-cultural imagery, racial/ethnic diversity, or social/racial justice in visual expression or in languages that are the primary tongue of your SAR participants. Do your best to address these issues before you launch your SAR. For example, we cull media from our international travels, such as in Brazil, where we have obtained publicly televised programs on HIV+ transgender sex workers; or in Germany, where we have purchased DVDs of fetish films and extreme BDSM behaviors; or in our journeys to world-class museums, where we ourselves document a wide variety of erotic/sexual expression that few can see in person, unless they also travel the globe. To us, being inclusive means showcasing the range and beauty of human sexual expression by all and about anything possible. You will want to do the same.

True Mission of SAR

In case you haven't gotten the message yet, the mission of SAR is life transformation for all who attend and participate in a SAR, with the goal of bringing that person toward greater tolerance, understanding, compassion, and acceptance of all forms of sexual expression. It is also a crucible in which you discover who and what you tolerate and do not, whom you can serve and cannot; SAR becomes the mirror in which you see your true self and reflect on what you have to offer those you serve, whether or not you consciously choose to serve that population. We lead SAR programs to evoke, not to teach, but learning is a definite by-product of all SAR events. Our mission for SAR is to create a safer, more tolerant, and joyful climate of "yes" around the world, where everyone can feel free to be themselves as sexual humans and express themselves in whatever way feels congruent with themselves. To that end, our mission is freedom.

Distinctions within SAR

There is a debate among sexological professionals who lead or have designed SAR programs in the past to delineate distinctions about how we define SAR: Is it Sexual Attitude Reassessment and Restructuring or merely a restructuring direction that the program follows? Our SAR model is both to help the attendees to *reassess* where they stand in their values/attitudes and beliefs and to *restructure* such aspects of themselves. Our model of SAR is designed to better serve the target audiences of our attendees, as therapists, healers, educators, or just as people yearning to explore who they are and perhaps redefine their sexual essence. However, other SAR programs skip the reassessment emphasis and work toward only a restructuring of values/attitudes/beliefs about sex and sexuality.

Another form of SAR, perhaps viewed by some as an Advanced SAR, is what we lovingly refer to as *SAR for Grown Ups*. This is known as our *Advanced Sexological Personal Exploration Xperience*, or ASPEX training program. We will discuss this advanced experiential program in Chapter 5. ASPEX has been conducted for the past two years in a private, nature-steeped retreat center in rural Poland, over a 5-day/night period in seclusion and away from all daily distractions that impair one's ability to focus, dive deeply into personal growth, and indulge in uninterrupted self-exploration. It is conducted in a safe container of a group of peers, under strict guidelines, and takes place in sacred harmonious alignment with each other. This type of SAR has an almost nuclear impact on personal change and sexually related self-awareness while promoting significant expansion that lingers.

Classical vs. Contemporary SAR

As you will find in reading the history of SAR in Chapter 2, its origins are well documented and bear out over time as a unique, impactful approach to adult learning. Both of us are graduates of the renowned institute in San Francisco, IASHS, where SAR was born. Back in the 1970s SAR was one of the original programs offered for sexologists at the newly established IASHS, founded by Reverend Ted McIlvenna, PhD, and supported by the revolutionary filmmaking of Laird Sutton, PhD, who created the concept and production of what were then named *Sexual Pattern Films* (Laird Sutton, 2016). This model for SAR forms the strength and tone of our current SAR model, as it includes the infusion of media, speakers from the Lived Experience, small group process, and experiential activities that drive one to shed layers of self-defensive mechanisms and melt into a state of openness, acceptance, tolerance, and *not knowing*. That suspended animation state of *not knowing* gives way to dramatic change for the individual in the SAR experience, regardless of where they began on their journey of self-discovery. The IASHS also focused on taking the SAR out of the classroom into the erotic/sexual venues of the region to provoke and heighten opportunities for further exploration, such as attending a Gay Pride event, frequenting a strip club, or visiting a local BDSM dungeon.

Specialty SAR

Finally, over the years of SAR history, specialty SAR programs have been developed based on a single topic. We will talk more about them in Chapter 5 and show you how a SAR may be defined by a single topic, such as the Silver SAR™ approach offered at Widener University for addressing the issues of sexuality and aging, while retaining some of the tried-and-true SAR principles discussed in Chapter 6 (SAR Leader's Tool Kit), which is your instructional manual.

SUMMARY

In the next chapter, we will take you down the winding, expanding, and exciting road of SAR history. You will learn about its origins, the profound and lasting vision of the founders of the IASHS SAR, and you will meet those who came after to create new SAR programs. We will go into depth about the current array of SAR leaders, with their unique styles and philosophies for SAR. In our investigation of SAR, we will present historical perspectives that inform the content and approach of SAR as we define, discuss, and lead you to understand the evolution of SAR as a key element in the training of sexology professionals. We will also share with you highlights from the very first SAR guidebook (Ayres et al., 1975), describing its appeal, its cultural and historic contributions as a reflection of its time (the Free Love Generation of the 1970s), and how and why it may or may not remain relevant for today's complex world.

References and Resources

American Association of Sexuality Educators, Counselors and Therapists (AASECT). (2016). AASECT requirements for sex therapist certification. Retrieved July 15, 2016, from https://www.aasect.org/aasect-requirements-sex-therapist-certification

Armstrong, T. (2016). Multiple intelligences by Dr. Thomas Armstrong. (n.d.). Retrieved July 15, 2016, from http://www.institute4learning.com/multiple_intelligences.php

Ayres, T., Lyon, P., McIlvenna, T., Meyers, F., Rila, M., Rubenstein, M., . . . Sutton, L. (1975). *SAR guide for a better sex life: A self-help program for personal sexual enrichment/education designed by the National Sex Forum*. San Francisco, CA: National Sex Forum.

Bair, J. (2016). Personal conservation. July 19, 2016.

Binik, Y. M., & Meana, M. (2009). The future of sex therapy: Specialization of marginalization? *Archives of Sexual Behavior*, *38*(6), 1016–1027.

Bowen, M. (1974). Toward the differentiation of self in one's family of origin. In F. Andres & J. Loris (Eds.), *Georgetown family symposium papers*, Vol. 1. Washington, DC: Georgetown University Press.

Brewster, M., & Wylie, K. R. (2008). The use of sexually explicit material in clinical, educational and research settings in the United Kingdom and its relation to the development of psychosexual therapy and sex education. *Sex Education*, *8*(4), 381–398. doi:10.1080/14681810802433903

California Board of Behavioral Sciences. (2016). LMFT license requirement. Retrieved July 16, 2016, from http://www.bbs.ca.gov/app-reg/mft_requirement.shtml

Crouse, J. S. (n.d.). Articles: Microaggressions: Political correctness run amok. Retrieved August 14, 2016, from http://www.americanthinker.com/articles/2016/07/microaggressions_political_correctness_run_amok.html

Dr. Patti Britton. (n.d.). SAR—Sexual Attitude Reassessment and Restructuring (October 22–23, 2016). Retrieved July 15, 2016, from http://drpattibritton.com/event/sar-la-oct2016/

Eck, J., & Lee, H. D. (2006). An analysis of the effectiveness of storytelling with adult learners in supervisory management (Doctoral dissertation, Thesis, PlanB (M.S.)), University of Wisconsin, Stout. [Abstract].

Fowler, F. L. (2012). *Fifty shades of chicken: A parody in a cookbook*. New York: Clarkson Potter.

Get the latest pornography statistics. (2013). Retrieved July 15, 2016, from http://www.covenanteyes.com/2013/02/19/pornography-statistics/

Gott, M., Galena, E., Hinchliff, S., & Elford, E. (2004). "Opening a can of worms": GP and practice nurse barriers to talking about sexual health in primary care. *Family Practice, 21*(5), 528–536. doi:10.1093/fampra/cmh509

Guyn, J. N. (2015). Through bedroom eyes©: The comfort and willingness of marriage and family therapists to discuss sexual issues with clients before and after attending a one day sexuality education workshop on the bedroom model© (Unpublished doctoral dissertation). IASHS, San Francisco, CA.

Hald, G. M., Seaman, C., & Linz, D. (2014). Sexuality and pornography. In D. Tolman, L. Diamond, J. Bauermeister, W. George, J. Pfaus, & L. Ward (Eds.), *APA handbook of sexuality and pornography* (Vol. 1, pp. 3–35). Washington, DC: American Psychological Association.

Harris, S. M., & Hays, K. W. (2008). Family therapist comfort with and willingness to discuss client sexuality. *Journal of Marital and Family Therapy, 34*(2), 239–250.

James, E. L., James, E. L., James, E. L., & James, E. L. (2012). *Fifty shades trilogy*. New York, NY: Vintage.

Laird Sutton. (n.d.). Retrieved July 15, 2016, from http://www.imdb.com/name/nm0840345/?ref_=fn_al_nm_1

Malone, L. (2015, March 15). Transgender suicide attempt rates are shocking. Retrieved July 15, 2016, from http://www.vocativ.com/culture/lgbt/transgender-suicide/

McIlvenna, R. T. (Ted). (1989). Personal communication.

Michaels, M. A., & Johnson, P. (2015). *Designer relationships: A guide to happy monogamy, positive polyamory, and optimistic open relationships*. Jersey City, NJ: Cleis Press.

Schoen, M., PhD (Director). (n.d.). *Trans the Movie* [Video file]. Retrieved September 5, 2016, from http://transthemovie.com

Sexual Medicine Society of North America, Inc. (n.d.). Retrieved July 16, 2016, from http://www.sexhealthmatters.org/resources/summit-on-medical-school-education-in-sexual-health

Shaw, J. (2012). Approaching your highest sexual function in relationship: A reward of age and maturity. In P. J. Kleinplatz (Ed.), *New directions in sex therapy: Innovations and alternatives* (2nd ed., pp. 175–194). New York, NY: Routledge.

Strauss, V. (n.d.). Has political correctness really 'run amok' on college campuses? Retrieved August 14, 2016, from https://www.washingtonpost.com/news/answer-sheet/wp/2015/12/03/has-political-correctness-really-run-amok-on-college-campuses/UCMAS. (n.d.). Retrieved July 15, 2016, from http://ucmas.ca/our-programs/whole-brain-development/left-brain-vs-right-brain/

Weir, K. (2014, April). Is pornography addictive? Psychologists' research is working to answer that question—and to identify ways to treat people whose porn use is interfering with their lives. *APA Monitor of Psychology, 45*(4), 46. Retrieved July 15, 2016, from http://apa.org/monitor/2014/04/pornography.aspx (p. 45 print version)

Xaviera Hollander. (n.d.). Retrieved July 15, 2016, from http://www.xavierahollander.com/

2

Historical Perspectives

"Sex is emotion in motion"

—*Mae West*

HISTORY AND EVOLUTION OF SAR

The history of SAR is a stormy and dramatic tale. The Hippie Era of the 1960s was a time when the Free Love Movement,[1] psychedelic influences, and volatile socio-political change were the norm. It is fascinating to recount the different paths that the originators of SAR took, both in San Francisco and beyond.

The textbook *The Sex Researchers* (2000) by Edward Brecher was required reading when we both attended our doctoral programs at IASHS, 14 years apart. He describes the origins of SAR from the National Sex Forum[2] in San Francisco, which was led by Methodist ministers Reverend Ted McIlvenna and Reverend Laird Sutton in the basement of the Glide Memorial Church. Both of these passionate clergymen felt that this new form of sex education was an outgrowth of their ministerial calling that emanated out of shared theological and philosophical perspectives. According to Brecher, McIlvenna's three basic intentions of SAR were to: 1) focus on attitudes and feelings of participants beyond the core of knowledge in sex education; 2) focus on the attitudes and feelings of SAR leaders being opened up prior to leading a SAR; and 3) place faith in a marathon experiential learning environment, up to 8 days, with a flooding immersion into explicit media,[3] speakers talking from their Lived Experience, participatory exercises (such as a nude swim), and small group process. Brecher posits that not only does the *sexual cinema verite* conjure feelings in the performers and in the viewer and show the meaningfulness of the real sexual acts in real time, but the speakers add a dimension where ". . . personalizing of forms of sexual behavior commonly found only in textbooks can be an eye-opening as well as emotion-laden experience for SAR participants" (2000, p. 377). Other researchers add that McIlvenna's ". . . rationale for using sexually explicit teaching materials is either to communicate information or to develop more accepting attitudes . . . (which can) help to develop accepting attitudes concerning one's sexuality and the sexuality of others" (Tepper, 1997, p. 168).

Early origins of the SAR at the National Sex Forum[4] (NSF) and the Institute for Advanced Study of Human Sexuality (IASHS) emerged from a multi-agency investigation in the early 1960s that focused on the sexual needs of youth, especially regarding their sexual identity and homosexuality. As IASHS librarian and graduate Gerald Zientara reflects, "(findings yielded that) . . . one cannot understand homosexuality without understanding human sexuality" (Zientara, 2015, p. 760). Reverend McIlvenna directed the San Francisco arm of the project. The findings from this pivotal study meant "The Forum would have as its main tasks the study of what helping professionals needed to know about human sexuality and the development of effective educational methodologies and design of innovative materials" (IASHS, 2016). As the website states, "In 1975 NSF sponsorship was transferred to the Exodus Trust, a California nonprofit trust which has as its sole and exclusive purpose to perform educational, scientific and literary functions relating to sexual, emotional, mental and physical health." Not only did the NSF give birth to the SAR training, it was the "largest supplier of professional educational material dealing specifically with human sexual behavior, (such as) . . . films, slides, audio and videotapes . . . used by more than 8,000 professionals and institutions throughout the world." Over the years 1969–1973, through liaisons with other key medical schools and through careful design of an interdisciplinary team, the Institute (IASHS) was founded in 1976 as the premier academic home for SAR. McIlvenna writes about the inclusion of films as the single most effective means of sex education: "In 1969 we started making our own films, which document what humans do sexually . . . We found that everyone reacted to the films on a deep emotional level regardless of academic background and professional training" (as cited in Weiss, 2010, p. 50). As you will soon learn, few data-driven, empirical findings have ever deeply informed evaluation of SAR efficacy.

Voices of the Originals ~ McIlvenna

An interview with 83-year-old Rev. McIlvenna revealed personal insights into the inception and evolution of SAR. Over time, it became clear that to be effective, SAR required media to add to the lectures that were given from a personal point of view (aka the Lived Experience). At first, the SAR leaders used commercial sex films available in the marketplace. The funds to acquire the first sex films for SAR came through a $10,000 grant from the Methodist church, which is a remarkable feat, attesting to Methodist minister Reverend McIlvenna's sheer dedication and commitment to SAR as an integral and necessary part of sex education. Using adult films or commercial porn did not produce the desired results of a shift in attitudes. In the context of the SAR, participants wanted to know about the people in the films and couldn't identify with those in the sex films. To address this gap, Sutton and McIlvenna created their own films, often working with friends and peers, to *develop a new genre of media with an intention for sharing authentic sexual patterns and allowing the viewer to connect and identify with the person(s) in the film. Although SAR began as a form of sex education, through experimentation with different designs, it soon evolved into an attitudinal restructuring. McIlvenna comments that people needed to self-assess their own sexuality, especially their fantasies, and look at what others do sexually. McIlvenna differentiates SAR from other modalities in sexology by saying that sex therapy helps show people "how to manage their own sexuality, not change attitudes" (2016).*

The original SAR Team members were also the creators of the NSF SAR-guide for a Better Sex Life[5] *(discussed in this chapter). Evaluations yielded a 96% success rate for the use of this self-guided manual and for the NSF/IASHS SAR approach. As this form of SAR progressed, McIlvenna and Sutton learned two things: (1) They validated the need to pull together a group of people for a SAR experience; (2) The concept of a* take-home SAR *did not work, as it lacked a shared group dynamic. In another series of SAR programs at universities as diverse as Drake, Boston, Vanderbilt, Northwestern, and others, McIlvenna cites that 10 major program evaluations were conducted. Comparisons were made between the sex education programs offered by the academic institutions and the SAR programs brought to them by his team. Out of 130 SARs, 119 of them showed preference over the SAR to the sex education offerings at those institutions.*

Voices of the Originals ~ Sutton

A recent interview with Rev. Sutton, now age 81, provided more insights into the development of the first SAR model. Admittedly, Sutton was heavily influenced by Marilyn Fithian and William Hartman (1972), whose work as sex therapists showed videotapes of sexually proficient couples to those seeking therapeutic treatment. Perhaps these authentic moving images formed the basis for what was to become Sutton's signature method for recording explicit sexual behaviors on film (Laird Sutton Filmography, 2016). Even today, sexual pattern films can be used for healing sexually dysfunctional activities or overcoming sexual ignorance. By using an immersion method of teaching,[6] SAR goals were to ". . . set people free from their bonds" (Sutton, 2016). The principles that guided SAR were (a) desensitization, using commercial porn films; (b) sensitization, using sexual cinema verite *that were made by Sutton himself; and (c) resensitization, often promoted through the intensive dialogue in group process. Additionally, for each subject covered in a SAR, these three principles informed how a topic was presented. Identifying media that would accomplish the goal of SAR of "learning to feel what's inside of yourself," as Sutton delicately puts it, was and continues to be one of a SAR leader's greatest challenges. Finding appropriate, timely, or topically correct media, whether to de-sensitize or sensitize the viewer, is often one of the most daunting tasks of designing and creating a successful SAR.*

The highlight of the desensitization process was known as the Fuck-orama, *which simultaneously projected 16 different film images onto a blank 20-foot high white wall in front of the students seated on the pillows in the SAR Room. Some of the films were selected for their shock value, others for their erotic impact. Content was mostly commercial porn or archival footage of anything sexual, including lions mating, trans persons on a swing, menstruation, vampirism, depictions of violent rape, animated shorts, comical sex, tepid lovemaking, and erotic art. The concept behind the immersion experience, as Sutton clarifies, was to bypass the thinking left brain and let the viewer transcend judgment or analysis. Instead, a gestalt was formed that left the viewer to* feel *its effect without cognitively encoding that effect (2016).*

Rev. Sutton shared personal insights into the effectiveness of SAR and how it was measured. Before the National Sex Forum's SAR evolved into that of IASHS, the SAR leaders would have a gut feeling *about whether the SAR elements were working or not. That sensing of tone in a group is a high level skill that we hope to teach you in this book. After IASHS began to offer SAR as one of it central components, self-evaluations would take place in the form of daily and extensive personal journals. These writings formed the basis for passing or failing the SAR course.*

Voices of the Originals ~ Zientara

Gerald Zientara has been a part of IASHS SAR for the past 27 years, ever since Britton attended her first SAR at IASHS in 1989. Zientara (2016) was commissioned as a community-based theatrical artist to design an experience as a celebration and integration of what took place in the SAR program at a turning point toward the end of the multi-day process. His background in ceremonial events and rituals, along with his participation in the California Men's Gathering, made him the perfect person to take on this unique aspect of the IASHS SAR. Known as the Sensorium, *this evening was a para-theatrical event, designed carefully to create a safe container for self-expression that combined theory and practice.* Sensorium *was considered to be a fulcrum for the culmination of the cognitive, affective, and experiential learning during SAR. Created to offer a break from the severity of the often* button-pushing *media and speakers on highly charged topics, it offered a community gathering and allowed for the expression of what had been learned thus far. Participants often went wild, felt liberated to dance, sing, shout, touch, go naked, or wear extreme representations of their sexual fantasies. (See the next chapter for Dunlap's story.) Zientara remarks,* Sensorium *was ". . . sex ed in a party-like setting . . . based on trust, communication and built on a premise that what happens to you is your choice. It is an empowering, transformative and bonding experience in a safe emotional space" (2016). One recent IASHS student remarked to SAR faculty that the* Sensorium *was the most powerful part of her education at IASHS, because it was visceral and changed not only her outward demeanor but her inner sense of self . . . the trajectory of body/mind/imagination was like a snapshot of the whole SAR (2016). As Zientara observes about SAR, "The framework (of SAR) is the perspective . . . helping participants to reframe their perspective is the secret of restructuring attitudes."*

BEYOND SAN FRANCISCO

In the early days of SAR, chairs of medical schools took the program back to their medical educational departments and offered SAR trainings for their students and the public, such as at University of Minnesota (UMinn) and at Rutgers University. As Weiss says in her lively summary of SAR history in Minnesota, ". . . the initial discovery of the SAR process and the impetus for bringing it to Minnesota came through the church" (2010, p. 25). In 1970, Rev. McIlvenna inaugurated the first SAR trial training in Minneapolis for a broad range of attendees. The program at UMinn was one of the seminal examples of the growth of SAR. Two of its primary leaders were Rev. Jim Siefkes, from the American Lutheran Church National Office, and Dr. Rick Chilgren, responsible for creating, implementing, and revamping the UMinn medical school curriculum in human sexuality inclusive of SAR. Even to this day, this approach to medical school education remains revolutionary, as UMinn is one of the few schools that require education in human sexuality, led by the Program in Human Sexuality (with Eli Coleman becoming the first funded University Chair of Sexual Health in 2007). Over time, the program emphasized the more clinical parts of sexual training, but the concept of SAR is intact. One of the key splits in the evolution of SAR at Minnesota is that one target group was seminary students and the other was medical students, each of which had different agendas and perspectives for SAR.

Rev. Jim Nelson of the United Theological Seminary in New York combined the two directions to address medical ethics and formed courses for both theological and medical students including a SAR (Weiss, 2010, p. 53). Later on, the Program in Human Sexuality in conjunction with United Theological and Luther Theological Seminaries offered Weeks of Enrichment for the more spiritually oriented practitioners which provided new philosophical and spiritual components to their SAR. Goals included "promoting acceptance of differences and a non-judgmental sexual attitude. To demythologize sex role stereotypes and performance expectations, while affirming a great range of human sexual fantasies and preferences were always the primary goals of every SAR production" (Weiss, 2010, pp. 56–57).

Shifting SAR from San Francisco to Minnesota meant that one of the first steps involved changing the title of SAR to *Sexual Attitude Reassessment*, as leadership resented any implications about reforming or reconstructing people's sexuality. "They preferred the idea of nudging people to simply *evaluate* their sexual attitudes and make changes by their own choice . . . [McIlvenna] believed that people needed help to *rehabilitate* unhealthy habits and *regenerate*, or rebuild healthy sexual attitudes" (Weiss, 2010, p. 43). We carry McIlvenna's message forward today.

TOPIC-SPECIFIC SAR MODELS

SARs that addressed a particular topic or population began to form in the 1970s as spin-offs from the UMinn program. One such was a *Disability SAR*, which was a "specialty SAR format for people with spinal cord injuries, cerebral palsy, and other physical disabilities" (Weiss, 2010, p. 49). Eventually, this SAR, led by Ted and Sandra Cole, who were part of the UMinn Program in Human Sexuality—and developed an entire disability program around the SAR—became a traveling program nationally within rehabilitation hospitals.

Other specialty SARs included *Family SAR*, developed by Pearl Rosenberg, one of the PHS, and led by Bill Seabloom, for teenagers and their parents in 1974. *Adolescent SAR* inspired his lifelong commitment to the treatment of adolescent sex offenders, as well as to better understanding adolescent and childhood sexuality. The *Family SAR* garnered positive evaluations, "with 87% reporting that they could discuss sexual matters more freely at home; and 82% felt the seminar had dispelled some sexual misconceptions for them. 96% of respondents said the SAR had been personally beneficial" (Weiss, 2010, p. 61). However, community backlash stopped this trend. Another SAR was created to serve sex offenders in a Minnesota correctional facility.

A SAR for SIECUS[7] was designed for recasting the goals and mission of the organization. SIECUS remains today a dedicated sexuality education and advocacy entity that actively promotes guidelines for comprehensive sexuality education in grades K–12, an initiative begun when Britton served as its Deputy Director from 1990–1993. In its Position Statements, SIECUS formally endorsed and continues to endorse the use of sexually explicit materials (SEM) for educational purposes, stating that ". . . when sensitively used in a manner appropriate to the viewer's age and developmental level, . . . (they) . . . can be valuable educational or personal aids, helping to reduce ignorance and confusion and contributing to a wholesome concept of sexuality. However, the use of violence, exploitation, or degradation, or the portrayal of children in sexually explicit materials is reprehensible" (SIECUS, 2016). Rhoades warns that some SEM could "reinforce myths and stereotypes about gender roles and erotic preferences" (2007, p. 10), a risk that one takes in showing explicit media of any kind.

Perhaps the most confounding type of Specialty SAR is the Advanced SAR. These would focus on kinky behaviors or, as Weiss puts it, "more dangerous or problematic behaviors and illegal sexual practices such as prostitution" (2010, p. 69). There were SARs devoted to the challenging topics of aging, death, and dying, and abuses to the human sexual self. Not that long ago, a SilverSAR™ was created, which we discuss in Chapter 5. One such Advanced SAR is proposed by Pillai-Friedman, Pollitt & Castaldo (2014) to focus exclusively on the topic of BDSM. As the authors state, "An advanced SAR designed exclusively with BDSM content may be a necessary next step for sexuality professionals who are planning to practice with clients who have interest in BDSM" (p. 203). They recommend including media, speakers, and even a visit to a dungeon to address the lone topic of BDSM in a SAR.

Finally, within a view of tantra, a sacred sexual pathway for enlightenment that can be used as a new model for sex education, Kuriansky states, "Tantric sex assists people in confronting their stereotypes and views about sexuality, similar to the popular SAR (sexual attitude and reassessment) courses with which sexuality educators are familiar" (2009, p. 195).

SARGUIDE FOR A BETTER SEX LIFE**: THE ULTIMATE GUIDEBOOK**

One of the lasting artifacts from the days of inception of SAR is the collectable book titled *SARguide for a Better Sex Life: A Self-Help Program for Personal Sexual Enrichment/Education*, designed by The National Sex Forum (published in 1975). Brown ink in small lettering appears on beige paper, while its pages are filled with imagery from the era: mandalas, delicate drawings of human forms, exercises for the reader to follow, explicit depictions of human sexual anatomy, and Persian erotic art. We each have our treasured copies of the original print version, and we possess a later version on enlarged white paper with the inimitable SAR logo on the front cover in tan and chocolate.

As the Preface states, "This SARguide is a workbook, an adjunct to the National Sex Forum's Personal Sexual Enrichment/Education program. PSE/E is a low-cost self-help program based on the SAR Process (Sexual Attitude Restructuring) developed by the Forum . . . It is a simple step-by-step process to open to you all the possibilities of sexuality; to enhance your senses; to give you joy, pleasure and freedom to feel" (p. 5). The guide includes a brief history and rationale for SAR, and takes the reader along the journey to self-awareness. Components include a calendarization of SAR events, sex history, informational segments on a variety of topics, a contract for commitment, and a journal in which to write thoughts, feelings, and experiences that inform the path toward enhanced and enriched sexual self-awareness and growth. Exercises are differentiated for those to do as home exercises, pre-workshop, or during breaks, with specifics such as "Taking Time and space for yourself, Learning to Breathe, Sensory Awareness, Kegel Exercises, Body Imagery" (p. 46) and an assortment of critical readings. Part of the power (and charm) of the workbook is the series of illustrations that show a range of aspects of sexuality, such as anatomy and physiology,[8] the sexual response cycle, acts of coitus, and masturbation. It normalizes and debunks myths about the highly charged topics of masturbation and fantasies.[9]

The *SARguide* addresses a wide breadth of topics: male sexuality, homosexuality, sensate focus, desensitization activities, female sexuality, lesbianism, bisexuality, androgyny, children, celibacy, disabilities, massage, and experimentation with new ways for sexual expression alone and/or with a partner, including the benefits of sharing masturbation. The manual is a cookbook for self-help and a roadmap for exploring the entire span of potential human sexual expression. For example, on massage: "Most of us have received very little instruction in the personal nurturing art of giving and receiving pleasure through touch"[10] (p. 106). Consensual and appropriate touch is discussed before the *massage exercise*.

On the topic of appropriate sexual terms, television, radio, and other media have very strict rules regarding the usage of words such as *cock, pussy, asshole*, and *fuck*. "One of the most effective ways of reducing the negative charge on a word or image is through repetition in a neutral context" (p. 77). To address the infinite possibilities for human sexual expression, our SARs present a wide variety of sexually explicit media, a message that is well promoted in the *SARguide*. Selected images and media include homosexual, lesbian, kink, and various sexual activities. As the book assures the reader, "Remember, there is no right way or wrong way to express your sexuality, only your way" (p. 77).

PRIOR RESEARCH ON SAR

Little research has been conducted about SAR, considering its vast presence since the 1970s. A few have looked at aspects of SAR, such as research on sexually explicit materials (SEM) (Weerakoon & Stiernborg, 1996; Koch, 2007; Rhoades, 2007) and one significant publication described below on SEM in the UK (Brewster & Wylie, 2008). Another researcher investigated the efficacy of brief group interventions including SAR (Barratt, 2008). However, most noteworthy and frequently referenced is the study by Wollert (1978), one of the few that described research specifically directed at analyzing SAR for its many components and potential impact. Wollert surveyed 11 SAR directors and provided an in-depth analysis of aspects of SAR that included format, participants' characteristics, organization of SARs, approaches to curriculum design, goals, and outcomes. As SAR leaders some 35 years later, we note that not much has changed in terms of the variables that constitute a SAR. Wollert states that explicit audiovisual materials delineate a SAR from more traditional forms of sex education programs, which remains true today. The multi-method SAR "generally entails a two-day series of media presentations, exercises, and some lectures, accompanied by several large and small group discussions of approximately 2 hours in length" (p. 254). SAR goals tended to focus on the acceptance of sexual attitudes and behaviors of oneself and of others (p. 256). Small group size was set between 8 and 12 by most of the SAR directors. In his study, Wollert found that group leaders were selected on the basis of their knowledge, group experience, and comfort with their own sexuality, with many serving in the mental health field or as staff of agencies offering SAR. The most difficult element of SAR to determine was and remains how to evaluate the effectiveness of this method of learning. As he states, "little apparent agreement exists concerning which participants benefit most fully from SARs, which specific techniques are most effective in achieving SAR goals, and what are the major concerns of SAR participants" (Wollert, 1978, p. 258).

In 1995, a cohort of researchers conducted an 18-year comparative analysis of 7,451 participants in SAR programs at University of Minnesota from 1973 to 1991. Findings included: 96.2% found the SAR beneficial personally and 1.5% rated the SAR personally harmful; of those, 1,237 rated the SEM alone at 89.8% helpful and .8% harmful; 91% reported that the SEM were appropriate for themselves and 93% reported that the SEM promoted emotional awareness (Rosser et al., 1995, p. 123). This was one of the most thorough studies on the content and impact of SAR. However, 21 years later, no updated study of this scope has been published.

Another, more narrowly, focused study investigated the one-time use of sexually explicit films (SEFs) in the context of disability and sexuality among professionals working with this population. Tepper concluded, "Health care professionals who learn to use sexually explicit films as a teaching method should, at minimum, attend a SAR as part of their training in the use of this method. A formal course on group processing is also recommended" (Tepper, 1997, p. 180). Tepper also commented that clinical impressions more often than not served to evaluate effectiveness of a SAR (p. 169).

A major figure in SAR is the Rev. Dr. William Stayton, who is a Baptist minister, prolific SAR leader, and noted sex therapist/researcher. By 1998, Stayton had led over 400 SARs to over 8,000 individuals. Even to this day he continues to offer SAR programs to an abundant variety of audiences. (Read more about him in Chapter 5.) Stayton's (1998) research defines four anxiety-triggering factors that contribute to professionals' feelings of discomfort and anxiety about the subject of sexuality. They include: sexual trauma coming from an "internal struggle between natural sexual interests and culturally sanctioned interests" (p. 26); sexual ignorance and the "proscription . . . that knowledge increases promiscuity and irresponsible behavior, (which is). . . unsubstantiated by research" (p. 27); sexual secretiveness, about which the author observes, "too often professional training exacerbates secretiveness, because sexuality is approached from a pathological perspective, thus increasing the professional's trauma and ignorance" (p. 27); and, finally, at the time of the publication of his article, he mentions that "one of the most neglected areas of research and clinical practice has been sexuality and the aging process" (p. 27). Stayton emphasizes repeatedly the need for training of SAR trainers and small group leaders. Stayton cites that even as late as 1996, studies showed that "medical students who participated in the implosion model . . . (using desensitization through explicit films) . . . were significantly more comfortable in confronting sexual issues in patients than those who saw no films" (1998).

Chuck Rhoades in his study on SEM (2007) gives practical solutions and illustrates the range of concerns for the ethical dilemmas one may face in the inclusion of explicit visuals in a sex education program. He cites the movement toward the creation and inclusion of SEM on the East Coast of the United States, by acknowledging the New York University program in human sexuality, led by Derek Calderwood, and one of its graduates, Mark Schoen, who has since become a positive force in adult sexuality education. As a filmmaker and founder of SexSmartFilms (2016), Schoen is a major contributor to the genre of sexuality educational media for adults, including his most recent documentary, *Trans the Movie*,[11] as noted in Chapter 1.

Brewster and Wylie (2008) published an informative paper about the values and practices related to SEM in the United Kingdom. The authors state that for psychosexual therapists who lack the skills and "comfort with the language of sex and attitudes toward it . . . illustrative materials can be useful to the therapist, not just to convey information, but also to develop familiarity, ease and acceptability in discussing sexual topics" (Barnes, 1994). The UK replicated the SAR approach as "a vehicle for the sex education of medical students and professionals" (p. 385) and used highly explicit audiovisuals, including "films depicting adult solo and mutual masturbation, oral, and vaginal sex, lesbian and gay sexual interactions, sex between older couples, and disabled persons engaging in sex." They also allude to the 18-year retrospective study on SAR described earlier, citing that participants found that "not only is SEM not harmful, but it may aid resolution of people's issues and concerns, as well as clarify their emotional responses to aspects of human sexuality" (Rosser et al., 1995, p. 126).

Former AASECT President[12] and noted sex therapist Barnaby Barratt has extensively written on sexually charged topics, including his paper on questioning whether workshops really work (2008). He challenges the notion that in a short term of less than four days adults can truly have "education that enhances their lives or that lasts beyond the immediate transitory effect" (p. 325). In his review of the literature and in his own research, he remarks that there is a strong suggestion that "there is an accumulated wisdom about SARs and other brief group interventions" (p. 329). The controversy over *saturation methods* or *implosion techniques* in behavior modification are his concern, while Barratt discusses that a shift has occurred away from shock value "toward the presentation of opportunities for attitudinal reflection and reappraisal" (p. 329). Barratt makes the striking point that much research shows that "the more favorably a communicator is evaluated, the more likely the communication to modify attitudes occurs" (p. 322), indicating that the influence of the presenter may trump the material being presented or the overall group effect. The author wisely admits that research about sexual attitudes is more difficult than in other realms of human life. Although most SAR evaluations rely on the narrative reflections at the close of a SAR or fulfilling a specific requirement post-SAR (such as one week or one month later), there is a need for more convincing data about the effectiveness of a SAR. He observes that most successful outcomes of small group workshops like SAR occur due to the ongoing nature of people's quest for more similar educational opportunities, thereby having a cumulative effect (p. 338).

SEXOLOGICAL WORLDVIEW

Perhaps the most refreshing and modern viewpoint about SAR in the current climate of sexual expression is that of Sitron and Dyson (2009, 2012), in which they propose admonitions and recommendations to completely revisit the purpose of SAR as a mechanism for shifting attitudes about sexuality to constructing a new sexological worldview. The researchers posit that "a new construct must be developed to measure the success of the SAR as a method of sensitivity training. . . (thus) . . . sexological worldview is demonstrated to be a more pertinent construct than attitudinal change" (2009, p. 158). They argue that for the profession of sexology to be viewed as its own discipline it must measure up to other disciplines. As they cite from AASECT guidelines (AASECT, 2005), "The objective of SAR is to give participants the opportunity to explore their attitudes, values, feelings and beliefs about sexuality and how these impact their professional interactions . . . (that) it is a highly personal internal exploration." They further note that these same guidelines promote greater understanding, comfort and respect for sexual diversity. Because of "the trend toward the use of evidence-based interventions in the training of professionals" (2009, p. 164), sexology has to defend itself as a viable discipline.

Sitron and Dyson allude to the widespread prevalence of the use of the Sex Knowledge and Attitude Test (SKAT) in prior studies that utilized this instrument.

As they comment, to date "there has been no standardization of the curricula used" (2009, p. 166), thus limiting past studies in the training of sexological professionals. Citing other research on SAR with and without SEM, no significant differences were found. What is so momentous for this study is that it approaches SAR not as a sensitivity or attitude-changing model, but rather a tool to "cultivate humanistic and pluralist professional approaches to Sexological practice" (2009, p. 170). They present the sexological worldview as a framework in which SAR plays a role to broaden the scope of participants' own sexological worldviews. As the authors define it, "Sexological worldview is the often unexamined but changeable perspective held by each person about the world around them with regards to sexuality; it is the result of the socialization process that is comprised of values, beliefs, opinions, attitudes and concepts specific to sexuality, including any and all sexual behavior and identities" (2009, p. 173). Their further research investigated whether the sexological worldview of individuals was more relativist or dualist, leading to an expansion of their definition to include: "Sexological worldview develops across a continuum with worldviews at one end being expressed as 'dualistic (right or wrong)' and at the opposing end as 'relativist (possible perspectives are endless and no one perspectives is right or wrong)' and varied expressions in between" (2012, p. 6). Their call for a shift in defining the purpose and efficacy outcomes of SAR is a relevant concern today.

SUMMARY

In the next chapter, you will read about each of our very first SAR experiences. You will gain insights into how our initiation into the SAR process has informed how we address and view SAR today. We guarantee that you will enjoy a few *aha*s and *aww*s along the way.

NOTES

1. "The name 'free love' has been given to a variety of movements in history, with different meanings. In the 1960s and 1970s free love came to imply a sexually active lifestyle with many casual sex partners and little or no commitment" (Lewis, 2016).
2. Originally it was named the National Sex and Drug Forum and later changed to National Sex Forum (NSF).
3. Laird Sutton's sexual patterns films formed the basics of the media, also known as *sexual cinema verite*.
4. Part of the Glide Foundation Urban Center in San Francisco.
5. Toni Ayres; Phyllis Lyon; Ted McIlvenna; Frank Myers; Margo Rila; Maggi Rubenstein; Carolyn Smith; Laird Sutton.
6. This is especially true with the use of media as an immersive experience.
7. The Sex(uality) Information and Education Council for the United States.

8. We offer an observational "show and tell" of genitals during ASPEX. Participants have the opportunity to view and have a greater understanding of the variety and differences of genitals.
9. At our SARs, we often open the introductions by asking each participant to reveal their deepest sexual fantasy as an icebreaker.
10. We introduce non-sexual massage into the ASPEX trainings.
11. *Trans the Movie* is widely used in SAR programs, especially when a speaker is unavailable.
12. Britton served as the President Elect under Barratt and as President from 2006 to 2008.

References and Resources

American Association of Sexuality Educators, Counselors and Therapists. (2005). Certification requirements of a sexuality counselor. Retrieved November 30, 2005, from http://www.aasect.org/counsel.asp

Ayres, T. (1975). *SARguide for a better sex life: A self-help program for personal sexual enrichment/education designed by the National Sex Forum*. San Francisco, CA: The National Sex Forum.

Barnes, T. (1994). Editorial. *Sexual and Marital Therapy, 9*(2), 107–109. doi:10.1080/02674659408409573

Barratt, B. B. (2008). Evaluating brief group interventions in sexuality education and enhancement: Do workshops really work? *American Journal of Sexuality Education, 3*(4), 323–343. doi:10.1080/15546120802371992

Brecher, E. M. (2000). *The sex researcher* (Expanded ed.). San Francisco, CA: Specific Press. Originally printed 1969, revised 1979.

Brewster, M., & Wylie, K. R. (2008). The use of sexually explicit material in clinical, educational and research settings in the United Kingdom and its relation to the development of psychosexual therapy and sex education. *Sex Education, 8*(4), 381–398. doi:10.1080/14681810802433903

Fithian, M. A., & Hartman, W. E. (1972). *Treatment of sexual dysfunction: A bio-psycho-social approach* (1st ed.). Long Beach, CA: Center for Marital & Sexual Studies.

Institute for advanced study of human sexuality. (n.d.). Retrieved July 18, 2016, from http://www.humansexualityeducation.com/mission.html

Koch, P. (2007). The what, why and how of group learning in sexuality education. *American Journal of Sexuality Education, 2*, 51–71.

Kuriansky, J. (2009). A new model for sexuality education: Teaching tantra. In E. Schroeder (Ed.), *Sexuality education: Past, present, and future* (Vol. 3, pp. 193–208). Westport, CT: Praeger Perspectives: Sex, Love, and Psychology.

Laird Sutton filmography. Retrieved from http://www.imdb.com/name/nm0840345/

Lewis, J. J. (n.d.). Free love and women's history in the 19th century (and later). Retrieved July 23, 2016, from http://womenshistory.about.com/od/sexualityandsex/a/free_love.htm

McIlvenna, R. T. (2016). Personal conversation. July 25, 2016.

Pillai-Friedman, S., Pollitt, J., & Castaldo, A. (2014). Becoming kink-aware—a necessity for sexuality professionals. *Sexual and Relationship Therapy, 30*(2), 196–210. doi:10.1080/14681994.2014.975681

Rhoades, C. (2007). Ethical considerations in the use of sexually explicit visuals as an instructional methodology in college sexuality courses. *American Journal of Sexuality Education*, *2*(4), 5–23. doi:10.1300/j455v02n04_02

Rosser, B. R., Dwyer, S. M., Coleman, E., Miner, M., Metz, M., Robinson, B. E., & Bockting, W. O. (1995). Using sexually explicit material in adult sex education: An eighteen year comparative analysis. *Journal of Sex Education and Therapy*, *21*, 117–128.

Schoen, M. (Founder). (n.d.). Sex smart films home. Retrieved July 24, 2016, from http://sexsmartfilms.com; Viewing: http://www.sexsmartfilms.com/premium/film/1164/45/33/trans#videoContainer

SIECUS position statements. (n.d.). Retrieved July 24, 2016, from http://siecus.org/index.cfm?fuseaction=Page.ViewPage

Sitron, J. A., & Dyson, D. A. (2009). Sexuality Attitudes Reassessment (SAR): Historical and new considerations for measuring its effectiveness. *American Journal of Sexuality Education*, *4*(2), 158–177. doi:10.1080/15546120903001407

Sitron, J. A., & Dyson, D. A. (2012). Validation of sexological worldview: A construct for use in the training of sexologists in sexual diversity. *SAGE Open*, *2*(1), 1–16. doi:10.1177/2158244012439072

Stayton, W. R. (1998). A curriculum for training professionals in human sexuality using the Sexual Attitude Restructuring (SAR) model. *Journal of Sex Education and Therapy*, *23*(1), 26–32. Retrieved from http://dx.doi.org/10.1080/01614576.1998.11074203

Sutton, L. (2016). Personal conversation. July 20, 2016.

Tepper, M.S., MPH. (1997). Use of sexually explicit films in spinal cord injury rehabilitation programs. *Sexuality and Disability*, *15*(3), 167–181.

Weerakoon, P., & Stiernborg, M. (1996). Sexuality education for health care professionals: A critical review of the literature. *Annual Review of Sex Research*, *7*, 181–217.

Weiss, K. E. (2010). *Sexual attitude reassessment seminars: A retrospective of SAR early years in Minnesota* (D. Boen, Ed.). Minneapolis, MN: Tasora.

Wollert, R. W. (1978). A survey of sexual attitude reassessment and restructuring seminars. *The Journal of Sex Research*, *14*(4), 250–259. doi:10.1080/00224497809550987

Zientara, G. R. (2015). McIlvenna, Robert Theodore (Ted). In P. Whelehan & A. Bolin (Eds.), *International encyclopedia of human sexuality* (Vol. II, H-P, pp. 760–762). New York, NY: Wiley Blackwell.

Zientara, G. R. (2016). Personal conversation. July 26, 2016.

3

Our First SARs

"Don't knock masturbation—it's sex with someone I love."

—*Woody Allen*

MY FIRST SAR, BY BRITTON (WINTER OF 1970s)

We all begin somewhere. For me, Britton, as a budding sexuality educator and clinical counselor for the mostly rural Planned Parenthood of Vermont (PPV), a tiny state in New England, I was clueless about how sex really worked and certainly even more naïve about things like the clitoris. Remember, the 1970s predated cellular phones and the Internet. Common terms like *snail mail* meant a catalogue on gardening. The new rage was owning a handheld cordless phone, if you could afford one, and this was long before icons like Samantha or Charlotte from *Sex and the City* created a universal awareness of sex toys like the "Rabbit" vibrator (Sex and the City and the Rabbit Vibrator, 2011). Blogging was not invented yet as a pastime or profession. Few of us had ever looked *down there* in a mirror and fewer knew beyond the birds and the bees (as in procreation). Plus, the SAR took place in my beloved home state of Vermont, where at that time current events and modern social trends emerged 5 to 10 years later than in any American metropolis.

My first SAR was a requirement for employment as a PPV Rural Outreach Worker in the 1970s. My role was akin to the barefoot doctors of China. I knocked on strangers' doors that appeared to be poor families that were in need of ways to manage their fertility. I brought them into the clinic to obtain counseling, to find them good advocacy for a healthier life, and to help guide them to begin using birth control. I would walk from trailer to apartment with my *Beautiful Book* and suitcase filled with various contraceptives in tow. It was my launch into the field of sexology, a field that I have never left, except for a brief stint as a Congressional Aide for James Jeffords as the lone Vermont US Representative to Congress. Even during that time I always maintained my footing either as staff or as a volunteer with Planned Parenthood, which eventually led to becoming the Associate Director for Education at Planned Parenthood Federation of America's national office in New York City for almost a decade in the 1980s.

The SAR was located at one of the most remote centers in northeast Vermont, known as the Northeast Kingdom with a population in 2010 at under 65,000;

back then it was a very low-population density region, which we jokingly called *the sticks* (Northeast Kingdom, 2016). Its reputation for being conservative made me a bit nervous. But once there among my peers I found my tribe of like-minded, openhearted, sex positive PPV workers.

Although I am going back now over fifty years, my memories couldn't be stronger about what I learned. There in the cramped clinic training room, we sat in stiff chairs with notebooks on our laps and watched hours of what I now know were Laird Sutton's groundbreaking *sexual pattern films* and other media. We saw men and women masturbating, couples engaging in full sexual intercourse, oral sex, anal stimulation, and lots of caressing. We also saw some of the famous and popular films made by the Glide Foundation (home of the National Sex forum), such as "Toad a Trois" and "Orange." The masturbation film of one of the women shocked me. For the first time, I observed there was a special place inside of the vulva called the clitoris; when rubbed by the woman herself she could produce a seismic release, the big O. Little did I know that this one particular film,[1] that is still shown today at the Institute for Advanced Study of Human Sexuality in San Francisco during their 6-day SAR program, would change my entire life view. Finding my clitoris was a revolutionary discovery!

Suddenly, I realized women could become liberated from needing someone else to rub them to ecstasy or even to experience a slight sexual hiccup. Instead, I was dazed and amazed and rushed to my hotel room that night to test-drive my new body part. It worked. Since that SAR I have appreciated not only my own sexual response to self-pleasuring through masturbation, but I have been able to advocate for others to do the same. Masturbation is liberation from dependency on others, regardless of your sexual identity or sexual orientation. It is our unique pathway to self-love, as Betty Dodson[2] defined it in her BodySex workshops, on her website (Betty Dodson & Carlin Ross, 2016), and in her many books.

At the SAR I also saw two gay men engaged in soft, gentle lovemaking. I witnessed a full array of explicit, non-shaming, non-fabricated, non-judgmental expression of the true human sexual experience, and I was hooked for life on spreading the good news: that sex is a healthy, natural, and celebratory part of being human. The Sexuality Information and Education Council of the United States (SIECUS) has promulgated this message for years, and eventually I would become the Deputy Director for SIECUS for two years, leading the charge for comprehensive sexuality education for K–12 grade youth and trainings in comprehensive sex education and HIV prevention around the country.

SAR influenced my life in other ways. When the HIV/AIDS epidemic hit home in New York City, one of the epicenters where the disease was prevalent among gay men, I was working at the national office of Planned Parenthood. I observed many of my fellow staff members affected directly or indirectly by the rising fears about contracting HIV/AIDS. We were watching friends and colleagues die from it, as well. To join their efforts to stem the tide of terror and to serve my friends in need, I volunteered as a safer sex educator at the Gay Men's Health Crisis. There I participated in SAR-like community programs for groups of 100 to 200 men learning about safer sex; as a member of the Safer Sex Brigade, I offered to design a template for the first all-gay male SAR, a program that never was implemented. My template was later used to design an all-women SAR in a Southern Planned Parenthood affiliate by one of its training staff. SAR had become engrained in how I viewed teaching about sex.

The most powerful SAR impact in my life was my first SAR at IASHS. I enrolled in the PhD program in 1989 while leading the national HIV/AIDS Prevention Teacher Training project for ETR Associates, funded by the Centers for Disease Control as a 3-year, pilot demonstration project. At IASHS, the SAR is over a weeklong journey of self-discovery, immersion into a huge collection of media on film[3] at that time, and an ongoing flood of speaker panels, showing us the infinite breadth of human sexual expression and engaging in expansive experiences. Speakers discussed their Lived Experience as a dominatrix, a stripper, a disabled veteran, bisexual advocate, or gay male activist.

One speaker in particular was a very active, HIV-positive, leader of the safer sex movement in San Francisco, David[4] (his real name). He walked to the center of the stage clad in all black clothing and spoke fervently about his passion for HIV Prevention and BDSM. David, an extremely handsome, dark-haired man in his 40s, was a very compelling speaker who was a beloved favorite at many an IASHS SAR and other classes. I listened but could not keep my eyes off his dominant hand, on which he wore a single black leather Italian racing glove with holes for the fingers as he whirled, whipped, and danced around. My eyes remained transfixed on that hand as he demonstrated his skills with a series of whips. I dreamed about the glove and told my friends in SAR that the sexiest (gay) man alive just affected me in ways I never imagined possible. This was my first exposure to the world of BDSM, one that has reverberated for a lifetime. The speaker panels endlessly unleashed mind-exploding new thoughts about human sexuality in all of its potential forms.

Fields trips to local clubs, marching in the Gay Pride Parade, getting naked in the swimming pool for condom relay races—all of these elements of an 8-day/8-night SAR resulted in becoming someone new.

One of the common themes for SAR anywhere is the formation of lifelong friendships. By day 2 of the 8-day SAR, I had noticed a handsome man we'll call Max, with a heating pad strapped to his lower back from a recent injury, sitting in front of me on the pillows on the bleacher-like seats in the SAR Room. The SAR Room remains today the only classroom at IASHS, one that has many fond recollections for any of us as graduates or faculty. Those pillows contained the DNA of hundreds of sexologists over the many years since the Haight Ashbury heyday when they were made. This particular day, during the safer sex negotiation exercise in which we got to practice with someone in the group, Max sidled over to me and said, sunglasses tipped up so he could pierce me with his brown eyes, "This is not a role play. Can we talk about having safer sex?" After five straight minutes of deep belly laughing, I thanked him for his asking me to participate in the practice session. That experience sealed our bond as friends for many years to come, as the beginning of an 8-year relationship that ended amicably. Such a personal connection with a fellow sexologist would not have been possible without the environment of openness and deep personal growth work that happened for me during this SAR. The hallmark of the IASHS SAR was the "Fuckorama,"[5] a multi-media event described in Chapter 2. My mentor and advisor, Laird Sutton, once told me that this is how to bypass the thinking part of one's brain and let the images bathe your mind. He was right. So many images cannot be analyzed, but felt. Feeling our feelings became the pathway to healing for myself, and for all of the rest of the SAR group. The re-entry into the real world outside of the SAR crucible is not always easy or smooth.

I also had what I consider to be the privilege to attend yet another 8-day/8-night SAR at IASHS devoted exclusively to the topic of HIV/AIDS. All of the speakers related to HIV, whether they themselves were activists, HIV+, safer sex educators, BDSM practitioners, spiritual leaders, crisis care workers, hospice nurses, medical doctors, or other roles that somehow tied in with the pandemic of HIV/AIDS. At the conclusion of that SAR, I knew that my life would be connected further to HIV prevention in any way it could. SAR was my gateway to self-awareness about my own core values.

Field trips included going ensemble with a group of fellow graduate students to the famed erotic venue, Mitchell Brothers. I spent my first trip to the club watching two females rub, caress, and fondle each other nude in the shower room. We then played host to women strippers on stage who shared a bawdy nude dance on each of our laps. Finally, I took advantage of being able to visit one of the very well known heterosexually oriented peep show venues in Little Italy, San Francisco. There men place coins in a slot to lift the window gate and watch sexy females strip, cajole, and touch themselves to simulated orgasm, while the men masturbate themselves to bliss in their private cages. These two SAR outside experiences alone expanded my horizons and made me a more compassionate and more tolerant sexologist in addressing the fantasy scope from my clients. I also learned to feel comfortable as a sex doc in a sexually explicit venue, which later on allowed me the ease to offer workshops and classes at one of New York City's most prominent male adult sex shops. SAR really affected my sense of permission to teach about healthy sex wherever we go.

MY FIRST SAR, BY DUNLAP (2005)

My own journey began as an actor in Hollywood. You may have seen me on television, in a few movies, and on many commercials over the past 50 years.

I am that guy about whom you say, "Gee, you look familiar." Because I am! This may seem irrelevant to a book about SAR, but it's very related in this way: Media is my world. Media drives the engine of SAR. My first SAR came late in life during my second career, while attending IASHS in San Francisco as a PhD student in the mid 2000s.

In 2002, I became enamored with the field of sexology. I was dating Dr. Britton then and found her profession to be nothing short of intriguing and compelling. Her cousin, Xaviera Hollander of Happy Hooker fame (Xaviera Hollander, 2016), was visiting the house in Malibu. After peering at one of my new film projects, she asked me to make a documentary on her life story as a famous sexual icon. Just before that, I realized that my career in Hollywood was taking a turn, as I leaned more into the world of positive sexuality. As a seasoned filmmaker of over 40 films so far (many of them about nature or science), I began to make my own contributions to the panoply of films related to explicit sexual themes. My initiation into sexology came as the producer and videographer for the soon-to-become cult classic documentary, *Beyond Vanilla*, on BDSM, kink, and fetish. That film changed my life in many ways. It brought me into contact with Dr. Britton and her peers, and it shifted my perception of sexual normalcy while expanding my acceptance of the almost infinite possibilities for experiencing extreme ecstasy through erotic power exchange. In that one film alone, I shot over 300 hours of explicit sexual behaviors on tape, interviewed over 200 BDSM practitioners in six major US cities, and altered my view for my life.

At the IASHS SAR in 2004, many transformative activities engaged my mind, body, and soul. That SAR changed how I view the world today. One of the exercises was to dress up as a way to truly express one's own sexuality. Being an actor, I had chosen a combination of film characters that I enjoyed watching on the silver screen. My black leather top bustier was from the "Rocky Horror Picture Show," made famous by actor Tim Curry. My black jeans came from "Midnight Cowboy," worn by actor Jon Voigt, now a star on Showtime network's television series "Ray Donovan." The last touch was full eye makeup from the imagery in *A Clockwork Orange*, based on the award-winning performance by Malcolm McDowell as Alex and directed by Stanley Kubrick. I made the choice of making up only my right eye, as it is the eye I use to look through the lens of my camera as a filmmaker and photographer. I realized I would never see the world the same way again. I was so right! My career as a filmmaker would never be the same, as well.

Previous works as director/producer included *Grandpa*, the love story of my grandparents. *Grandpa* earned me an Emmy Citation and was selected for the Martin Luther King Film Festival, as well as for an airing on PBS. Next came a film short that emerged to become a cult classic of its day: "Anton," which was the first depiction of a gay interior designer ever made. "Anton" aired on the Showtime network and won as a selection for Directors' Fortnight at the Cannes Film Festival and in over 30 other international festivals. This was my first real foray into making media about sexuality, a theme that has led me deeply into the heartblood of SAR today.

Years later, in 2001, I produced with director Claes Lilja the revolutionary documentary, *Beyond Vanilla*, including theatrical releases in New York City, San Francisco, and Los Angeles. To have a documentary show at commercial movie theaters is a statement of the hunger for this type of subject matter shown on the big screen, similar to what a SAR offers. It gave me an insight into the practices of BDSM, kink, and fetish in a way that few others get to view or feel with all of their senses wide open. I am often interviewed as a sexological expert on BDSM even today, and serve as a regular source for ABC News. Often clips from *Beyond Vanilla* are part of our SAR media exposure, and this single documentary is shown worldwide at other SARs.

My SAR experience focused my dedication to sex workers and sexual surrogates. One of my classmates was Cheryl Cohen Green, who enlightened my views about the importance of sexual surrogacy. She later became the subject of the Oscar-nominated movie *The Sessions* for her original work in Surrogate Partner Therapy (SPT). She also happened to attend classes years before at IASHS with Dr. Britton, for whom the concept of SPT became a pivotal force for awareness of this adjunctive type of physical care for talk-only clients seeking sexual help and relief from their problems. The seed for my next film about Xaveria Hollander emerged from my SAR as I understood that this Madame was far more than just a sex worker, but also a sexual revolutionary. That theme infused the entire making of the next documentary, *Xaviera Hollander: Portrait of a Sexual Revolutionary*. Indeed, she changed the world's perception of prostitution through her books that took readers behind the scenes and showed the enjoyment and empowerment that sex workers may get from their work. In addition, she has written over 25 other books on sex and has been that famous "Call Me Madam" columnist for *Penthouse Magazine* for 35 years. Sex work and sexual freedom are themes that her life reflects and that serve to inspire me in much of my own approach to sexual healing.

SAR is a bonding experience. For me, in the SAR Room lifelong relationships were formed and remain today. One of my classmates, Elise Turen, was a leader in the trans movement and influenced my thinking about trans identity from the start. As a CIS-gendered woman born a biological female, her involvement as a trans therapist and advocate, along with her doctoral dissertation (chaired by Dr. Britton) on internalized trans phobia, led to a breakthrough in treatment care for trans clients in her extensive Los Angeles private practice. She is co-founder of the Los Angeles Transgender Center and trains staff at the Los Angeles GLB center. Turen is also now the leader of our local SAR team to secure speakers for our trans panel, plus share her own views, at every one of our Los Angeles–based based SAR programs. During SAR *free time*, Turen and I shared our souls and commitment on what we would do to educate and ultimately to change the world sexually. We also became the study group known as *the pod*, which morphed into the now-popular LASA (Los Angeles Sexological Association) that offers monthly sexology discussions and speaker sessions for anyone interested in learning more in that context.

A profound friendship was born in that SAR room with a trans man we'll name Jon. He was a new grad student at IASHS, who had flown across the United States to be at the SAR. He did not know anyone else in town. To support his quest to explore his new gender expression as a man, he asked me to accompany him to a very popular gay male drinking hole just a few blocks from IASHS. I agreed to go as his date, and it was a night to remember for us both; this his first foray into being taken as an out gay man, and, as a visible straight guy from Hollywood, it was my first time visiting a gay bar with my male date. Finding camaraderie and advocating for trans rights began for me with this one trans man and has not stopped since.

One of my fondest memoires was the *Fuckorama*. Even the name had me a bit tentative. The *Fuckorama* left me shaking. This display of multiple films included animals having sex, blowjobs, breasts, penises, and every orifice thinkable for penetrations. It was overwhelming. It did, however, let me breathe out, let go of my previously held judgments, and melt into the process.

My SAR included a trip to a public BDSM dungeon known as The Power Exchange in San Francisco, a well-attended milieu for local kinksters. We also attended one of the world's largest Gay Pride parades, where I proudly walked with the group called *Straights for Gay Rights* under a huge banner in the sun along the roadway. Another favorite SAR experience was floating naked in a pool with four naked women holding me up so I could float. Although this was non-sexual, it was a liberating moment for me in my sexual development as a shy adult male in his 50s. It brought me back to memories of when I was born in water, with my father delivering me in that tub. The odd thing is that I was born only five blocks from the location of the Institute, in a blackout, and raised a Roman Catholic by my family and later by nuns. Literally, this was a baptism for my new life yet to be lived.

Finally came the finale of the IASHS SAR, the Sensorium, where I was blindfolded and escorted through a maze of sensual experiences, such as fur, warm, wet, fans, touch, tickle, taste, sounds, giggles, breathing, erotic, safe, free. The final day of SAR is to bring you back to the real world. It is the deconstruction of the entire 8 days of SAR as a way to transition back to your former life. How do you talk and act around *ordinary* people again after such an expansive experience with your peers? That final day was at the home of the leaders of IASHS, the McIlvennas, where we were lavished with time in their swimming pool, fine food, and caring company, as we moved into a more normalized state of being. My first SAR was unforgettable and indelibly left a lasting impression that has fueled my commitment to develop and lead SAR programs worldwide that can produce the same remarkable results for others. I hope I do so.

SUMMARY

In Chapter 4, you are going to read about our legacy as worldwide SAR leaders. First, we begin with our programs in the United States, and then we take you around the world to view the different elements and components from our SARs in The Netherlands, Czech Republic, Germany, and Poland. You will also be taken inside the SAR rooms to discover special educational tips, stories of SAR breakthroughs, and illustrations of how to maximize success for your own SAR. Don't stop now!

NOTES

1. "Margo" by Laird Sutton.
2. Betty Dodson and I remain good friends, and she was one of the seminal mentors that informed my career. In her mid-80s now, she continues to write blogs and host workshops.
3. The entire collection of thousands of films is now digitized, save a larger repository of media housed in several warehouses that are part of the Exodus Trust.
4. Sadly, David died of AIDS not long after that SAR. We all wept for days.
5. Sometimes also referred to as the "sexorama."

References and Resources

A Clockwork Orange. (n.d.). Retrieved July 16, 2016, from http://www.imdb.com/title/tt0066921/?ref_=nv_sr_1

Betty Dodson with Carlin Ross Better Orgasms. Better World. (n.d.). Retrieved July 16, 2016, from http://dodsonandross.com/

Beyond Vanilla. (n.d.). Retrieved July 3, 2016, from http://beyondvanilla.net/

NortheastKingdom. Retrieved July 3, 2016, from https://en.wikipedia.org/wiki/Northeast_Kingdom

The sessions. (n.d.). Retrieved July 16, 2016, from http://www.imdb.com/title/tt1866249/?ref_=nv_sr_1

Sex and the City and the Rabbit Vibrator. (2011). Retrieved July 16, 2016, from https://www.youtube.com/watch?v=o-RozcHd08kXaviera Hollander. (n.d.). Retrieved July 15, 2016, from http://xavierahollander.com/

Xaviera Hollander: The Happy Hooker. (n.d.). Retrieved July 16, 2016, from http://thehappyhookerdocumentary.com/

4

Our Lived Experience

43 SAR Programs Later

"It is bad enough that people are dying of AIDS, but no one should die of ignorance."
—Elizabeth Taylor

Since 2007, our method of designing and delivering a SAR has expanded and shifted over time. The same will be true for you as a SAR leader. Here is a summary of our experiences in the United States and some of the highlights from each of our significant SAR events held in foreign countries.

2007–2009: INAUGURAL SAR

Our very first SAR was led for a group of graduate students. As an accidental occurrence, we were testing the waters in an academic setting to determine if this type of educational approach to adult learning would pan out. It certainly did. Britton was teaching Human Sexuality (42 hours, 3-unit course) at The California Graduate Institute[1] (CGI) that began as a requirement and then developed into a full program of 5 courses for 11 units that led to a State of California *Certificate in the Treatment of Sexual Disorders*. The other courses included Sex Therapy Methods; Sex Therapy Clinical Practicum; Human Sexuality; and Sex in Cinema, co-taught with Dunlap. The program drew from our training as clinical sexologists, our doctoral work at IASHS, and years of sexuality education and clinical expertise that enhanced our graduate-level teaching skills. The first series of SAR courses for CGI included some noteworthy speakers, many of whom came from being lecturers in the Human Sexuality class. For example, Nina Hartley, adult film star, presented on her matrix of understanding human desires; Sharon Mitchell, former adult star and founder of the Adult Industry Medical (AIM) clinics that provided HIV and STI screenings for the adult industry (International Encyclopedia of Human Sexuality, 2015), spoke about testing and the epidemiological trends in managing HIV among XXX performers; various experts on BDSM discussed their practices; another speaker shared about her work in Surrogate Partner Therapy; and a former escort and advocate for sex work talked about her book *From Cop to Call Girl* (Almodovar, 1994) and her activist work toward decriminalizing prostitution. Those were just a few of the spectacular presenters at our SAR programs at CGI. Of course, small group process and watching hours of explicit sexual media formed the foundation, as well.

SMALL GROUP PROCESS

A key component of SAR is the small group process. Having qualified group leaders is a value that we hold high. To accomplish having a roster of local group facilitators we began to train a group of professionals who worked with us over the years at CGI. (You can learn how small group facilitators should be trained in Chapter 6). We believe in having group leaders who share our view of SAR. We train our small group leaders to possess an in-depth approach to small group facilitation, including a good sense of group process, knowing how to structure the discussions, and being inclusive and comprehensive in a short amount of time. They, too, need to feel comfortable to share authentically about what affects them as role models for personal disclosure, and be able to handle difficult situations or participants. Ironically, several of the small group leaders we have worked with over those years were those very same student peers from IASHS that attended the PhD program with Dunlap.

We recall one such SAR. On day 1 of the SAR, a young man in the front row, Dan, who was just completing his PsyD, slouched backward in his chair, dressed in flip-flops, cut-off jeans, and a tee shirt, with a shy look on his face. Occasionally, he would cover his eyes with one hand. He winced at the media, seemed intrigued by the speakers, and held back in the discussions that ensued. Finally, as the second day of SAR started, we walked up to Dan and asked if he was doing all right in the SAR process. He said he was okay, and could he talk to us afterward? At the conclusion of that SAR, he admitted that this was the first time, as a well-trained therapist and specialist working with teens, that he had completely opened up and changed his world view about sex. Dan began to cry, holding my hand, and said, "This SAR has changed my life. I'll never be the same again. Without it, how could I possibly be a good therapist to my clients? And by the way, I think I'm going to take your other classes!" We sighed and laughed. A year later, Britton became Chair faculty for his doctoral dissertation that focused on compulsive sexual behavior among young men, inspired by the SAR experience that gave him the courage to pursue his dreams.

2010–2011: OTHER LOCATIONS IN LOS ANGELES

In 2010, we began to offer SAR events at other locations. We were colleagues at the Institute for Sexual Health (Institute for Sexual Health, 2016), now defunct, a sexual health and sex addiction treatment facility in Los Angeles. Its director had studied at a well-regarded postdoctoral sexology program and was keenly aware of the need for SAR for his staff and other professionals working in the sex addiction field.

We also began to host our own SAR programs in Los Angeles, often held at hotels that offered extreme attention to privacy. They featured lobby environments where speakers could sit and wait to enter the SAR training room and good accommodations, as we tend to serve lunches for multi-day SAR events. The Culver Hotel[2] became our training annex for all SAR and other sexology training programs (Culver City Hotels, 2016). Staff were not shocked when they would bring in a fresh pot of coffee or remove stale water glasses in the midst of explicit films displayed across the wall or an MTF (male to female trans person) speaker in early transition who could be easily misread. Often we would invite a full panel of heavily tattooed and visibly pierced BDSM experts. They appeared at the hotel fully dressed in black leather and hauling equipment that was not your usual fare for a corporate meeting in the upstairs conference room of a charming local hotel. Culver Hotel remains a hub for entertainment as the home to SONY Pictures as well as frequent productions of television shows and movie shoots, sometimes while we have hosted a SAR. It's a rather small and welcoming space that we continue to use for SAR trainings. A safe and intimate space and respect for the people coming to a SAR, regardless of their role, are a must.

At one point, we moved the SAR events to a penthouse apartment at a nearby Ramada Inn. It also housed some of the participants attending the SAR and Clinical Sexology weeklong training, so it had a homey feel. It was important to us that the ambience radiated warmth, acceptance, and safety. Those criteria will be discussed in more detail later in Chapter 6.

Composition of Participants

Los Angeles is its own international hub (think LAX[3] airport) and drew attendance from all around the globe and across Canada and the United States. Others flew in from India, New Zealand, Portugal, Greece, Taiwan, Mexico, South America, UK, and European nations. Of course, most participants hailed from Southern California from a wide variety of disciplines.

SAR students included a medical doctor from India, who at an early SAR we led, began his shift in career focus from this very first training to eventually becoming an AASECT Certified Sex Therapist. He would stand up at discussion times, clad in flowing Nehru outfits, wave his arms in the air, smile, and bow, and then pontificate to the audience with statements such as, "Goddess Dr. Patti. This training is changing my understanding of the entire field of human sexuality. You are the moon and the stars and you have opened my soul to the possibilities of all that we can do. Bless me, Dr. Patti!"

A female gynecologist from a large medical care system, also a sex researcher on the terribly disabling condition of fistula, attended not one but two of our SAR programs. She wanted to get up to date on trending sexological issues and to feel the sense of freedom that SAR promoted for her own path as a sexual being. Another stellar yet shocking experience occurred with one of our own local Sex Coach University (2016) students. Josh appeared in SAR as a heterosexual male, living with a CIS-gendered female, and came from an American Native Indian tradition. His exploration of sacred sexuality and polyamory had begun to shift his values. At the end of the small group process, Josh stood up, clasped a large walking stick that he had clung to all during SAR. He began to sing-chant in a native language about his personal transformation. He wept and fell to the floor. Afterward, we learned that he had realized at this moment, after exposure to the transgender speaker panel and with this opportunity for self-exploration, that his true gender identity had been compromised all of his 26 years. Through this one SAR, he found the courage to accept his true gender identity as a *she* and is now undergoing full gender transition to become the first female transgender certified sex coach. What an amazing journey this can be!

Nurses, naturopaths, disability experts, social workers, psychotherapists, MFT interns, religious leaders, courtesans, art models, sex addiction counselors, sex workers, bodyworkers, energy healers, tantra specialists, sex educators, military personnel, youth advocates, and all other types of clinicians have attended our SARs. In their evaluations, they unilaterally remarked how they gained the knowledge, awareness, and expansion of their own perceptions about the sexual lives of humans. They realized that they had been stretched as containers for holding a safe space for their patients, clients, or students. SAR was the center of the sexological universe for personal and professional growth for so many at our Los Angeles-based events.

Los Angeles Speaker Selection

During those SAR events, we became friendly with other experts and hired speakers from the Center for Positive Sexuality (2016) in Los Angeles. Many have been some of our favorite speakers on BDSM, fetish, and kink. They could be counted on to show demonstrations embracing foot worship, knife play, spanking, flogging, whipping, gagging, electric stimulation, and other forms of erotic power exchange. One BDSM demo featured a duo in a highly charged consensual scene that involved her being dominated into submission. The dominant male placed clothespins on her tongue while she remained on her knees, blindfolded, in rope bondage with her hands behind her back. This woman happened to be a highly educated psychologist whose doctoral work was addressing the positive mental health aspects of this kind of BDSM exchange. It was sizzling to observe and not a breath could be heard in the room! After the scene, she remarked that the dominance/submission exchange created a serenity and peace she longed to feel, while it also gave her a path to regain her grounded center of self. The CPS continues to be a resource that we admire and engage for our SAR programs to date.

We also have cultivated a lifelong relationship with Elise Turen, Co-Director for the Los Angeles Gender Center (2016), mentioned in Chapter 3 as one of Dunlap's fellow doctoral students at IASHS. Her genuine knowledge and caring spirit toward the trans experience, along with her superior expertise about trans issues, lend credibility to what our SAR offers each time. For the many years in which Turen has served as both a speaker and sometimes as a small group leader, she has shown dedication to our SAR approach. She has delicately yet firmly pushed for positive outcomes among participants seeking to better understand trans itself. Dr. Turen has taken on the role of securing our trans speakers for all of the years of our Los Angeles–based SAR events.

We have hosted SAR speakers of all dimensions of the trans experience, such as male to female (MTF), female to male (FTM or F2M), gender queer (GQ), questioning queer (QQ), and gender fluid (GF). Our speakers have ranged from pre-op to post-op, to living full time in the gender of their identity at various stages of transition to just beginning to shift, and they always share the deepest part of their story from a heartfelt perspective. Several of the speakers and other prominent figures in the GLBT movement in Los Angeles have been repeaters, showing up at different stages of their own movement toward their authentic gender expression and identity. Often they too gather support from the room full of clinicians and educators as part of the unified field of experience that SAR provides. At times they may bring their significant others or their children, all of whom share about the impact of trans presence on their lives.

One story stands out, that of Jake, a late 20s trans man in his early transition. Jake is a well educated doctoral level psychologist. He appeared at the SAR dressed as a man, with short blonde hair and facial acne. He was vulnerable and generous in sharing that the injections of testosterone (common for most FTMs) had given him full blown adolescent acne and that he had just undergone *top surgery*. He proclaimed, pointing to his bare and manly chest, "I feel like a teenager again." Thanks to the safety he felt in the SAR room, with great pride and some hesitancy he gingerly took off his shirt and revealed to the group the scars on his chest from the recent removal of his breasts through a double mastectomy. That was a special moment, realizing the painful journey that most trans persons go through to become authentic. We have also had the other side of the spectrum, including a trans woman in her 60s who speaks regularly about her transition through post-op, and how in her mind she does not identify nor want to be associated as a trans woman. As so many say in the SAR, "I'm not a this or a that. I'm just ME."

We have had trans women with prominent dark chest hairs protruding from their white silk blouses, with deep bass voices and visible 5-o'clock shadows. Trans women have also shared the stage who were *Vogue*-magazine-cover beautiful and indiscernible from their CIS-gendered sisters. We have had trans men whom one would never know were born in female-identified bodies at birth, as their presentation is so masculine in facial hair, body mass, vocal qualities, and affect. We have been the host of many trans persons who share a dreadful and powerfully moving history of the suffering in their evolution to the present moment; others delight in showing off who they are today in their new attires, new hairstyles and full make-up, new mannerisms, and often with a new lover at their side who simply adores them for who they are. Many of our speakers have admitted their failed suicidal attempts or lifetimes of depression, reclusion, and anxiety (Vocativ, 2015).

At our most recent SAR in Los Angeles, we recognized that, thanks to the mainstreaming of discourse about the insurgence of trans persons' coming out, more and more of our speakers are younger and more confident in their choice to transition at an early age. This is an exciting moment in the history of trans. Gender-reaffirming surgeries are more readily available to those who can afford them, many insurance plans now have coverage, especially through the Affordable Care Act or Obamacare (2016), by redefining such surgeries as medically necessary (Della Costa, 2016). The global cultural climate seems more open to acceptance of the trans phenomenon than ever before. Turen often provides updates from her attendance at major transgender-oriented conferences, such as at WPATH (World Professional Association for Transgender Health, 2016), the governing body that sets criteria for appropriate transgender health care standards worldwide. She shares international views and burgeoning changes in language, treatment approaches, best practice standards, social trends, political movements, or other aspects of serving the trans community in Los Angeles and beyond.

The Danish Girl (Hooper, 2015), a major Hollywood film about the first transgender surgery starring Eddie Redmayne and Alicia Vikander, garnered Oscar nominations for the leading actor performances without any resistance from the Motion Picture Academy about its theme. Trans is one of the must-have speaker elements of any SAR worth leading. We will talk more about that in Chapter 6.

Los Angeles Field Trips

During all of our SAR programs, even while at CGI/TCS, we have consistently offered a field trip event on the evening in between the two full days. The field trip is always optional, as certain participants from the local region do not keep that time slot open, compared to SAR participants who fly in for the event. At a recent SAR, a nursing mother regretfully chose to skip the field trip to a local dungeon; personal issues can occur that prohibit attendance at all that a SAR may offer. It is not rare to have an international student attend an SAR who has never been to an erotic or sexual venue at all. Our field trips have included a local BDSM club, a private BDSM dungeon, a pole dancing studio, and a sex toy boutique.

External events become critical experiences for some of our students to engage in what they have seen presented during the SAR by our expert speakers. Often a person will become mesmerized, even affirmed in their desires, when watching, say, the Master/Mistress wield a flogger or whip to willing volunteers. Those who have buried BDSM fantasies can act upon them at the safe space of the club or party, with highly articulated rules of engagement or etiquette. Most clubs of this nature have their own policing, monitoring, and enforcement policies. An example is having an *Open Doors Only* policy, with signs posted, to assure that people using any of the rooms (where penetrative sex is not permitted) feel safe in the setting. One of our regular SAR BDSM presenters also was the on-site club Master. His role in guiding students from SAR into the actual physical or emotional experience of BDSM pain-pleasure play often changed their entire lives as sexual beings. We frequently receive comments that describe their experience, such as "I've always thought I could be a submissive . . . the night at the club let me find that part of me and I never want to stop!" Or "Being flogged nude, in front of a group of my friends, transported me into a new dimension. I've never felt that kind of trust before. I'll be back, for sure."

Structure for Los Angeles SAR

We used to offer a 2.5-day SAR and have traditionally stayed with our model of two consecutive days, sometimes running by request a shorter SAR with an evening that precedes a shorter day after. One such event was a SAR for 2015 Woodhull Sexual Freedom Summit (2016), discussed later in this chapter. You will learn about the role and value of field trips in planning your SAR in Chapter 6.

INTERNATIONAL SAR EVENTS

2012: Amsterdam, Holland (The Netherlands) SAR

Venue

Our first foray into delivering an International SAR was in 2011 at the home (also a bed and breakfast of world acclaim) owned by Xaviera Hollander (aka the Happy Hooker). Situated in one of the finest neighborhoods in Amsterdam, The Netherlands, she offered a setting where many guests could be housed on premises and provided with Dutch delicacies and meals. Xaviera was the concierge to obtain some of the most amazing speakers imaginable, including herself, as she spoke about her life as a famous sex worker and author. She also served as Host Coordinator, a role we highly recommend that you secure early on in the planning process if you go outside of your home town to run a SAR (more about that in Chapter 6). Her specific duties included finding alternate nearby housing, organizing private or tourist excursions, local transportation, field trips, and of course the roster of speakers.

What made this location so special was the fact that it housed a huge erotic art collection, crowding every available wall space, and had the potent presence of Xaviera herself as its host. Her gentle, attentive husband Philip prepared the food and assisted with outside lodging and information about public transport, along with an occasional cup of hot coffee. One of our American SAR couples was erroneously double booked at their bed and breakfast. Philip valiantly helped them relocate to a new hotel at midnight the day before the SAR began. As a social worker in Amsterdam, Philip also possessed the skills to serve as a soothing presence, with perfect English, when a participant felt a need to process an emotional upset away from the SAR main room.

Venue plays a large part in the tone and ambience of a SAR. In this case, being located for the media, live presentations, discussion, and daytime meals in the home of a famous sexual icon lent an immediate air of acceptance of sexual diversity and eroticism. Xaviera's home also offered a chance for intimate networking, shared meals on the patio and dining room area, and an upfront peek into the lifestyle of someone who has fought many battles against political and social bigotry, targeted hatred, and personal threats to her life. Her reputation as a former prostitute, despite her becoming a leading supporter of the theatrical arts in Holland and a prolific writer, haunts her even today. The stories she would share, in casual passing with the SAR participants, enriched their perspectives of the issues surrounding sex work then and now. It also happened that the day our SAR began, April 20, was the international holiday for Cannabis Liberation Day (2016). That cultural backdrop helped to liberate the thinking among some of our attendees, coming from other countries where the legalization of marijuana had not been enacted. This was the perfect setting to expand perceptions and talk about sexual freedom!

Composition of Participants

The composition of the participants varied as much as Dutch culture itself. Psychotherapists, healing arts professionals, a medical doctor and his nurse wife, tantric educators, energy workers, escorts, sexuality educators, students at Sex Coach University, all provided a broad spectrum of where the impact of SAR could have a lasting effect on their work in the world of sexology. An American BDSM *Shibari* (Art of Contemporary Shibari, 2016) rope bondage expert and her *slave* occupied the backyard cabana, proving an ongoing exposure to the mistress/slave relationship for all to see. Several of us stayed upstairs in the rental bedrooms of the house where we hosted 24 participants from as far away as Michigan, New Jersey, North Carolina, California, Austria, Germany, Poland, England, Belgium, and Portugal.

Small Groups

Often the measure of a small group flow is how conversational that group becomes and how quickly this happens, such as how animated is the sharing and the depth of emotional outpouring. This SAR had three small groups of eight each, one led by Dunlap, one by Britton, and another by a colleague who was a Polish sexologist and founder of the Warsaw-based Sex Positive Institute, who exhibited an excellent grasp of spoken English and brought her friend Lina, a polyamorist from Warsaw. Lina's great breakthrough came when she had an emotional confrontation during one of the processes that triggered early memories and guilt about her poly lifestyle. It was only after Dunlap encouraged her to share in her native language of Polish that Lina was able to express her deep emotions and find a plateau for self-healing an old relationship wound. Such an emotional shift is something that often happens in a foreign language setting, where English is not the primary language of attendees. You will want to account for the presence of different languages as we often do, having simultaneous or synchronous translation on site or other means for coping with multiple languages when you run an International SAR.

Speakers

Speakers included the mistress Lady L and her female slave, who revealed how their 24/7 dynamic as live-in DS (Dominant-Submissive) relationship was formulated, with the rules they followed and the list of consensual behaviors in which they engaged. Lady L also showed the group how *Shibari* bondage is done at an expert level and riveted the audience with her rope-tying acumen and its sheer physical beauty. Xaviera spoke about her many books on sex that she had published, her career as the author of *Penthouse Madame* for 35 years, and how prostitution has become regarded in The Netherlands today, which naturally led up to one of the field trips to the Red Light District.

Field Trips

People will come to your SAR for various reasons. One is for adding on vacation play time. If you intend to offer an International SAR, you may want to emphasize the importance of shared personal time on excursions. Before the SAR opened, we offered a special tour of the Tulip Gardens annual festival, *Keukenhof* (2016). This is a national treasure of a park that was in spectacular full bloom at the time. What we discovered was that being with SAR participants a day in advance, in the relaxed state of touristing, allowed for trust and camaraderie to blossom (pun intended) before the formal SAR began. Casual, friendly conversation enhanced the bond among our students who arrived early. Similarly, post-SAR, we invited one of our SAR couples to join us on a personal tour of the outlying towns that Philip provided in his private car. We traveled along the beauty of the Dutch seaside to the town that made Edam cheese a household term, and along the streets and canals of Amsterdam. The possibility of being in a different environment from home and sharing new adventures, great food, and jolly conversations allowed an expansiveness for us and SAR visitors that is rare to accomplish in daily life. Of course, thousands of photographs and hundreds of trinkets later, those memories live on.

During the SAR, the main speaker event was held in conjunction with one of the field trips to a local and very popular sex shop. The shop was not only a place to purchase the latest lube or European sex toy or BDSM accoutrements but it also had a huge lecture room with hooks in the ceiling for suspension play, common to BDSM play spaces. One of the speakers was a tall, cross-dressed 60-something male, wearing a hot pink satin outfit of a ballet tutu over fishnet black stockings in hot pink pumps, with a bustier top in white cotton. He wore a shoulder-length blonde wig and over-smeared red lipstick, pursing his lips as he swayed his hips to walk across the lecture space. Xaviera shouted commands for him to sit, stand, or preen, emphasizing her role as a dominant, informing her own sexual preferences and complementing her natural personality.

Another speaker was a Dutch female submissive (one of Xaviera's *slaves*) who agreed to be tied up with rope then suspended from ceiling hooks at about a five-foot height to hang in the air, arms and legs tied together behind, a ball gag in her mouth, her eyes covered with a blindfold. She expressed a sense of surrender as she swayed back and forth over the chairs of the audience. She later shared with the group how the suspension scene allowed her to relax and feel intense pleasure along with heightened excitement.

The final presentation was one we will never forget. For this event, in secret prior to arriving in Europe, Dunlap had negotiated with Lady L from the United States to be a back-up submissive. He agreed to assist with holding the slave while Lady L masterfully whipped her naked breasts with a long tail whip, until her slave could not endure any more pain for their mutual pleasure. Dunlap wore a black medieval mask with holes cut out for eyes and mouth, bare chested, in tight black leather pants with a belt. Lady L whisked his belt off and secured it around his neck to engage him in submissive response to her, pulling him toward her. He looked menacing. As this scene unfolded, Britton was sitting in the front row of the audience of SAR students. One of the highlights from the SAR overall was the moment when Britton let out a shriek of surprise when Dunlap emerged as an active player in the scene, dressed in all black and masked. Xaviera commented that with all of the experiences we have had as sexologists, she never expected to see Britton so shaken up. It all ended in a good laugh and a major learning outcome for the audience about the profound effect of erotic power play among consenting adults, ourselves included. Sometimes leading a SAR means participating to assist in the process, even if the activity is not part of your normal sexual or erotic outlets.

Two other field trips made this SAR a special one, given the cultural and social climate of Amsterdam, one of the most liberal cities in the world regarding sex, drugs, and tolerance for diversity. The Red Light District (RLD) (2016) is known throughout the world as a site to visit to witness sex workers dancing and cajoling from the windows above the street and to hire them for legally sanctioned sexual services. Young women, old women, women from all backgrounds at some time might find themselves working the RLD in Amsterdam for the sake of art, money, or their own pleasure. Our group walked through the district on a privately led tour, thanks to Xaveria's connections, and also interviewed many of the *working girls* to hear their stories. Things are changing in Amsterdam regarding the legalized and decriminalized status of prostitution. It became a huge point of discussion back in the SAR room to deconstruct how our participants felt seeing and talking with the prostitutes of RLD.

Another brief field trip was to the famous Sex Museum Amsterdam (Martinez, 2016). At the door stood a rather unappealing animated statue of a man in a trench coat that mechanically opened at passers-by, giving a flasher's taste of what was inside. Visiting the sex museum also provided much-needed discussion about the history of pornography, historical objects for masturbatory pleasure, representations of erotic art, and where art fits into the conversation about sexuality in general, a common theme at most of our SAR events. Visiting a museum or a gallery or other public spaces where explicit eroticism is shown, if at all available, is a recommendation we make to all SAR leaders as an enhancement event for your SAR. (More about that in Chapter 6.)

2013: Vancouver, British Columbia, Canada SAR

Venue

The site for SAR in Vancouver was one of the most unique yet. Our Host Coordinator was a lovely Sex Coach University (SCU) student and also a Masters in Psychology student in Vancouver. She lived in a beautiful condo complex slightly outside of the heart of the city. Her complex had a well-lighted and spacious conference room that could have its windows darkened with moveable shades. The room also came supplied with a high-definition television system that enhanced our media and had excellent sound quality, all considerations for your SAR. A nearby sandwich shop provided easy access to morning hot coffee for staff, quick snacks, drinks, and lunches. Not all SAR events have 5-star lunches, and yours will depend on your budget and available food sourcing. Although it was a bit outside of the city center where we stayed in a hotel, using either expensive cabs or cheap metro subway/train lines helped our participants to find their way.

Composition of Participants

This was one of our smaller SAR programs, with only 12 participants from the Pacific Northwest of the United States and all across Canada. Many of them were SCU students; some were counselors and psychotherapists in training, community-based sex educators, or HIV/AIDS counselors who desired a SAR experience. As a reminder, both SCU and AASECT require SAR for certifications, so this SAR garnered many who attended for the fulfillment of those requirements. All spoke English, so translation was never an issue, although at times you will find that cultural translation, when you are in a different cultural norm or country, may be necessary. We will discuss cross-cultural observations later in Chapter 7.

Field Trips

This SAR had a single field trip designed to enrich our participants' awareness of a wide range of sexual expression. Advertised widely as the Sex Expo, in a gigantic convention center in the harbor side of Vancouver, the venue allowed for socializing and networking after the event. Our group arrived at the end of a long day on the Saturday evening. This Sex Expo, the largest in North America, was packed. In one area people were hanging on ropes in spider-web patterns, in all different angles and heights of suspension and innumerable levels of undress with lines waiting to be suspended next; this was a quiet area for silent observation. Another area had loud speakers booming, featuring talks by top adult stars, such as Ron Jeremy[4] (who seems to appear everywhere we go), and offering opportunities to speak in person or take photos with the stars or grab their autographs. Our group loved that option. Primarily, this was a sex toy convention, showing the newest sexual enhancement products of the day. Some of the students made purchases, while others of us just used our palms to test drive the buzzing, vibrating, sensual tools on display at several of the unique booths in the large hall. It was a very connecting and bonding experience, as being in such an openly erotic environment was not an everyday occurrence for most of our attendees. In addition, many sexological organizations (such as local classes or national organizations) featured booths that taught about rope bondage, floggers, electrical stimulation, or tantra, where anyone could sign up. Several of the booths sold erotic costumes, BDSM gear, and other couples' enhancement accessories. Many of the students stayed in the local neighborhood to indulge in drinks and great eats at a variety of local restaurants and got to know each other better. Over a full hour was devoted the next day to sharing about the results from attending this amazing event, including some amusing stories about buying new toys, trying out the demos of floggers, or meeting a favorite adult performer.

As a tip, if you are thinking in advance about SAR dates, be sure to check with competing events that may draw participants away from enrolling in your SAR. It occurred to us later on that perhaps scheduling the SAR on the same dates as a world class Sex Expo may have deterred greater enrollment in our SAR. You will want to find out about any potentially similar events, such as a tantra festival, an erotic film festival, a noteworthy sex expert workshop, or other SAR programs blending or overlapping the same dates in your geographical region before you commit to dates.

Speakers

Our speakers included persons within the trans spectrum, a polyamory advocate, and a BDSM expert. This SAR had a moment in which something special happened that surprised us all. One of the participants was a trans man from the United States, who had agreed not to share his gender identity in public with the group as one of our trans speakers. However, that soon changed. Our Vancouver Host Coordinator (VHC) had a difficult time finding speakers willing to come out and share their story. She did find one local trans woman as our speaker, Lu, an older person who had to hide her secret identity to protect her professional reputation as a public figure. Lu lived a life hidden away from her authentic expression except at speaking events like our SAR. And Lu was a poor speaker, hard to hear and not well organized in the messages she wished to present. Once she finished her presentation, our trans man stood up, applauded her, delicately faced the audience then said, "I have never come out like this before. But this is such a safe place and powerful experience for me. I want to tell you the truth about myself. You may not have figured this out, but I'm a trans guy myself . . ." That moment produced a flood of cheers and tears.

Our other speakers included a BDSM master with an enormous collection of tools packed in two suitcases that required a handcart to bring them into the room. He demonstrated many of them with an extremely enthusiastic line-up of volunteers from the audience, who had particular fascination with the Tesla Wand, pulsating its purple electrical force field. It was a riveting and engaging presentation.

Our last speaker was a surprise, as well. It was our first time to have a speaker on polyamory, one who had become a cult figure in the Vancouver region. Peter had been persecuted for his choices as a poly man, living consensually with a wife and other partners. Again, the emotional takeaways from all of these talks made lasting impressions on the entire SAR group. Speakers can change the dynamic of a SAR and create the intention to dive deeply into the feeling self. It never has failed us yet. The Lived Experience says it all.

2013: Prague, Czech Republic SAR

Prague, in the Czech Republic, is known as the "Paris of Eastern Europe." Many Hollywood and foreign films that are allegedly shot in Paris are made here. The famous Charles River Bridge with the padlocks from lovers chained to the sides, the gorgeous dramatic Wenceslaus clock tower square where you never want to leave your café seat, and the charm of old world Europe with its delectable cuisine and elegant architecture add to the juxtaposition of modern life. Parts of

Prague all blend in perfect harmony. It is no accident that Dunlap loves Prague so much; his great grandfather was a famous Czech opera composer and Dunlap is half Czech. The charming and seductive spirit of Prague makes it a perfect place for a sexological event such as SAR. We will be going back to Prague in 2017.

Venue

Our Prague Host Coordinator (PHC) was a media host who openly talked about sexuality on her popular show and was one of our SCU students. The PHC was actively involved in the communities of polyamory, BDSM, kink, and other elements that make for a good SAR. Because of her comfort with sexuality in all forms, and due to her excellent networking skills, the PHC was able to meet a lot of the needed criteria for a venue and speakers.

Our venue was a charming, smallish, modern, well-appointed hotel located outside of the center of the old city, making it affordable and offering amenities that enhanced our stay. The restaurant at first appeared to be a pedestrian diner. Later it turned out to be our favorite place to eat all three meals a day. The hotel provided us with privacy by giving us the entire restaurant, with two wooden long tables and benches or chairs for seating around it for our two small groups to process during the lunchtime meals. No one else was allowed in or near the fairly open dining area while we ate. When you lead your SAR, be aware that having food in the training room can create a mess. Having a separate dining area makes for a clean training environment and less time for clean up before and after lunches. (Envision salad oils and coffee spills on the necessary paperwork!)

We stayed in a lovely, spacious room within the hotel where the SAR was held. As another tip, if you are leading a SAR outside of your home location such as at a commercial hotel, be sure that you have space, comfort, and an ambience to let you get your rest and feel relaxed when you are not on tap to lead the SAR or chaperone a field trip. Extreme self-care is important for all SAR leaders and small group facilitators, as well. Also, your room may become meeting central for emergency staff check-ins that are often a required part of leading a SAR that takes participants deeply into their experience. (More on that in Chapter 6.) Our room at the hotel was one of the best yet, giving us quiet, space, and an escape haven.

Composition of Participants

Compared to the prior International SAR programs, this was perhaps the single most comprehensive representation of global views, in terms of countries of origin and culturally diverse perspectives. Two of our participants were ultra conservative Orthodox Jewish women active in their religious communities, both mental health professionals from Israel. One of them was a leader in sexuality education for her peers and came to this SAR to learn how to replicate it. The other woman was motivated to learn more about sexuality for herself, as a recent divorcee. Both were eager to learn and they became two of the more vocal, friendly, and interactive members of the group. Each day they would ask how others were doing, what they thought or felt, and vociferously shared their innermost challenges and joys.

Of course, approximately 50% of the group was Czech, many of whom did not speak a word of English. This was quite frustrating for them and for us, as part of the SAR process is our own opportunity to dialogue in person. Often we become a sounding board for participants to share their most intimate personal emotional confrontations that may ignite during the SAR event. Without a translator standing by our side, being so available was nearly impossible.

One of our SCU students was a woman from Florida in her late 50s. She brought her husband, as is often the case for some of our married attendees. They love to travel to a desirable foreign location where they can attend a SAR and also explore as tourists. Many of them launch afterwards into vacation mode if the timing is right. As owners of adult stores in the United States, this couple was extremely sex-positive, knowledgeable, and aware of the potential range of human sexuality. We made an exception and invited her husband to attend our evening event in the hotel conference room where we held our SAR. Unlike other SARs, the evening presentation was more of an extension of the day's media, lectures, and demonstrations, rather than an outing.

Other participants came from Switzerland, Germany, United States, and UK. As usual, our group consisted of medical practitioners, mental health counselors and therapists, sex workers, sexologists, body workers, life coaches, sex shop owners, and sex toy home party consultants.

Dunlap and the PHC each led one of the small groups in Czech language, with simultaneous translation for the group. Britton led the third small group in English, with some who struggled but somehow stayed current in English with the personal observations, emotions, and cultural views that were being revealed. The group in Czech felt separated from the whole group, which was true. Having a language barrier not only can create a divide in the experience of unity at a SAR, but can also trigger deeper emotions already smoldering. Examples include being excluded for one's sexual orientation or preferences, feelings of shame about sexual ignorance in a conservative cultural ambience, or any other emotional baggage that a participant may bring into the SAR. At times, too, we have felt a wave of resistance from our being Americans, as in some international locales being American is not well received by everyone.

The Czech group also pushed back at having to watch a variety of sexually oriented media, which they termed all-porn. Perhaps also melded with the language differential in the whole group lectures, the group tension reflected confusion about the purpose of media in this particular SAR. For example, watching the segment of gay male sexuality was not understood as having educational value, and the lack of control over the precise translation left us helpless as leaders to differentiate porn from other explicit media. This can happen to you, even if you are not traveling to a far-off location. In Chapter 6, you will learn about how media plays a role in SAR and how to select and then access the best media for your SAR goals.

The pervading sense of exclusion or other-ness formed the basis for a powerful and pivotal discussion during SAR about how to create inclusivity and bring about integration when one (or more) feels different. That theme is prevalent at all of our SAR programs, as presenting the group with the alienation of, say, a trans person, or a closeted GLB employee, or a BDSM play partner can resonate with the same emotional charge. You will want to be sensitive to this potential problem if you lead a SAR with different languages and/or cultures, and find mechanisms for resolving the tension it can create for you as the SAR leader and guide. It will fall upon the small group leaders to be in a flow of communication with the SAR leadership. Feelings may be expressed in the container and safety of the small group that may not come out in the whole room. If you are the SAR leader, make sure that these types of feelings are being addressed and not left to simmer.

At this SAR on the evening of our first day, we spent hours as a leadership team in our room that night discussing if we should recommend that certain members of our SAR Czech delegation leave the SAR. We were prepared to offer them a refund for their tuition, given how angry and upset they felt. What happened in the night in between was part of what we observe to be the *magic arc* of SAR. The next morning, the integration and dripping down of emotions and cognitive reframing for the participants in question had emerged into a positive shift in their tone. The small band of unhappy Czech participants realized that some of their resistance was reactivity to the highly charged situation of learning about sex/sexuality/explicit sex in front of an international group of peers and not speaking the primary language. For the first time, they discovered their boundaries, owned their values, and acknowledged their choice to join the group as equals. Such profound shifts occur regularly at a SAR, but sometimes they don't make it. Just because a participant may judge or resist the SAR does not mean the SAR is not well designed or led. A situation of this kind underscores the need for careful screening of applicants to join a SAR. Furthermore, you will need to possess strong leadership and counseling skills and deftness in handling your participants if attempts are made to stage a rebellious response. In Chapter 6 (your Tool Kit), we talk in depth about how to handle difficult participants and situations.

Speakers

Our good fortune was in our PHC. She was a highly visible and active member of the kink community in Prague and contributed as a speaker from her own Lived Experience. As a woman in polyamorous relationships, she stayed with her husband and another male partner in separate dwellings. As a submissive for rope bondage and domination, the PHC gave powerful lectures and demonstrations on the art of rope bondage, polyamorous negotiations, and the nuances of being a BDSM/kink advocate in the Czech Republic.

Another speaker was a young Czech woman, fairly new to the BDSM scene, who lectured with a slide show of images from one of her recent adventures in a thicket within a dense forest. There a group of fellow BDSM players had created a suspension device on a tall tree, on which they gently and slowly hoisted her up with meat hooks threaded in her back region, which she called her *wings*. In the suspension experience she claimed that she could *fly*, a term that is often and commonly described in the process of transcending pain in BDSM. The images penetrated the comfort zone of the entire room. This dramatic representation of the pain-pleasure continuum, and the trust that was evident in her engaging in this extreme form of heightened sensation, made a real difference in the group's taking away a refreshed knowledge of the depth of possible explorations in erotic power exchange. The depictions of her process, and her discussion of how she does not consider this to be BDSM but a spiritual practice, changed many a view in that room. Taking off her blouse and showing us her back, devoid of much scarring at all, served as a testament to the skills used on her body with her consent. In closing, she said with a half smile, "I will do this only one more time. Three times will be enough."

Another powerful encounter was a *Shibari* demonstration with a volunteer who was another of our SCU students and also a speaker, Fran. Her contributions over five different International SAR programs reverberate even today. She self-identifies as a therian, a person who is half human, half animal. A therian (2016) expresses sexuality through costuming (in this case wolf ears, tail, and paws), animal behaviors (pawing and clawing and making wolf sounds), and ideological concepts (who am I truly) that drive the expression and form an integral part of her marriage. Her polyamorous marital home is her *wolf pack*. Fran volunteered to try out being tied in front of the group. We all gasped in unison when she melted into the rope cage that the Master created, restraining her from movement of her arms or hands, and resulting in a change in her facial expressions that resembled a holy visage at peace. Again, the sense of peace and calm emerged from the bondage as Fran proclaimed, "This is what I've been looking for. I feel so at home, so at peace. Here I am all tied up and unable to move and yet I've never felt so free." For Fran, this one moment was the turning point in her life to pursue a BDSM expression as a daily part of her living as a sexual human, with her husband back home in Germany.

Field Trip

Unlike most SAR events, our field trip was not on the night of day 1. We wanted Prague to offer an integrated excursion to the museum on day 2, allowing ample time to return to the SAR room for a debriefing. There was certainly a lot to talk about! If you ever visit Prague, you must not miss seeing the world-acclaimed Sex Machines Museum (2016). The Sex Machines Museum is a repository for some of the most valuable and historically relevant artifacts of BDSM, sexual pleasure devices, and art depiction.

We always bring still or video cameras and ask permission to document our tours of galleries, museums, and other settings where erotic or sexual art is on display. Some of those pictures or videos become part of our media collection to show at SARs and on our websites. A tip for you is to imagine that anywhere you travel you search out any sexually indicative media content and curate your own. (More about that in Chapter 6.)

At the museum, some of the highlights included images, devices, artful depictions, and informational explanations that helped our group to gain knowledge and confront their biases. One such example was on a wall, showing a priest's white robes with holes cut out at the genitals; a 6 foot × 6 foot free-standing wooden box where two small people could fornicate inside and be viewed through peep holes along the outside walls (hence the name *peep show* began); a series of penile extenders or vulvas decorated in latex and leather, with grommets and baubles all over them dotting an entire wall; historical collections of ancient vibrators in all shapes and forms, even some electrical stimulation machines from the early 20th century; and an entire large high-ceiling hall displaying paraphernalia from Nazi Germany, with full size body bags floating from the top and glass cabinets filled with kink head gear (such as pig or dog faces in leather) or apparatus devices used for breathing in times of war, all surrounding the view. In addition, a video viewing room showed old 8-millimeter footage of classical European porn of its day; fine art images of Hollywood movie stars like Marilyn Monroe and others were tucked on the walls that housed a barrage of photos, drawings, pen and ink, and gauche art. Upstairs in a private room, the owners allowed us to peek at some of the collection under consideration, including a tableau of Barbie and Ken dolls in compromising positions and more ancient handheld masturbation machines. The place was exploding with content that enriched our SAR and allowed our group to discover parts of the origins of human sexual expression that offered unique creative outlets for sexual thought and erotic energies over time. Few get to see this type of sexual art, as it is well hidden in certain parts of the world and not very accessible for most sexual/erotic art enthusiasts.

2014: Berlin, Germany SAR

Venue

Our time in Berlin was unique in not having a SAR in the home city of our Host Coordinator. For this event, we hired two of our staff from our pool of European

SCU students, both veterans of SARs that we had led. Fran was a speaker at other SAR events and was seeking expansion of her own erotic boundaries. Jill was exploring coming out of her own shell and regaining traction as a participant in the world of consensual dominance and submission. Both were dear to us, as their appointed temporary surrogate parents. We knew we could trust them to find an appropriate venue, riveting speakers, and a juicy field trip in one of the more edgy sex-friendly cities, Berlin. East Berlin had become a vibrant arts center and they were able to locate an affordable, spacious, reputable apartment in the center of the district, with easy access by public transportation and situated near a hostel for cheap housing for our students who required that option. We also rented out the extra bedroom to one of our mature couples who were repeating a SAR, knowing they would respect the space and contribute to making the SAR and prep time easy and enjoyable. We were not disappointed.

As a tip, if you are going to share housing and use the same site for your SAR training, be aware of setting firm boundaries about your needs for privacy, rest, and quiet. We found that having younger students come in and out of the apartment front door at all hours was tiring and took away from our time to prepare and adjust to the 9-hour time difference. Sharing with people who had become close friends created an urge to jabber. Having to regulate clean up time, help keep flow with prep time, manage the doorbell and the arrival of a group of participants in your living and working space, and just plain keep the space in order made our stay a bit of a pressured one. In the future, we will insist on our own quarters, not sharing with others, as being a SAR leader is a huge job that takes focus, energy, and leadership, with *on-time* and *off-time*. Another issue for us was the need to create an open space for smokers. As avid non-smokers coming from an American tradition of healthy, smoke-free environments, this issue caused us tension.

Our apartment had a beautiful terrace, open to a wide view of other modern residential buildings. The space was huge, with three bedrooms, two private full bathrooms, a generous shared living room and a large open sitting/eating/food preparation area to make our own meals or warm up catered foods being brought up for the SAR. Best of all, it had an enormous well-lighted dining room at one end of the suite with windows looking out to the city scape below; nearby, the second bathroom worked well for a crowd who needed to meet their creature comforts without strain. This was a perfect setting for an intimate SAR. For our SAR lunches, the restaurant in our rental building offered an elegant, catered gourmet luncheon extraordinaire.

Composition of Participants

This SAR was even more international than the prior one in Prague. Students came from as far away as China, all over Europe (Austria, Monrovia, Czech Republic, Germany), various parts of the United States, the UK, Russia, and

Germany. At one point we realized that we had small groups speaking in Russian in one corner, German in another, Mandarin in another, with the generic talking being done in English. This was a true polyglot SAR! Interestingly to us, one of the participants returned after attending our Amsterdam SAR.

As a PhD sexologist with his own private practice in the United States, Bobby expressed that coming to our SARs was a refresher for him to keep going in his own career development and that personally it served as a reboot for his erotic energies to flourish. Bobby also felt a sense of community, a common theme we hear at most of our SAR programs. Others in attendance were popular media figures, therapists, bodyworkers, sex educators and scholars, healers, and dancers, along with our regular troupe of Sex Coach U students.

We even had a US military specialist from a European base, Vern, who attended as a curious seeker to expand his sexual landscape. When he returned home from SAR, Vern reported that he felt the loss of the sense of freedom and community. Vern had discovered that the BDSM expression compelled him to learn more, even if he were to risk being found out and threaten his career. SAR often pushes the envelope of personal courage for attendees to be authentic to themselves, regardless of the risks involved.

Speakers

Despite Berlin's reputation for being a hub of sexual free expression, finding speakers across the sexual spectrum was not as easy as one might think. We did get lucky and found a German man and an Austrian woman who were willing to come out and share their expertise.

Our first speaker was a shy, unassuming female escort in her 40s, who offered a wide range of bodywork services to male clients. Her demeanor was distant and she was careful not to reveal her true identity, as she was a closeted sex worker. The stories of her passion for her work impressed the group.

The highlight speaker was a male dominant and frequenter of the local BDSM community. Tomas had appeared in some of the most successful female erotica that was distributed worldwide and was produced by a UK female director. That director, Petra Joy, was connected to one of our dear friends, Candida Royalle (2016), who (sadly) passed away from cancer in 2015. Candida's pioneering work as a filmmaker leaves a legacy today in porn/erotica made by a woman, for women and couples, and from a woman's perspective. One of the chosen directors in her series of films was Petra Joy, one of whose film clips was part of the current SAR media montage. Participants expressed a big splash of delight to have our speaker note his and our connections with other sex-positive outlets. Tomas' presentation dove deeply into discussions about the German scene of BDSM. In his live demonstrations, he offered to volunteers two different ways to experience the dominance-submission role and an exposure to erotic pain/pleasure. One of our own staff, Jill, volunteered her buttocks to be spanked ferociously. Her response to the hand-hitting caused a flair of excitement in the SAR group, as Jill had not claimed this part of her own erotic map for years. Such a moment in the presence of a group of near strangers left her breathlessly in ecstasy. She joyfully showed to anyone who wished to see it the morphing of a fresh red spanking pattern of his hand to a bright purple bruise mark.

The other most memorable scene occurred with one of the male sexologists from the United States. Bobby agreed to submit to the dominant master, who grabbed him by the back of his pony-tailed hair on his neck, told him to close his eyes and get on his knees. Tomas moved the submissive Bobby all around within the circle of standing viewers, and commanded him one at a time to open his eyes to take a snapshot of each person he saw. His instructions were to then say "I am a camera." Afterwards, this event prompted a lively discussion with the group about this form of relinquishing control. Bobby began to cry, disclosing that for the very first time in his 65 years of life he had been able to totally let go and submit. That single 10-minute experience changed his life, according to his ongoing revelations. This is the power of SAR.

Field Trips

Berlin is home to one of the most famous sex educators and sex-positive advocates in the entire world, Beate Uhse (2016). She was comparable to the revolutionary Planned Parenthood founder Margaret Sanger (2016), by promoting contraception and sex education in the 1940s, then opening the world's first sex shop in 1962. Although her highly successful sexuality-related businesses live on, Uhse died in 2001. She left behind one of the world's kinkiest museum collections (established in 1996), according to ABC News in 2010. Making this a daytime field trip as a required part of the SAR meant that everyone could visit the sex museum. Our students raved about the contents of this exquisite erotic art museum, which became part of a documentary on erotic art around the world that we have now shown at sexological conferences and describe in Chapter 7.

Attached to the Erotic Museum is the Berlin Sex Shop, where one's shopping fancies and fantasies are easily met. We ourselves are always on the lookout for new SAR media materials, so we bought a few DVDs (in American player format) and shared in the discoveries our students were making as they passed by the copious shelves of uniquely European or German-made sex toys and devices. This excursion formed the basis for animated discussions back in the SAR room.

That night, another field trip was designed to offer a real time experience of a BDSM play space, or dungeon. We, as the SAR leaders, often delegate the role of chaperone to our staff assistants. Instead, we opted to rest and stayed in the apartment, stocked with food, healthy drinks, and the audiovisual equipment at our disposal. We loaded in our new DVD acquisitions only to find that we had hit the jackpot for SAR media! One of the DVDs was produced by a famous fetish director, and featured scenes all in stark white or black latex, set on gynecological tables in sterile white rooms, and severe-looking medical equipment to probe, squeeze, examine and pinch the subjects of domination. One of them made us wince, as it was a female on the exam table, with her labia open, then pumped to an enormous size, then paddled with a flat metal spoon. Because we are not fans of watching blood play (a controversial topic for some SAR content), we were happy to discover that only saliva and natural body fluids emitting from the vaginal openings were on display.

The second DVD is one we cherish and show now at all SAR events. The DVD offers an intensive look into a dominatrix's dungeon, decorated like a Bavarian castle. It begins with a man in a dog mask, being punished with a horse crop, then moves inside the castle where activities include cock-and-ball-torture (CBT) by an old Remington typewriter, CBT with two live cactus plants, and more. Dunlap gasped watching the media, and I regaled at having found such SAR-worthy depictions of the sexual range of creative, inventive SM fare. Perhaps our greatest find was a short film called "Skin" (see the list of genres of films in Chapter 6) that showed a couple unravel their sensual/sexual relating in Morphsuits.

Post-SAR Field Trip

A post-SAR event is not the normal design of our SAR programs. However, when we can offer an excursion or other erotic or sensual experience, we do so. This trip was no exception, as Berlin houses a world-class public natatorium that requires full nudity and openness. European culture is very comfortable with the natural state of nudity; most of Europe is friendly to topless beaches. Spas dot the landscape and are how Germans often spend their leisure time and enhance their health. We visited the natatorium with several of our students, staff, and our male SAR speaker. Options included floating weightless in the blue-lit salty waters of the pool, settling into a small hot tub with coursing bubbles, lying nude on the many lounges while chatting with friends, or indulging in the uber-heated steam room with water poured on the rocks at specific intervals. The experience created a sensual, freeing, and bonding experience together that we'll never forget.

One of the unexpected pleasures of being in Berlin was a dinner meeting with the staff of Finland's prominent agency in the sex positive movement. They were also leaders within the World Association of Sexual Health (2014), which offers biannual congresses for sexologists (including ourselves) to present their work and scientific findings. Our Helsinki friends provided unique perspectives that lent an air of cultural diversity to our European experience. If you can attend one of the world WAS congresses, your ability to provide a more cross-cultural view on sexuality will enrich your SAR.

2013–2016: Warsaw, Poland SARs

After the two years of offering International SAR events in Holland, Canada, Czech Republic, and Germany, we moved our SAR to Poland, which for the past four years has been our International SAR home. Our Polish Host Coordinator is a renowned Polish sexologist with an American doctorate, who herself works as a psychologist, sexologist, and sex-positive advocate. Her own organization and retreat center at the Warsaw Sex Positive Institute (2016) is the site of many workshops, speeches, networking events, and our own SARs since 2013. Without her drive and dedication to enriching the training opportunities for her peers, our role as change agents would not have been possible. We have literally trained over 150 clinicians, healers, and sex educators in Poland, enabling them to provide better sexological services and sexual counseling to the Polish citizenry. Many of them are top-level scholars, psychologists, therapists, professors, and researchers who were yearning to expand their repertoire and vision for sexual wellness in their part of the world. Their experiences at SAR and other clinical sexology trainings (and of course our SAR for Grown Ups, discussed in Chapter 5) have given them fresh perspectives, deeper knowledge, and increased compassion for those they serve.

Venue

Our first SAR in Warsaw was at a rented space in an accessible part of the city at a single dwelling that housed a highly regarded group therapy practice. The center was used for healing arts and had an ambience that organically promoted vulnerability and personal disclosure, perfect for SAR. The building was well designed for our needs: a pleasant entryway where the registration table was set up; several individual small rooms on two floors, large enough for small group work; a large kitchen/dining area with a refrigerator and coffee maker, conveniently located on the lower level for the snacks, beverages, and catered lunches (this SAR featured freshly made Mexican tacos catered from a roadside truck); easy parking on the street; a spacious large central room for the whole group sessions; and a beautiful back yard garden area for breaks and smokers (a necessary evil). We rented their flat screen television and projector that cost little, as the center held frequent community events there.

Two problems occurred with the media and the window coverings, two critical areas that you must guard against. We were forced to use a computer for broadcasting the media, rather than a high-definition DVD or Blu-Ray player, causing a reduction in the quality of the picture. (In Chapter 6 we talk more about what you will need as requirements for showing your media.) The gigantic sliding glass door walls to the garden let in too much light for the media showing, and no curtains were suitable to darken the setting. The healing environment, the quiet location, and the soothing presence of the manager of the therapy center joining the SAR as a vocal participant helped to make this a wonderful venue.

At this first Poland SAR, we had a group of about 20 participants, some of whom were also our speakers. Mostly Polish, attendees were lively and engaged. Polish culture has a long embattled history of repression and oppression politically with communism and from their heritage as a mostly Catholic country. We learned quickly that cultural memes around repressive sexuality had to be broken. The new thoughts of sex-positivity, sexual diversity, and inclusivity that we brought as SAR leaders were much needed and desired, as a gentle sexual revolution was already rising.

Our subsequent SAR programs were held at the Sex Positive Institute (SPI), located in a swank neighborhood not that far from our apartment and with a host of amenities: a spacious three-floor home that offered small group rooms, a full working kitchen, an entryway for sign-ups and paperwork, an intimate main setting for whole group sessions, an outdoor garden area, and ample toilets. Food was catered in for the lunch breaks, while coffee and snacks were available at all times. The PHC is a good manager and assured that more than one volunteer or staff was always present on site to meet participants' needs. One of the benefits of being in our *own* space was that the walls were decorated in exhibitions of vibrant erotic art displays, and the space belonged solely to SAR for the weekend of its use. SPI has a casual living room ambience, making it easy to form private conversations and encouraging networking among peers. No negotiations were ever necessary to keep others out or to keep us safe within. SPI in Warsaw became the home of our International SAR with little preparation required over the three years of its location. The standard array of handout materials was retained, speakers were invited back, and organization of the arrangements for food, small group leadership assignments, media equipment, and all other repeating tasks became automatic over time. Of course, we have not spoken yet about marketing promotion, advertising techniques, assuring minimal enrollments for break-even budgets, or other management strategies, but we will do so in Chapter 6.

One incident occurred which taught us a lot about preventing venue disasters. Even if you work with a Host Coordinator, she or he may not be able to determine the workability of a selected venue to the level you would like. One example, which sounded in advance like the perfect setting for our 3-day clinical training following a SAR, turned out to be not quite up to par. The PHC secured a cheaply priced space in a friend's working loft in the center of a popular shopping district in Warsaw. It had plenty of space for the 18 participants, with its windows taped over with black garbage bags and some stark hanging light bulbs for lighting. It was early spring in Warsaw, where temperatures vary widely. What PHC did not know was that the frigid space never went above 32 degrees Fahrenheit upon our arrival and into the morning session. The men and women of the group all huddled together on slouchy couches in blankets they managed to grab from their own cars. At lunch, Britton screamed for a portable space heater to be brought in when she saw the discomfort and actually saw one person's breath visible in the room! Britton's feet were freezing, and at lunch the time was spent shopping for warm socks and picking up a take-out lunch of Polish pastries from a nearby café. Once the heater warmed us up, everything was fine. Keep an eye out to assure safety, access, comfort, temperature control, air handling, and privacy in any space you rent. Not being able to personally scout out venues for your SAR may bite you later. Be sure to establish clear criteria and do your due diligence as much as possible. More about that in Chapter 6.

Finances

One of the cost-saving aspects of hosting a SAR in a country with a low economic base is that your costs will be reduced against your currency, in most cases. Even if you only travel to the neighboring state, this could be true. In our case, the PHC offered complimentary private housing each time we visited Warsaw. She had the privilege of being co-located in a beautiful apartment building with a close family relative next door who traveled frequently. His absence during SAR events gave her the chance to move to his apartment and liberate her own for our stay. You may not have that luxury but will discover low-investment options in Chapter 6, where we talk about creative housing options such as apartment rentals, sharing with friends, resorts, or an Airbnb. We find that you will need to have private, quiet, and rejuvenating space, as we have mentioned, to keep your energies high and to focus on your goals of delivering a successful SAR.

The added factor of the poor economy, as compared to the US dollar, made pricing the SAR a difficult issue. Even to this day, our pricing for a SAR in Poland differs vastly from elsewhere. You will learn to target your tuition fees for SAR according to the cultural norms of your location. (See Chapter 6.) We advocate for you to create a matrix of different tickets for pricing your event. Some will be at full price, others at discounted rate for students or low incomes, and others can provide a volunteer or work/study role to service your SAR needs. It will be up to you well in advance to negotiate with your Host Coordinator or among your SAR planning team to determine the best price that yields both ample participation of a diverse group and also a net profit for your efforts. A SAR, after all is said, is an income-generating event. Net gain from SAR will not buy you a castle in the Alps or a home in Bel Air, California (home to the Hollywood royalty), but if planned correctly, should garner enough profit to pay all of your expenses, compensate you, your speakers, and staff, yielding some extra for marketing the next one. SAR is traditionally not a profitable money-maker! So let that thought go, if that's what you thought this book would provide for you.

Then again, if you lead a huge SAR of over 50 attendees (ours average 20) and have a reasonably low-cost space in which to house a SAR of your own, high profits may be possible. (For example, if you have 20 participants paying an average of $400US each, that is $8,000US income. However, most US hotels will cost you about $2,400, including the two days of lunches and coffees. Add in the cost of three-speaker panels at $150 each and two co-facilitators at $500 each (one for every 8–10 participants); handouts and supplies may average $150, media equipment rental at $500 or more, and a field trip may cost you entry fees of $200, for total expenses of $4700 (US dollars). This formula does not factor in your costs for lodging, food, travel, or any marketing costs. It is not uncommon to stay at the hotel where you lead a SAR, adding on the cost of your lodging and hotel meals. Assuming you offer a SAR in your own home city, ignoring possible expenses for hotel extras, your net profit is $3300. If you offer an International SAR with a Host Coordinator, you will also have to address the net profit split. We will go over various methods to plan and calculate your SAR income, expenses, and profits in Chapter 6.

Another expense at the Poland SAR is the cost for translators. Polish is a difficult language for us to master (we have learned only four words in 4 years and one of us was a linguist!). English is not ubiquitous as a primary language, so if you are offering an English-language SAR in a country with a different primary language, you will need to budget for this task. We have had a series of different translators, ranging from some of our multi-lingual SCU students to professional United Nations status translation experts. Having translation is a must if you intend to capture the nuances of personal sharing in small groups, host large group lectures in a language that you cannot grasp, or need to have a personal one-on-one with an emotionally challenged participant. Not hearing the actual guest speaker lectures in English was a problem for us on two accounts—the speakers on polyamory and the BDSM duo, which we will discuss later in this chapter. We also enhanced our fatigue level at having to simultaneously monitor the talks, follow the group interactions, and understand the content of the presentations while attempting to follow the constant hum of simultaneous translation in our ears at the back of the training room. It can be draining to work in a multi-language SAR. We discovered that in Czech and Polish, the differential in word length requires finding your stride as a speaker and accommodating their language pattern in the moment.

Composition of Participants

The recruitment for Polish SARs took many a turn over the three years. Much of it was led by the PHC through her regular website promotion, announcing special events, and handing out pamphlets we had constructed for the many networking events and conferences she attended in Europe. An uncanny opportunity also arrived when Britton was selected in 2014 to give the prestigious keynote address to a delegation of over 200 sexologists at Jagiellonian University. The annual sexology conference was thrilled to host her talk on sex coaching for aging clients. "The Jagiellonian University is a research university founded in 1364 by Casimir III the Great in Kraków. It is the oldest university in Poland, the second oldest university in Central Europe and one of the oldest universities in the world," according to a Google search and the Wikipedia website (2016).

That single presentation was so well received that it garnered ongoing interest in SAR and other programs, such as a 3-day clinical sexology training and the SAR for Grown Ups, known as ASPEX, for years to come.

At all of the Poland SAR programs, students arrived from a world spectrum, such as Tanzania, UK, Kenya, Austria, Germany, the United States, Luxembourg, The Netherlands, and Canada. Attendees ranged from a public health HIV expert/researcher, to a highly respected sexual medicine physician, to a Christian missionary for the Maasai people of Tanzania dedicated to bringing sex coaching to their world, to an international school teacher and vocalist.[5] The roster included sex educators, nurses, sex toy shop owners, university students, sexological bodyworkers, psychologists, therapists, activists, and other healing arts professionals. Such diversity brings the gift of unique personal and professional perspectives that are readily shared in the SAR small and large group process, making it a true chance for offering life-altering, divergent viewpoints about sexuality.

Speakers

In the first SAR, we were graced with two Polish speakers with facility in English who provided insights for the group. One spoke about her work in sacred sexuality through her vast training in Dark Tantra and sexual magic. The other had just returned from a utopian polyamorist community in Portugal that celebrates free love to avert global wars. Both of these powerful speakers and beautiful women enlightened the group with their views, many of which the participants were hearing for the very first time, evoking a barrage of clarification questions. We also have been the host on two occasions to a married couple who discuss and show a wide variety of their own handcrafted leather, metal, and rope BDSM equipment and demonstrate their practices in a unique, signatory way. The husband sets up a teepee of three thin tall wooden poles and binds them together at the top with rope; the wife then surrenders as he ties her up inside the teepee with rope, suspends her considerably large body of about 150 pounds under the top of the structure, then elevates her to different angles and levels, while pouring hot red wax on her body. Although they speak only in Polish and it was almost impossible for us to hear their dialogue, the sheer effect of the physicality of their demonstrations left a lasting effect on the SAR. We found it an interesting fact that for our first two years of SAR in Poland, this was the only Polish couple willing to come out as BDSM practitioners to speak about their Lived Experience in a public setting. As a tip, if you are working in a setting beyond our own network of potential speakers, it is not always possible to find those willing to speak on controversial topics. This may determine how you structure your SAR outline, as we cover in Chapter 6.

Two other presenters left a lasting memory; one was a *sissy boy* male in his midlife, cross-dressed in a woman maid's outfit, wearing high black pumps, a wig, and make-up. He talked about being a slave to dominants who liked to punish him and direct him to do things for them. His discussion with the SAR group in Polish held them spellbound.

This past year we had a speaker whose effect has not stopped reverberating for us. The man was in his mid-50s and had become a fairly well-known icon for his fetish practices, which he had recorded and broadcast on YouTube. His fetish (and singular erotic pathway for his sexual arousal) was the act of being trampled upon. Not only did he enjoy having women stomp on his chest, genitals, thighs, and even cover his nose and mouth with their feet, but he especially derived sexual/erotic pleasure from being walked over by horses. His complex fetish was a ritual: He would dig a hole in the dirt on a pasture, remove the dirt, then ask someone to cover up his body with the dirt, placing rubber tires around his feet and face for protection. He then closed his eyes and a volunteer (whom he had negotiated with prior) rode or used a rope to usher a horse to step over his body, carefully allowing the animal to slowly secure footing as it bore its full body weight across his; finally, he would be dug up and out of the grave. He played footage showing this practice to gasps and sounds of "Wow" all over the SAR room. This was one of our most unusual SAR fetish revelations—one that is hard to forget! During the SAR, he asked for female volunteers to walk all over him, which created a stir of engagement for all.

Another of our all-time favorite speakers was on transgender. We witnessed an amazing evolution for one person over 4 consecutive years: Year 1, our trans speaker Paul was a beginning university student in psychiatric treatment in Warsaw for his transgender condition, a signal of the conservative values in Poland that are not trans-friendly, as he told the group. He appeared as a male, clad in a nondescript outfit of jeans, teeshirt, and butch-cut short hair, wearing plain glasses. His voice was pitched high and he spoke from a very angry position as a trans man with little to no support. Year 2, we noticed a transformation within Paul. He had become more self-confident, and he had found a trans community in which he was now active as he spoke strongly for trans rights. Year 3, what once was a trans man now appeared as a female we'll call Monica. The trans talk that year was startling, as Paul/Monica remarked about how they had found that within himself/herself they were *both* a trans man and a CIS-gendered woman and another person as well, without gender adjectives. By our final year, Paul/Monica had become a beautiful woman in her presentation of her gender identity to our SAR, dressed in soft feminine blouse and skirt, with coiffed hair, pretty make up, and glamorous stylish glasses. Monica possessed a poise not seen before, as she talked about the two other identities residing within herself. She revealed that she had transcended labels and identities and had found total freedom to just be a person. Over the years, we learned about her transition in terms of her trans identities but also how she had grown psychologically, socially, romantically, sexually, and in her career path. Paul/Monica is one of our favorite speakers, thanks to her continuum of bringing about evolving knowledge and understanding of true trans experience. Paul/Monica remains a significant contributor to the emerging world of sexual freedom that SAR promotes.

Field Trips

We have never attended any of the field trips in Poland, so all we know is the responses we observe and hear in the SAR room on day two. Day 1 evenings are a time for socializing, expanding horizons of erotic possibilities, and often putting sexual theme into action. Venues have included going to a famous Warsaw strip club, joining the activities and being a part of a citywide march for the empowering Slut Walk, visiting and shopping at a series of adult shops, and frequenting a local BDSM play space that held a private party for our SAR group this past year. The comments in the SAR group the next day illustrated the power of field trips, as new erotic encounters created new friendships and sexual outlets. SAR can provoke sexual energy, and arousal is no stranger to a SAR. You will have to master working with those sexual/erotic energies in and outside of the SAR room to become a good SAR or small group leader. (More about that in Chapter 6.)

Special Request: Woodhull Freedom Summit SAR

One SAR we offered in the United States was not one of our regular home-based SAR programs. This SAR was for the national Woodhull Sexual Freedom Summit (2016) in 2015, held at a beautiful hotel in Alexandria, Virginia. SAR served as a pre-conference workshop and added to the draw to attend this significant sexual advocacy and educational event. Britton is a former National Board Member and currently serves on the Advisory Council for the Woodhull Freedom Foundation. This SAR was more of a fundraising event than an income-generating one. We offered to cover minimal expenses together and to share the net revenue with Woodhull. Proudly, we were able to write a check to Woodhull for a contribution to sexual freedom, SAR style.

Venue

Because the hotel was set up for the conference in advance of SAR, there were few arrangements to be made. We worked with the Woodhull Host Coordinator (WHC), also the Executive Director of Woodhull. She arranged for all conference requests and was cooperative and supportive. Issues included securing a large enough room for the main session with two breakout rooms; audiovisual (AV) equipment for media; inviting speakers from the local region and/or from among the Woodhull *family*; and meal accessibility during the second day of SAR. We scheduled a Wednesday evening from 7 p.m. to 10 p.m., followed by Thursday from 8 a.m. until 5 p.m. In the beginning stages, we had hoped to offer a field trip to a dungeon that was under renovation, which never manifested.

The venue was a huge ballroom with horrible temperature control; some attendees complained bitterly about how cold it was and we spent considerable time as leaders informing hotel staff repeatedly about our dilemma of ice cave or sauna. This will happen to you! It became important to be transparent with the group and assure that we were on top of the temperature control management. As add-ons to the ballroom, the two small rooms were perfect for lunch at round tables in privacy. The only other holdup was producing lunches from the hotel café, which had been given ample notification about our needs, and which was perilously slow in delivery. Even with that handicap, lunches were delicious, affordable, easily accessed, and did not interfere much with the time allotted for small group process. The other advantage of tagging a SAR onto an existing major conference was that the participants at the Summit could arrive in time for an Early Bird special discount for attending both SAR and the Summit. That type of alliance will help you in marketing your SAR programs and enhance enrollment if you are invited or suggest yourself as a SAR leader for other relevant events. Along with that option, many noteworthy conference speakers turned out to become our speakers on site, as well, resulting in one of our very best SARs!

Speakers

Buck Angel (2016), older trans man and world-famous adult star, agreed to fly in early from Brazil, where he was making one of his international appearances. His contributions as a riveting trans male speaker were well received. Another trans man, Alex, spoke from his early stages of transition as a young *out* trans activist, providing a balance to Buck's long history of living full-time as a trans male public figure. We did not have another trans speaker lined up in advance, but a beautiful surprise occurred. One of the conference volunteers was an older trans woman who had been sitting at the registration table and evidently was a part of the local trans community. Boldly, we approached her and invited her to speak about her own trans journey, which she happily agreed to do. Having the juxtaposition of a very famous porn figure and a fairly integrated resident of Virginia (who happened to also be trans) helped to normalize the trans experience. This also provided insights into the nuances, challenges, emotional ups and downs, and courage it takes to be an out trans person. Buck Angel also is on the Woodhull Board of Directors, and he is someone we admire and respect greatly.

The previous evening was comprised of our own SCU graduate, Fran, recently relocated to Virginia from Germany. She spoke openly and deftly about her experiences as a polyamorous military wife, as a sexological bodyworker, and of her expression of therianism (mentioned earlier in this chapter). Nina Hartley (2016), celebrity adult star, host of multiple adult sex educational DVDs, and vocal sex-positive advocate, was another featured guest lecturer. She is a powerful presenter, whose views on sexuality and whose positive approach to sex ed and advocacy always leave a mark on the listening audience. This was not unlike other occasions when we felt so fortunate to have Nina as one of our speakers. She, too, is on the Woodhull Board and is a highly regarded friend and colleague.

Perhaps our greatest challenge was in finding good speakers on BDSM. One male/female duo, who speak locally on BDSM, volunteered to present on their overview of what is BDSM, how the encounters or scenes are structured, and showed a demonstration of a power exchange between themselves. Once again, we found ourselves in a conservative locale in which the BDSM speakers chose to use fake names (their BDSM scene names) to protect their high-level employment identities.

Hardy Haberman (2016), another Woodhull Board member whom we admire and trust, spoke from his perspectives as a Leather Man in the gay male communities. His sharing of the Lived Experience added just the right dimension of understanding to complement the team presentation to the group, including demonstrations of accoutrements they had brought to show. In a mere 1.5 days, we covered several topics, enjoying the sense of freedom this SAR provoked and provided against the backdrop of a sexual freedom conference that was about to launch hours later. If you have the chance to piggyback your SAR with another conference, consider doing so. You benefit from embedded marketing, cost savings, on-site management details being covered for you, and a chance to participate in a conference yourself that you might otherwise not attend. It's a win-win all around.

Society for the Scientific Study of Sexuality (SSSS) Pre-Conference Workshop

In November of 2016, we had the privilege of being asked to provide a SAR as a Pre-Conference workshop attached to the annual conference of SSSS (Society for the Scientific Study of Sexuality, 2016) in Phoenix, Arizona. Although we had been asked to deliver a SAR for other national sexology conferences before, this was our first time to be available to offer one in conjunction with a noted and well-attended sexual science meeting. This SAR met the 10-hour requirement for AASECT CEs against our better judgment for what should be the optimal length of 15–16 hours for a SAR. However, having an evening session before the all-day SAR, on the day that the conference opened with its evening plenary, proved to be a successful formula. We had no indication of the background for the group as the SSSS conference staff managed all registrations. However, we learned during group introductions that there were sexuality educators, a cohort of sexual medicine physicians and nursing staff from one exemplary medical program, a few sex therapists, and sex coaches in the mix. Our 16 participants came from all over the United States and Canada.

It took months of preparation to find a local colleague who would act as our Arizona Host Coordinator (AHC), who secured a local (and what turned out to be a very famous) BDSM dungeon meeting space to host our group off-site for the evening portion of the SAR. We enjoyed seeing our participants squirm with delight at the dungeon upon our arrival. There we were shown the list of etiquette rules for the opening segment, followed by demonstrations of different sensory techniques at three different play stations, along with refreshments and a grand tour of the enormous warehouse-style facility. The next full day allowed for personal sharing, media, and experiential activities, but most prominent was the speaker panel of three older trans women of African American heritage, all of whom were eloquent and moving presenters about their arduous journeys to becoming accepted as trans women in a hostile community. This particular SAR left us weeping with compassion and relieved that despite not being able to vet our speakers ourselves, the riveting stories they told fulfilled our dreams to provide a high-level SAR that changed attitudes, values, and beliefs, while opening the hearts and minds of a diverse group of sexology professionals. Once again, SAR showed the humanity of all who deserve our attention in sexology.

Living the SAR Life

One of the most challenging participants we have had in a SAR was not due to her resistance, but thanks to her own remarkable life and how broadly she participated in the infinite realms of sexual expression and identity. There was seemingly nothing that Eye had not done or tried. Every SAR topic possible was one she knew, without grandstanding with the SAR group. Instead of trying to present new information or engage her in fresh experiences, we engaged her instantly as SAR assistant. Her contributions elevated that Los Angeles-based SAR, as she openly shared from her unique perspectives as a real-life expert, one who represented the Lived Experience of so many aspects of sexuality. Eye was polyamorous and lived in a sexually open commune; she participated in BDSM, having brought equipment with her on the flight to Los Angeles to play at the local dungeon. She showed her set of specially handcrafted elk-skin floggers before she demonstrated them at the BDSM club later that night on Dunlap (don't worry, with his consent). Eye had participated in the realms of sexual magic and shamanic practices; but beyond the sexological possibilities, she was also earning a mainstream master's degree in counseling/therapy and had already opened a private practice where she worked with trans clients and focused on the kinky population. Eye was involved with many sex-positive organizations, and remains today one of our *SAR Stars*. Her life *was* a 24/7 SAR all in itself.

SUMMARY

In the next chapter, you will learn about how to get ready to design and lead your own SAR, following our suggested guidelines. In it we will cover our version of what should constitute SAR criteria and share some of our sticky points about SAR. We will also provide you with distinctions between Basic and Advanced SAR, including an overview of our own SAR For Grown-Ups. In Chapter 5 you can read about taboo topics and decide how you want to proceed.

NOTES

1. It has since been acquired by The Chicago School of Professional Psychology.
2. The Culver Hotel is an historic site where many past celebrities of Hollywood fame, and the entire cast of Munchkins from *The Wizard of Oz* (made in 1939), have stayed; it was the "movie making mecca in the 1920s."
3. Los Angeles International Airport.
4. Well-known adult star and frequent presenter on pornography.
5. Three of whom were Sex Coach U students.

References and Resources

Affordable Care Act USA. (n.d.). Retrieved July 16, 2016, from http://www.hhs.gov/healthcare/about-the-law/read-the-law/

Almodovar, N. J. (1994). *From cop to call girl*. New York, NY: Avon.

Amsterdam.info. (n.d.). Red light district Amsterdam. Retrieved July 16, 2016, from http://www.amsterdam.info/red-light-district/

Art of Contemporary Shibari. (n.d.). Retrieved July 16, 2016, from http://www.artofcontemporaryshibari.com/?page_id=29

Beate Uhse. (n.d.). Retrieved July 16, 2016, from http://www.beate-uhse.ag/index.php/the-story.html

Buck Angel documentary. (n.d.). Retrieved July 16, 2016, from http://www.imdb.com/title/tt2387132/

Cannabis liberation day festival. (n.d.). Retrieved July 16, 2016, from http://www.dutch-passion.com/en/news-and-development/cannabis-liberation-day-festival-june-16th-Amsterdam-free-admission/

Center for Positive Sexuality. (2016). Sex positive education & research. Retrieved July 16, 2016, http://positivesexuality.org/

Culver City Hotels. (2016). Experience a historic, boutique hotel in Culver City, California. Retrieved July 16, 2016, from http://CulverHotel.com

Della Costa, C. (2016). These insurers offer transgender health care coverage. The Cheat Sheet. N.p. Retrieved July 16, 2016, from http://www.cheatsheet.com/personal-finance/these-insurers-offer-transgender-health-care-coverage.html/?a=viewall
Hardy Haberman. (n.d.). Retrieved July 16, 2016, from https://en.wikipedia.org/wiki/Hardy_Haberman
Home. (n.d.). Candida Royalle. Retrieved July 16, 2016, from http://candidaroyalle.com/
Hooper, T. [Director]. (2015). *The Danish Girl*. Universal Studios.
The Institute for Sexual Health. (2016). Providing psychological services and training for professionals in clinical sexology including sex addiction and compulsive-abusive sexual-relational disorders and is the founder of the sex addiction induced trauma model. Retrieved July 16, 2016, http://theinstituteforsexualhealth.com/
Jagiellonian University. (n.d.). Retrieved July 16, 2016, from https://en.wikipedia.org/wiki/Jagiellonian_University
LAGC. (2016). Retrieved July 16, 2016, http://lagendercenter.com/
Margaret Sanger. (n.d.). Retrieved September 19, 2016, from https://en.wikipedia.org/wiki/Margaret_Sanger
Martinez, M. (2016). Visit the world's 12 sexiest museums. Retrieved July 16, 2016, from http://abcnews.go.com/Travel/worlds-kinkiest-sex-museums/story?id=10081617
Nina Hartley. (n.d.). Retrieved July 16, 2016, from https://en.wikipedia.org/wiki/Nina_Hartley
SexCoachU. (n.d.). Retrieved July 16, 2016, http://SexCoachU.com
SexMachinesMuseum official site. (n.d.). Retrieved July 16, 2016, from http://www.sexmachinesmuseum.com/
Sex positive institute. (n.d.). Retrieved July 16, 2016, from http://en.sexpositiveinstitute.pl/
Sexual health and sexual rights for all. (n.d.). Retrieved July 16, 2016, from http://worldsexology.org/
Society for the Scientific Study of Sexuality. (2016). Retrieved November 28, 2016, from http://sexscience.org/Therian. (n.d.). Retrieved July 16, 2016, from http://www.urbandictionary.com/define.php?term=therian
Tulip Gardens. (n.d.). Retrieved July 16, 2016, from http://www.keukenhof.nl/en/
Whelehan, P., & Bolin, A. (Eds.). (2015). *International encyclopedia of human sexuality* (Vol. 1, A-G, pp. 63–64). Oxford: Wiley Blackwell.
Woodhull Sexual Freedom Summit. (n.d.). Retrieved July 16, 2016, from https://www.sexualfreedomsummit.org/
World Professional Association for Transgender Health. (2016). Retrieved July 16, 2016, from http://www.wpath.org/

Part Two

Designing Your SAR

5

Preparation Time

What You Need to Know and Do as a SAR Leader

"The difference between pornography and erotica is lighting."

—*Gloria Leonard*

Chapter 6's SAR Leader's Tool Kit is a guide for you to use in planning ahead. In the next chapter, you will begin to conceptualize your design and assure that all parts are accounted for. It takes time, vision, hard work, and good planning to produce a SAR. For now, let's take a look at the options for a successful SAR and how you will fulfill your vision. SAR guidelines have varied over time, from the IASHS in San Francisco as the birthplace of SAR in the 1970s with its 80+-hour programs, to criteria that have been developed by several constellations of other experts on committees at AASECT (and elsewhere). These experts are dedicated to setting professional standards of excellence for SAR. To date, no specific criteria from the AASECT Board of Directors have been finalized. When you are ready to mount your SAR and if you wish to offer AASECT CEs, you will want to stop by their website and obtain the necessary guidelines for meeting their criteria to offer CEs to your groups.

BASIC SAR

What is a Basic SAR Model? There has been discussion over the years among professionals in sexology about how many hours meet requirements for a SAR and what constitutes the basics. In our thinking, a Basic SAR is what we offer at this time as our main model for an average of a 16-hour SAR. Others claim that 10 hours, what AASECT currently requires as the minimum number of hours for a SAR, is ample. We disagree. Our gold-standard SAR is structured with approximately 40% in media, 40% in speakers from the Lived Experience, and 20% in small group process. This model takes place over a 2-day[1] span with an overnight stay (as a requirement) and limits attendance to a maximum of 24 people. In addition, we always offer an evening field trip, as you have read about, to round out the experiential aspects of what SAR should provoke for participants.

Remember that field trips are always optional. Occasionally you will want to integrate the field trip into your daily activities. We discussed what we provided for Prague in Chapter 4. Ultimately, it is the participant's choice as to whether or not to indulge in a possibly triggering experience, such as seeing consenting adults in compromising acts, positions, or encounters, or even allowing sensual play with themselves. Participants have complained (very rarely) about the quality of an adult venue such as a local strip club for the noise factor or cost of alcohol, or about the actions of certain BDSM practitioners who appeared to be ignoring boundaries in their sadistic play, or about not being able to get a sizeable enough discount at a sex toy boutique. We are clear from the onset that we literally have no control over external venues, and yet we offer them anyway.

ADVANCED SAR

Some SAR leaders prefer the model of offering an Advanced SAR, again a term that has no universally agreed-upon definition. The concept of providing a more extreme experience is one that may have merit, for those in sexology who have already attended a Basic SAR and are seeking a refresher course. Advanced SAR may also apply to those professionals working in the field of human sexuality who have years of experience and exposure to a wide range of sexual expression, yet have never attended a SAR. After researching our key sources, few of them are offered in the United States.

Our good friend Bill Stayton continues to offer SAR programs at the Basic and Advanced levels. He customizes the SAR for each group, such as for churches, medical professionals, psychotherapists, families, all-gay, all-lesbian, all-transgender, or any constellation that may ask him to design a SAR. Basic SAR includes six standard components that are tailored according to the unique needs of each audience, as follows: self-pleasure or masturbation, body image, sexual orientation, gender expression/identity, aging, and disability. Often he will ask the group to define what is normal or natural sexuality for them. Next he shows them a variety of media, then asks them to compare the viewing experience to their definitions of normalcy, eliciting their feelings and attitudes. Stayton remarks, "Our regular SAR covers everyday things that everyone has to cope with. Our Advanced SAR is more extreme and follows my driving construct that the Universe is a sexual turn-on." Topics cover sex in its many dimensions, such as with animals, with animate or inanimate objects, and the role of spirituality (2016). We love how this approach normalizes sexual behavior and expression in such a gentle and accepting paradigm. Another major aspect of these SAR programs or SAR-based classes addresses Universal Sexual Rights as a pivotal landing place for self-assessment of values, attitudes, and beliefs. Stayton presents topical material, then asks participants to evaluate, "Where among the World Health Organization's statement of Universal Sexual Rights does this topic fit?" We ourselves promote the World Association of Sexual Health (WAS) Declaration of Sexual Rights that was last published in 2014.

Another significant proponent of the combination of both Basic and Advanced SAR is Chris Thrasher, a Stayton protégée. After having attended over 15 SARs since the 1990s, including the 2-day mini-SAR at IASHS, and conference-attached SARs for AASECT or SSSS, he replicated Stayton's methods. In his opinion, none are outdated or ineffectual today. Most notable is his role as the Director of the Center of Excellence for Sexual Health at Morehouse School of Medicine from 2003–2015, under the leadership of former US Surgeon General David Satcher. Thrasher led SARs as a part of the 10-month-long residency fellowship program for training medical professionals, in which SAR has since been abandoned as a component of the required program content. It was under Surgeon General Satcher's leadership that *The Surgeon General's Call to Action to Promote Sexual Health and Responsible Sexual Behavior* (n.d.) was published, bringing to prominence sexual health for Americans. As the website (Office of the Surgeon General, n.d.) states about this landmark 2001 publication: "This Call to Action provides an evidence based foundation for developing a public health approach to sexual health and responsible sexual behavior." These same themes of sexual rights are human rights and an approach toward sexual health infuse most well-constructed SARs today.

DESIGNER SAR

Similar to an Advanced SAR, a Designer SAR format may be offered. One outstanding program is the Silver SAR™, which is a specialty SAR designed to serve those who work with the elderly that addresses only sexuality and aging as its theme. This is one of the types of target-specific approaches to SAR that could be applicable for both professionals and consumers alike. Co-creator/leader[2] Wayne Pawlowski (2016) remarks that most of the participants on the three such SilverSAR™ programs thus far were sexology professionals, despite its aim to serve long-term care facility providers and staff. One of the barriers to attracting that genre of professionals to attend a SAR is the lack of time in their busy schedules and the lack of priority importance given to meeting the sexuality needs of their residents. Sadly, serving sexuality needs of older persons in most elder-care facilities is not a high priority, and remains one of the unmet need areas in sexology overall. Much of the content of a SilverSAR™ is like any other SAR, with an emphasis on self-awareness, attitudes, and beliefs around aging. Components include: how participants feel before and after about their own status of aging; watching media images of age-gap relationships, bodily changes over time, and different constellations of coupling; LGBT issues related to aging; the ravages of Alzheimer's and other debilitating diseases; institutional issues for residential care around intimacy, sex, and relationships; and the presentation of a special film[3] that we ourselves have seen years ago, about an aging woman in a nursing home environment with a need and desire for intimacy and emotional connection. SilverSAR™ is a wonderful chance for participants to explore their values, attitudes, and beliefs focused on this one theme of aging and sexuality in its many dimensions.

SilverSAR™ programs to date were located at Widener University in Pennsylvania. The university houses the Sexuality & Aging Consortium (SAC), which provides a wide range of services as a leading force for advocacy, education, training, policy development, and "support for professionals and students interested in sexuality and aging" (2016). Leadership of the SAC also presents an all-day institute on sexuality and aging as a significant component of the Woodhull Sexual Freedom Summit. In the 1980s, Britton designed the format and content for an all-gay-male SAR for the Gay Men's Health Crisis in New York. In addition, ideas have been presented to offer a SAR focused exclusively on BDSM or Trans, including media, speakers, field trips, and small group facilitators from those respective communities.

One such Designer SAR stands out, which was conducted in 2013 for Walter Reed Military Medical Center's (2016) Working Group for Sexual Health and Intimacy for Wounded Warriors. Led by sexologist Miletski, this is a touching example of customizing the essence of SAR to de-sensitize and re-sensitize professionals working with a specific population. In this SAR model, Miletski focused on staff who address the physical and mental sexual health needs of returning veterans of war. Her approach to this specialty SAR included multiple self-awareness exercises, such as getting the group to begin talking about sex and mining childhood memories of learning about sex, with discussions on masturbation, sexual orientation, body image, and most notably sexuality and disability as the core of their work. As she puts it so aptly, "Focus on what's important. Start with the basics, establishing a comfort level and openness. Gradually take the participants into deeper levels of interest with an escalation toward out-of-the-box topics, such as polyamory, paraphilias, and confrontations around significant body image issues." This gradual approach often only happens in the luxury of longer times for a SAR, not with today's inherent pressures of time constraints in providing a wide variety of content in short formats. Miletski adamantly agrees with us that 10 hours for a SAR is insufficient time in which to adequately process what is required of a SAR experience.

Another form of a designer SAR is offered by Stephanie Mitelman, a well-respected Canadian sexuality educator. Having offered SAR programs for over a decade, she relies on a speakers-only format with a heavy infusion of small group process dialogue time. When asked about this approach and why she never included the viewing of media, she responded, "It never occurred to us to do it any other way." As she emphasizes, ". . . videos are one-directional with no interactivity and no opportunity for participants to ask questions. In the safe space of her SAR people can ask all the questions that they were never allowed to ask before, without feeling dumb or politically incorrect" (2016). Attendees also have a chance to speak with the presenters and pose questions to have them elaborate on their story, creating a free exchange of ideas and experiences. That freedom is what SAR is all about.

NUDE SAR

Another approach to consider is offering a clothing-optional experience. IASHS elaborate and elongated 6- or 8-day SAR programs include time for sharing conversation and learning while being *au naturel*. Being naked yet non-sexual in front of your peers can be the last frontier in the de-armoring of the sexual self. Nudity is not inherently sexual. In fact, naturists who enjoy socializing, playing athletics, eating meals, and relaxing in nudist resorts often report how de-sexualizing the experience can be. The ability to feel our natural self, in our skins, without pretense or the defenses of make-up, clothing, and socially prescribed details of an assumed role through our visual presentation, are often the results of shared nudity in a public setting. That is not to say that a commercial nude or clothing optional resort cannot be intended to ignite sexual desire and serve as a place to meet like-minded others. One example is Hedonism clubs in Jamaica, which feature the *nude* and *prude* sides of the resort. Guess which one Advanced SAR leaders might prefer. Noted researcher and sex therapist Marilyn D. Story studied social nudism in depth and presented in one journal that "Much popular belief connects nudism with sexually permissive behaviors, but researchers have shown that social nudists have strict sexual conduct rules and that social nudists mentally separate nudity and sex, seeing nude bodies as 'natural' and 'pure' rather than sexually arousing . . . (my research) results illustrate that the sexual implications of nudity vary among people and that there is no direct relationship between nudity and sexually permissive behaviors" (1987, abstract). Barkan (2015) also describes that the origins of social nudism actually rest on the assumption that clothing provoked sexual or erotic meanings to nudity, declaring "that modesty and shame were a social imposition" (p. 829). Nudism could act as a remedy for these conditions, evidence that we find to be accurate from our own experiences both as individuals and as professionals.

SAR FOR GROWN-UPS

Our own Advanced model is our SAR for Grown-Ups, or, as we call it, *Advanced Sexual Personal Exploration Xperience* (ASPEX). As Britton's website (2016a) states for its deliverables:

> *ASPEX is an experiential personal journey of sexual self-discovery. The week-long experience will accomplish the following outcomes:*

- *Expand our boundaries about what we feel about sex, sexuality, and sexual expression*
- *Enrich our acceptance of sexual humans—oneself and others*
- *Illuminate our fundamental sexual needs as persons first then as clinicians or educators for others*
- *Empower us as sex-positive change agents*
- *Lavish ourselves with joyful shared connection and a pathway to personal sexual ecstasy*
- *Enable Sexual Self Realization as the ultimate result*
- *Experience emotional clearing of past wounds*
- *Engage in the exploration of female/male genitals and SRC*
- *Discover how to move into a state of personal embodiment*
- *Learn sensual movement and touch for personal liberation*
- *Acquire a plethora of techniques for freeing the sexual self*
- *Discover a community of like-minded, openhearted, soulful peers*
- *Meet world leaders in personal growth, erotic exploration and sensual awakening*
- *Explore BDSM practices in a safe supportive environment*
- *Learn specific tools for self soothing*
- *Gain high level tools for freeing the old blocks to sexual bliss*
- *Enjoy a natural setting and healthy lifestyle*
- *Find means for enlarging your network*
- *Learn to describe your own work and how to maximize its impact*
- *Be available to treasure being in the present moment and much more . . .*

ASPEX follows Britton's MEBES© model as its theme and uses the shamanic MEBES wheel as the center of all process work in the space: MIND—learning what you need to know; EMOTIONS—exploring your feelings: BODY—recognizing your sexual patterns and awakening your body; ENERGY/SPIRIT—accessing energy and evoking spirituality.

Our FOCUS includes the following elements: debunking myths; de-shaming; unraveling personal blockages; liberating body-based sexual energies; building sexual intelligence; finding balance in giving/receiving; soaring into sacred space; touching spiritual freedom; exploring touch in safe space; unleashing sensuality; finding your sexual voice; and joyful play.

This training is a journey in self-discovery toward sexual self-realization, through mini-lectures and demonstrations, self-awareness techniques, personal journal writing, dyads, small and whole group discussions, experiential exercises, playful art expression, movement and dance, sounding, shamanic drumming and journeying, sexologically-based bodywork and sacred ceremony. Using the MEBES mandala wheel system, you will discover sexual healing for yourself and how to apply this system with your clients or your own sexual experience. Expert speakers will present their areas of specialization during three of the 5 days. Nudity will be part of the event. No sexual touching without consent will occur without permission of participants involved. This is an advanced training. No one will be permitted to attend without an approved application. No one is permitted to participate who cannot attend all 5 days or the full training. No late arrivals or early departures are allowed to protect the integrity and safety of the 'container' for this group.

We have led two consecutive ASPEX events at a rural retreat center in Poland. In 2017 ASPEX will be offered in the Czech Republic. Newcomers and return students find profound healing and personal enrichment in this predominantly experiential (not didactic) weeklong learning opportunity.

HIGHLIGHTS FROM ASPEX (ADVANCED SEXOLOGICAL PERSONAL EXPLORATION XPERIENCE)

The venue of a rural retreat setting promotes healing, growth, intimacy, relaxation, and letting go, all tenets of ASPEX. Being in physical residence together in one building and sharing all meals at the communal table helps to promote a feeling of extended family and intense bonding and, for many, establishes lifelong relationships. An average of 20 professionals have attended ASPEX thus far each of its two years. People have come from the UK and Eastern European regions, Africa, United States, and Europe. Attendees represented the disciplines of sex education, mental health, and healing arts professions, along with somatic practitioners, tantra leaders, sacred movement experts, and dance therapists.

Interactions are intimate, including disclosure of past deep wounding for a full day of emotional clearing. Non-sexual, therapeutic bodywork is available on site, as often massage therapists are members of the paid staff. Having clothing-optional participation in exploratory activities promotes a more advanced arena for growth and expression than a Basic SAR might otherwise offer. Examples include the guided trust walk through the woods or the genital self-viewing process that occurs after comprehensive lectures on sexual anatomy along with body awareness exercises. This form of education shows the uniqueness within the spectrum of human sexual anatomy. We have had volunteers as live nude models for a *Full Monty* and *Vulva Parade*, enlightening others and providing a rare chance to view others' human genitals in the safe container of an educationally relevant setting that honors and respects all personal boundaries.

One of the highlights of ASPEX is a replication of our doctoral-level training offered at the IASHS. In respect for our students, like at IASHS, we as faculty are dedicated to creating ample time for any activity that takes a person into a vulnerable introspective state. At ASPEX events, we lead a whole-body Mirror Activity for all participants who choose to do so. Each person (nude or semi-clothed) steps up to the mirror on the wall in front of the entire group; they then state what they see and like about each part of their own body in the presence of someone who is standing next to them as a supportive figure for this potentially frightening process of personal disclosure. The Mirror Activity often produces sobbing or other catharses. It can be transformational, liberating the innermost self-loathing to melt into positive self-acceptance. The Mirror Activity forms one of the cornerstones for sexually related client work on body dysmorphic disorder (2016) and helps to restructure harmful self-deprecating inner dialogue about body image.

That said, much of the discussions prior to engaging in any nudity or touch is part of a detailed workshop and flowing conversations on consent for touch. This workshop is based on the work of Betty Martin, using the Wheel of Consent template (2016), and was taught by an expert from the UK who studied her methodologies. Consensual negotiations frame the appropriate behaviors and set the tone for healthy boundaries. The element of consent opens up the possibilities for pure exchanges, authentic growth, and enhancement of pleasure. Movement classes, art expression, and dynamic discussions in small groups add to the dimensions of personal sexological exploration. Pre-assigned ASPEX *buddies* help to create a sense of community and avert isolation among attendees. Part of the curriculum at ASPEX invites outside experts, such as a BDSM half-day teaching and laboratory experience, a dance and movement personal trust exploration segment known as Biodanza (Dance Biodanza, 2016), and sensual touch activities. All of these are governed by extensive talk, sharing of boundary-setting, and liberation for pleasure. ASPEX is not for newcomers to the field of sexology. Rather, it is a one-of-a-kind enrichment environment in which significant personal and professional growth can rapidly change a person's realization of their authentic sexual self.

Our Graduates Speak Out

"ASPEX is a transformative, powerful, healing experience, one that deserves a place in your annual calendar. ASPEX for me is 5 days of extreme self care—a chance to heal and rejuvenate myself . . . In 2016, ASPEX had a huge impact on my life—I was able to release old anger that I was carrying with me. I felt so safe and cared for in the container of the group. Once I was past this block, it's like the world opened up anew—I felt myself getting curious again, and I felt myself getting back in touch with my sexual self—my source of great personal power and pleasure!" **Sarah Martin**, Certified Sex Coach, Warsaw, Poland

"ASPEX was a well-structured training that involved deep self-discovery in the context of safe and nurturing environment. It proved that, getting embodied results in better relationships with ourselves and, ultimately, with others. What touched me most was the presence of people of very different ages and backgrounds. All were willing to share their experiences, struggles,

challenges, insights, and the things that they are proud of. ASPEX is intense learning and role-modeling which has great transformational impact" **Natalia Flak**, Couples Therapist, Sex Coach, www.e-sexcoach.pl

"ASPEX was a journey deep into my sexual soul. Dr. Britton is an exquisitely powerful guide and healer. The experience of ASPEX touched each of us and connected us to ourselves and each other in beautifully profound ways, each uniquely our own and deliciously ours as a community" **Celina Criss, PhD**, Sexologist/Sex Coach, Munich, Germany

TABOO TOPICS

Before you dig right in to design your SAR in the next chapter, think well about some of the more controversial, if not taboo, topics. These may seem like relevant topics to include, but adding them into your repertoire of media, and perhaps inviting speakers who can express their paraphilic proclivities, could backfire against you during or after the SAR. You will want to test out whether or not you add in topics such as zoophilia, adult-child sexuality, or the infamous *snuff films*. Let us unpack this.

Bestiality and Zoophilia

One of the most negatively charged topics is *beastiality* or *zoophilia*. Our good friend and respected sex therapist, Hani Miletski (2002, p. 6), defines the two terms this way:

I use the term "bestiality" as "any sexual contact between a human being and a non-human animal," and the term "zoophilia" as "an emotional attachment and/or sexual attraction to an animal." A "bestialist" is a person who engages in sexual relations with animals, and a "zoophile" is "a person who has an emotional attachment and/or sexual attraction to an animal."

Miletski (2002, pp. 46–49) studied this population for her doctoral dissertation and discovered that the exact percentage of people who have erotic/sexual leanings toward or sexually active behaviors with animals is difficult to determine (Beetz, 2004), based on the stigma and fears surrounding disclosing this part of one's sexual interests. In an interview with Miletski about the need to show explicit media footage of zoophilic practices at a SAR, she claims, "I view this as a sexual orientation. It is not some fetish or unhealthy behavior. It is how a person is wired . . . and it is much more common than you may think" (2016). "Writing in the 1940's, famed sexual researcher Alfred Kinsey estimated that 8% of men and 3.6% of women had engaged in some sort of sexual act with an animal . . . (while) . . . a later study in 1974 by Morton M. Hunt put the prevalence of men and women having intimate relations with animals at 4.9% and 1.9% respectively" (Health24.com, 2015).

"There is no federal law which explicitly prohibits sex between humans and animals" (Lectlaw.com, 2016). Legal rulings are governed by state or country. Check your local laws to assure you are within the rules of your jurisdiction. In our home state of California, it is a misdemeanor to use animals for a human's sexual gratification, with up to 6 months jail time and a $1,000 fine for doing so if caught. Most states in the US pose hefty fines and jail terms for a variety of definitions of human-animal sexual encounters for human pleasure.[4]

Although ownership of zoophilic pornography is legal within California, transporting it across state borders is not. We have been strongly advised by legal advisors not to transport anywhere media that may contain explicit imagery of human-animal sexual contact. According to the extensive page on Wikipedia, in the (liberally minded) state of California, it is legal to possess zoophilic pornography, legal to sell it within state borders, and illegal to engage in interstate sales. Zoophilia itself is deemed illegal but the videotaping or photographing of zoophilic pornography is legal. Due to its controversial nature, it may be difficult to ascertain if this is a topic for you or not.

One research study (Cerrone, 1991, p. 29) showed that bestiality is frequently found in rural areas due to a wide variety of circumstantial factors, such as young pubertal men in rural settings who may encounter their first coital experience with farm animals, often replicating the size and feel of humans (Beetz, 2004, pp. 20–21). (We are not promoting this, merely reporting it to you now, as Kinsey would report on what he collected as data.) You may or may not agree about including SAR media footage of human-animal sexual contact even though it is one of the paraphilias in human sexuality. It is difficult to obtain unbiased examples of this genre, with a few exceptions.

Here is one example: Aside from the legal risks of transporting zoophilic explicit footage, in our local SARs we used to show (with permission) a 1970s documentary of an adult woman in Scandinavia who is documented engaging in penetrative sex with her farm animals. Her pets consisted of a large dog, a boar, and a black stallion, none of whom were muzzled or fully restrained. We have shown clips from this film (reduced to several minutes from its original 90-minute length) to groups of psychologists who found great compassion for the humans who seek out animal lovers, often because they lack opportunity or are psychologically or socially underdeveloped to find companions of the human species. We have taught other professionals who balked, complained, and threatened us for promotion of animal abuse. The zoophilic portrayals generated painful push-back among participants who resented being forced to watch animals in sexual encounters with human partners, without consent.[5] Thus, we stopped showing this important aspect of human sexual expression. It became too stressful for the audience and especially taxing for us as SAR leaders. You will have to formulate your own decision as to what you show and how you will respond to fallout.

Sex with Vegetables

Whether or not it was folklore or an old law on the books when Britton attended IASHS in 1989, another controversial topic was the act of penetrating human sexual orifices with vegetables. Many of us as sexuality educators from the 1970s may recall a hand-mimeographed booklet that circulated throughout the Planned Parenthood network, *Why Cucumbers Are Better Than Men*, now a book at Amazon (1983). Having sex with vegetables is probably as normal as commercial farming or the home garden plot, but it was said that inserting an ear of corn into a female's vagina in pornography was potentially risking violation of California's agricultural law. To date, that information is not available online. Stay clear of ancient or current laws that may pose a legal threat if you are caught showing such behaviors, as we have seen in the 100 hours of explicit pornographic footage that we were required to watch and analyze as part of our doctoral training. In her book *Simple Sexy Food™* our friend and expert talks about the historical origins and common uses of aphrodisiac foods and erotic cooking, including the vegetable ingredients necessary for preparation of sexually evocative meals and libations (DeVillers, 2012).

Violence and Snuff Films

An enormous amount and variety of fetish media exists in the world today, some of which appear to be disgusting and appalling, such as blood sports or scatological play (aka behaviors eroticizing poop or feces). On occasions we may show clips of each, often disguised in clever lighting or post-production special effects such as in *Beyond Vanilla,* Dunlap's groundbreaking documentary on BDSM/kink/fetish.

Perhaps the most frightening and alarming of all possible media is the genre known as *snuff or murder media,* which to us ranks near the top of the list of media to avoid. We to date have never found such media, nor do we wish to include it in our roster of media montages. A debate still exists about whether snuff films, in which people are murdered on camera for the viewer's sexual gratification, exist. Whether they do or not, that topic raises too many concerns, legally, ethically, and morally. Assume (as we do) that such a film would be illegal, subject to seizure and prosecution. It is best to avoid this genre altogether. The patterns of sexual serial killers are something for the psychology communities to try to understand, but few of us as sexologists are going to ever want to watch the behaviors live or in depictions thereof. Some of you may work as criminologists, forensic sexologists, or therapists, and you may want to treat those killers as your patients. If so, watching media may enrich your understanding, or not. In the 1990s, Britton was an expert witness for a case against an adult store owner in which it was claimed that pornography in his stores contained and promoted imagery linked to violence. Her study found that the ubiquitous R-rated genre of *slasher* films, such as *I Spit On Your Grave* (Zarchi, 1978), showed far more violent depictions than porn. Her findings revealed that less than 1% of the porn in her extensive study contained any pseudo-violent images or behaviors. The content of much media today that is broadcast on the Internet for free, on television, and in films contains far more explicit violence than most adult entertainment even today. We try to avoid violence in media, with rare exceptions, such as clips from the American version (Fincher, 2011) of *The Girl with the Dragon Tattoo*. From this film, we have shown both the male-female rape and the female-male rape vengeance scenes for their shocking effect. These two clips make for rousing SAR discussion material!

One horror story told to us by a trusted colleague was about a SAR in which the SAR leader showed an alleged *snuff film*.[6] While it was playing, the SAR leader dashed out of the training room, remarking that she could not handle the material. To us, she abandoned the room for her own mental health while leaving her attendees bankrupt of correct role-modeling and appropriate leadership. Her role was to create a safe container and to manage it. If materials are upsetting, too extreme, or make you sick, think about having a small group facilitator keep watch over the group or avoid showing that media altogether. Leaving the SAR room sends a message about your values, but nothing about theirs. SAR is not for the faint of heart or for sissies. (Unless, of course, we are talking about sissy boy play, as we did in Chapter 4.) Sometimes your selection of media will shift over time, and trial and error will be your guide.

Adult-Child Sex[7] / Child Pornography

One of the most dangerous topics to include in a SAR in the United States is that of adult-child sex or children in sexual depictions (often called *Kiddie Porn)*, by showing explicit imagery either in print or video formats. Laws dictate legal behaviors and vary widely, especially with children under 10 years of age (NDAA, 2016). As cited from the *Citizen's Guide To U.S. Federal Law On Child Pornography*: "Images of child pornography are not protected under First Amendment rights, and are illegal contraband under federal law. Section 2256 of Title 18, United States Code, defines child pornography as any visual depiction of sexually explicit conduct involving a minor (someone under 18 years of age) Jul 6, 2015."

Visual depictions include photographs, videos, digital or computer generated images indistinguishable from an actual minor, and images created, adapted, or modified, but appear to depict an identifiable, actual minor. Undeveloped film, undeveloped videotape, and electronically stored data that can be converted into a visual image of child pornography are also deemed illegal visual depictions under federal law (U.S. Department of Justice, 2016).

The laws in the United States are clearly stated, and child pornography is illegal and censored in most parts of the world, with serious consequences for producers, distributors, or users of child pornography in any forms (Wikipedia, 2016). Anyone who intends to enter into this dangerous topic zone should consult their own attorney, as no depiction of minors' sexuality is legal in the United States, and the age of legal adulthood varies from state to state. Images that depict underage performers using adult actors can be construed in this category of illegal materials (DeWitt, 2015, p. 964). As faculty at IASHS, we have been specifically trained as Certified Erotologists in a post-doctoral course on the handling of sexually explicit materials. Even with that one layer of protection, we do not show still or moving images of children being naked or in seductive poses or in sexual acts (illegal in California[8]). Instead, we may consider inviting a speaker panel to discuss the impact on adults from viewing or engaging in acts with children. In some less developed societies, adult-child rites of passage continue to be common parts of adolescence and part of those cultural norms. But norms are changing and laws are expanding to protect children globally. If you are thinking of having a SAR that features the topic of adult-child sex, kiddie porn, pedophilia, or relevant aspects of children and sexuality, we suggest that you proceed with care and caution.

One of our respected peers, the Rev. Dr. Stayton, who is mentioned earlier in this chapter, does in fact show childhood sexual depictions as part of his methodologies. Having served as an expert witness in many legal cases that involved pedophilic behaviors, especially with priests and clergy caught in sexual acts with youth, he emphasizes that a SAR is developed to allow individuals to assess their values and boundaries. He shows a wide range of depictions, such as explicit sculptures from his travels to Italy that are banned in the USA, portraits, pictures, paintings through the ages (including from the Sistine Chapel), pictures of youth from a *nudist colony*, and magazines from the extensive legal collection at the IASHS, while escalating imagery into more and more explicit levels. He challenges SAR participants to ask themselves, "Where do you draw the line? Where does this become harmful to children or youth?" (2016). What is so astounding is that some don't ever draw a line, and others do so at different markers along the spectrum. Stayton's premise is that everyone needs to know where they draw the line, including members of a jury, court judges, lawyers, or sex experts. Materials that were lawful in the 1970s and 1980s may not be lawful today, so this is a risky area in which to engage your audience. Only you can decide whether or not to enter into this arena and for what purpose.

GRIEVANCE POLICY AND PROCEDURE

If you are offering Continuing Education (CE) credits, or even if not, you will want to develop a clear statement of your Grievance Policy and Procedure. You may want to post it on your website as part of your pre-enrollment process. One example from Maze Health is beautifully articulated on their SAR website page (Maze Sexual and Reproductive Health, 2016), which addresses complaints about a possible ethical breach as a provider of AASECT CEs. This *SAR in the City* (labeled as Sexual Attitude Realignment) was led by another IASHS doctoral graduate, Bat Sheva Marcus, PhD (2016):

Grievance Protocol and Procedures
If you feel that a class or course or presenter has acted in violation of the AASECT Code of Professional Ethics please follow the following procedures:

- Participants are encouraged to talk directly to those with whom they have issues, to facilitate resolution without recourse to further procedures whenever possible.

If resolution is not achieved:

- Submit a complaint in writing to the event coordinator: Bat Sheva Marcus, Maze Women's Sexual Health, 2975 Westchester Avenue, Purchase NY, 10577.
- The Continuing Education director, will review this complaint with the other two workshop coordinators.
- If it is possible and the participant would like to attend this meeting in person, that opportunity will be made available. If not, the complaint in writing will be reviewed.
- If discussion is needed with counsel, that will be arranged.
- Within 30 days a written response will be provided.
- If the grievance is not adequately resolved, we encourage you submit your complaint in writing to your professional association: AASECT via their website: www.aasect.org/contact

Please note that innocence will be presumed unless proved otherwise and confidentiality will always be respected.

If you do not feel the course fulfilled the description as advertised and you would like a refund, please send your written complaint, (write us). A full refund will be provided and you will not receive the CEC credits.

Here is our own (Britton 2016b):

In the event of a complaint or grievance by a participant, Dr. Britton (as an AASECT Individual CE Provider) will:

a. work with the AASECT office to resolve the issue;
b. engage in a discussion with the participant to attempt to resolve the issue(s) related to the grievance;

c. offer a partial refund for the tuition based on the level of the complaint and how much of the event they attended overall;
d. if warranted, offer a full tuition refund;
e. in addition, Britton will offer alternative measures for assisting the participant to resolve the grievances they raise, such as offering a one-on-one mentoring session, additional resources on a case-by-case basis, and/or referral to alternative CE garnering events by Britton in lieu of the one offered. Furthermore, Britton will make recommendations for competent mental health professionals that may be able to provide more in depth psychological care for the aggrieved participant.

This has never occurred in nine years. However, we are prepared to handle such a situation should it happen. You should be prepared, too.

LIABILITY PROTECTION

You should secure your own professional liability insurance in case of injury on the premises. Policies must be in place, in the event that someone claims that your SAR has (re)traumatized them, that you ignored their complaints or wishes, or that you did not address their concerns that emerged in the SAR. Of course, there really is nothing you can do to prevent someone from having their own personal baggage accompany them into the SAR room and create harm for them and you. That is why we are so insistent on careful screenings through an application process before they are accepted as a participant at a SAR. SAR is for the healthy and stable person, not someone fresh out of rehab, coping with a sudden flood of re-activated memories of highly charged somatic or mental traumas, coping with a health/family/personal real-life crisis, or who is there begrudgingly just for the credits. There is no such thing as 100% prevention of someone reacting to the SAR and blaming you for it. SAR is designed to bring about a response. The media, field trips, and speaker panels are selected to push buttons that enable your participants to feel their feelings and confront their attitudes, values, beliefs, and boundaries. Small group is the container to allow them to process any upsets and feel more protected than in the whole group. You are going to want to be prepared and well trained to handle even the most volatile of personalities in SAR.

SAR ONLINE SURVEY 2016

In 2016, we conducted an online survey on Qualtrics.com, asking a series of questions to determine similarities or differences in comparing SAR training programs. Some were selected because they advertised Continuing Education programs on the AASECT website; others were previously well known to us.

After inviting 17 such SAR leaders worldwide, their insightful and customized responses are contained in the summary below of findings with highlights from their unique characteristics as SAR providers.

Among the 14 responders were (listed alphabetically) these SAR providers: Stephanie Buehler, Eli Coleman, Bat Sheva Marcus, Hani Miletski, Stephanie Mitelman, Sara Nasserzadeh, Wayne Pawloski, Justin Sitron, William Stayton, Chris Thrasher, Linda Wiener, Gerry Zientara, and Yi-Li Lin of Taiwan. Survey results showed a similarity among all SAR providers, with some exceptions, such as: the exclusion of media for the SARs offered by Mitelman; speakers were not present for Miletski at her Designer SAR for Walter Reed; and Coleman no longer uses SGFs as leaders for the small group process at his SARs. Highlights indicated that the average length of a SAR is 2 days, with a range from 1 to 5, often with a 3-hour evening session before an 8-hour full day. Over 63% offered SGFs, with 4 of 11 requiring participation at a previous SAR, some training by themselves, and others with no training required. Venues ranged from hotels with conference rooms to clinical suites, offices, and even two at homes. Most covered a full range of sexological topics, including trans, group sex, porn, fetish play, aging, polyamory, masturbation, hetero/homo/bisexual expression, and sex toys. Overall, respondents featured 45% media; use of speakers ranged from 10% to 90%; small group time ranged from 25% to 75%, with an average of 42%. Approximately 75% of them offered a field trip experience, such as to sex clubs, dungeons, or sex shops. Most used a quantitative Leikert-like assessment and many used pre-post testing, but not all. Over half required a post-SAR self-evaluation narrative to be sent back to the SAR leaders. Only 50% have a standing grievance policy and procedure. As you can see, SAR design varies widely, yet preserves the universal themes and content overall.

SUMMARY

In our next chapter, you are going to find the essence of what you need for designing and leading a SAR of your own, using the SAR Leader's Tool Kit. The Tool Kit serves as a handy workbook inside this book that will allow you to approach your SAR comprehensively and eventually manage it all. You will learn how to structure, plan, and dive into the nuances of 21 variables that relate to a successful SAR. We hope you are ready to spend some time and have fun!

NOTES

1. When possible, we offer a 2.5- or 3-day model or a week-long Basic SAR.
2. Co-creators also included Anita Hoffer and Joan Garrity.

3. "Rose by Any Other Name" (Allessandro, 1979; see Resources at end of chapter).
4. Is it almost impossible to determine if the animal in a sexual act with a human is experiencing sexual pleasure or gratification or what constitutes animal cruelty.
5. Consent by animals is probably impossible to determine; however, one measure is the animal behavior shown, such as the absence of biting, kicking, or outright killing the human in the process.
6. Britton's mentor and faculty advisor Laird Sutton at IASHS vehemently proclaimed that snuff films are a myth.
7. Also known as Pedophilia as a sexual orientation; a set of erotic or sexual behaviors.
8. And in many other locales if used or interpreted for erotic or sexually stimulating purposes.

References and Resources

Allessandro, R. [Director]. (1979). Rose by any other name [Video file]. Garden City, NY: The Center. Retrieved August 5, 2016, from http://dan-keller.com/tricepts/rose.html

Barkan, R. (2015). Nudism (A. Bolin, Ed.). In P. Whelehan (Ed.), *International encyclopedia of human sexuality* (pp. 828–830). Oxford, UK: Wiley Blackwell.

Beetz, A. M. (2004). Bestiality/Zoophilia: A scarcely investigated phenomenon between crime, paraphilia and love. *Journal of Forensic Psychology Practice*, *4*(2), 1–36. Retrieved July 16, 2016 from doi:10.1300/j158v04n02_01

Body dysmorphic disorder. (2016). Retrieved July 16, 2016, from http://www.mayoclinic.org/diseases-conditions/body-dysmorphic-disorder/home/ovc-20200935

Britton, P. (2015). Personal [doc].

Britton, P. (2016a). Home. Retrieved July 21, 2016, from http://drpattibritton.com

Britton, P. (2016b). Training events. Retrieved July 12, 2016, from http://drpattibritton.com/events/category/training/list/

Cerrone, G. H. (1991). Zoophilia in a rural population: Two case studies. *Journal of Rural Community Psychology*, *12*(1), 29–39.

The Cucumber Group. (1983). *Why cucumbers are better than men*. Lanham, MD: M. Evans and Co.

Dance Biodanza. (2016). Welcome. Retrieved July 16, 2016, from http://www.dancebiodanza.co.uk/dorset-school-of-biodanza/welcome-to-the-dorset-school-of-biodanza/

DeVillers, L. (2012). *Simple sexy food™*. El Segundo, CA: Aphrodite Media.

DeWitt, C. (2015). Pornography, laws regarding (A. Bolin, Ed.). In P. Whelehan (Ed.), *International encyclopedia of human sexuality* (pp. 960–965). Oxford, UK: Wiley Blackwell.

Fincher, D. [Director]. (2011). The girl with the dragon tattoo. Columbia.

Health24.com. (2015). Bestiality is much, much more common than you think. Retrieved July 16, 2016, from http://www.health24.com/Sex/Sexual-diversity/Bestiality-is-much-much-more-common-than-you-think-20150218

Lectlaw.com. (2016). Zoophilia & the law—laws around the world affecting zoophiles. Retrieved July 16, 2016, from http://www.lectlaw.com/files/sex13.htm

Martin, B. (n.d.). The wheel of consent, Betty Martin. Retrieved July 16, 2016, from http://bettymartin.org/videos/

Maze Sexual and Reproductive Health. (2016). Grievance protocol. Retrieved July 16, 2016, from http://www.mazehealth.com/sar-in-the-city/grievance-protocol/

Miletski, H. (2002). *Understanding bestiality and zoophilia*. Bethesda, MD: Hani Miletski.

Miletski, H. (2016). Personal conversation. August 24, 2016.Mitelman, S. (2016). Personal conversation. September 14, 2016.

NDAA Web file [Pdf]. (n.d.). Retrieved July 14, 2016, from http://www.ndaa.org/pdf/ Sexual Offenses Against Children 2013.pdf#page=4&zoom=auto,-98,774

Office of the Surgeon General [US]. (n.d.). *The Surgeon General's call to action to promote sexual health and responsible sexual behavior*. Retrieved July 15, 2016, from https://www.ncbi.nlm.nih.gov/books/NBK44216/

Pawlowski, W. (2016). Personal conversation. August 3, 2016.

Sexuality and aging consortium. (n.d.). Retrieved July 14, 2016, from http://www.widener.edu/academics/schools/shsp/hss/sex_aging/about.aspx

Stayton, W. (2016). Personal conversation. August 31, 2016.

Story, M. D. (1987). A comparison of social nudists and non-nudists on experience with various sexual outlets [Abstract]. *Journal of Sex Research, 23*(2), 197–211. Retrieved July 14, 2016, from http://dx.doi.org/10.1080/00224498709551357

Thrasher, C. (2016). Personal conversation. September 2, 2016.

U.S. Department of Justice. (2016). *Citizen's guide to U.S. federal law on child pornography*. Retrieved July 14, 2016, from https://www.justice.gov/criminal-ceos/citizens-guide-us-federal-law-child- pornography

Walter Reed National Military Medical Center. (2016). Retrieved August 26, 2016, from http://www.wrnmmc.capmed.mil/SitePages/home.aspx

World Association of Sexual Health. (2014). Declaration of sexual rights. Retrieved September 1, 2016, from http://www.worldsexology.org/wp-content/uploads/2013/08/declaration_of_sexual_rights_sep03_2014.pdf

Zarchi, M. [Director]. (1978). I spit on your grave. Cinemagic Pictures.

6

The SAR Leader's Tool Kit

21 Elements to Make Your SAR a Success

"The message society gives young people about sex is clear: Sex is dirty; save it for someone you love."

—Marty Klein, Sex Therapist (Klein and Associates, 2014)

INSTRUCTIONS FOR MAXIMIZING YOUR SUCCESS

We have identified the basic 21 elements that allow you to design and lead a successful SAR. Hopefully by now you have a well-grounded concept about SAR from what you have read in the previous five chapters. Creating a successful SAR is not a paint-by-numbers game. Think of this Tool Kit as a broad canvas, where you get to add in your fine line brush strokes and even change the pattern to fit your unique vision for SAR. Design is a dynamic and organic process. As you explore the Tool Kit, you may wander off to a new format or create elements for yourself that we haven't even dreamed of yet. Be creative and utilize that old homage, "Take what you can use and leave the rest behind."

Here is a list of the 21 key elements for a SAR, organized for you to implement and to achieve great results:

- ***Element 1: How SAR Works***
- ***Element 2: SAR Purpose***
- ***Element 3: Planning and Preparation / Event Management***
- ***Element 4: Budgets and Income Projections***
- ***Element 5: Logistics for Venue Selection***
- ***Element 6: Field Trips and Erotic Venue Options***
- ***Element 7: Curriculum Design: Content and Structure***
- ***Element 8: SAR Learning Objectives***
- ***Element 9: Topic Selection***
- ***Element 10: Media: Selection, Editing, and Legalities***
- ***Element 11: Speaker Selection: Revealing the Soul of SAR***
- ***Element 12: Materials and Supplies***
- ***Element 13: Student Journals or Notebooks***
- ***Element 14: SAR Leaders***
- ***Element 15: Small Group Facilitators***
- ***Element 16: Creating "Safe Space" (and Other Demands:***

- ***Element 17: Small Group Process and Takeaways***
- ***Element 18: SAR Evaluations***
- ***Element 19: Damage Control: Preventing SAR Fallout***
- ***Element 20: Your Ideal SAR***
- ***Element 21: SAR Readiness Checklist***

Element 1: How SAR Works

Looking through the Lens of SAR

SAR is an experiential training designed to challenge your values, attitudes, and beliefs (VABs) about sexuality and allow you to examine your sexological worldview. Not for sex ed or for clinical skills, SAR is ideally conducted by trained leaders to embrace a constellation of content in our model that includes: a) 40% media; b) 40% speakers/panels; c) 20% group process that is led by trained small group facilitators over a 2-day, 16-hour timeframe. SAR covers a broad range of sexuality topics and often includes off-site field trips to enrich the SAR experience and to promote a greater sense of community, bonding, and authentic sharing with peers. Participants learn to move out of their heads into their embodied feeling selves to discover a new awareness and freedom that serves them and those they affect as professionals in the interdisciplinary field of sexology.

Element 2: SAR Purpose

Setting an Intention to Create Your Vision

Your SAR purpose is going to drive the intention of your SAR. Why are you doing this program? What is your ultimate goal? How would you describe outcomes from the training itself? Those outcomes are different from the participant learning objectives, which are the students' learning takeaways. SAR is unique in the world, in part due to the fact that it is not sex education, sex therapy, or clinical skills training. Rather, SAR is a rare opportunity for self-exploration that is designed to allow people who work anywhere or in any capacity with human sexuality to understand their personal values, attitudes, and beliefs about sexuality. SAR is not necessarily a profitable money-making workshop, but is often reported to be a life-changing educational, experiential event. Once you become qualified to lead a great SAR, you begin to build your credibility in the world as a SAR leader extraordinaire.

Sample Purpose Statement

> "The goal of SAR is to explore personal and professional boundaries and allow participants to (re)evaluate or (re)assess, expand, and ultimately reconstruct their values, attitudes and beliefs about sexuality and sexual expression."[1]

ACTIVITY 1: *What is the primary purpose for your SAR? Write your answer here: (100 words max)*

ACTIVITY 2: *These are our screening questions: Try them for yourself now!*

1. What are your specific dreams, goals, and expectations for outcomes from attending this training? What are your certification requirements? Why are you here?

2. What is your current or future professional involvement in the field of sexology? [Examples: therapist, sex educator, bodyworker, graduate student, MFT, nurse, minister . . .]

3. What are your professional philosophy, values, and educational experiences regarding sexual expression, clinical treatment, and sexuality education?

4. What areas for personal growth do you hope to address during your training experience?

Now: List your own screening questions here:

1.

2.

3.

4.

What else do you need or want to know before you press the "Accept" button for their deposit or full payment?

(Other:)

Element 3: Planning and Preparation / Event Management

Careful Planning Yields Better Outcomes

There are many things to keep track of well before you place your first advertisement, create a website, post a flyer, or network among your peers about your SAR. Here is a description of what you must address before you offer your SAR. Use the checklists and Activity sheets provided in the categories listed below as you go through these important pre-SAR elements to keep track of your own tasks and to get them done well and on time. Think of them as apples in your barrel. Let's begin now.

1. **Defining your role**. Decide months in advance before you begin to talk to anyone about your SAR plans if you are going to be your SAR leader, which implies that you are ready to run a SAR business or offer SAR as a one-time or ongoing component of your other training, therapy, or educational business offerings. Maybe this is your own SAR, like ours, which is only one aspect of a larger scale business model. Or instead perhaps you are hired to design and conduct a SAR for someone else or for an organization, such as leading the Pre-Conference SAR for the well known and highly attended annual conferences of the Society of Scientific Study of Sexuality (SSSS), AASECT in the United States, or the World Congress of Sexology (WAS, 2016). Either way, there are what may seem like a gazillion moving pieces to planning and managing the event itself, before, during, and after.
2. **Naming your SAR**. Don't begin to promote a SAR as simply **SAR**. Make it sizzle! We use different titles[2] to differentiate our domestic from our international SARs, and none is merely called a SAR in any of our promotional avenues. You must decide if you are offering a Sexual Attitude Reassessment, or Restructuring, or both (as we do). Decide on a compelling name to draw enrollments. Examples include the SilverSAR™ described in Chapter 5, **Shake It Up!** (Wiener, 2016), or **SAR in the City** (Maze Health, 2016). In today's competitive marketplace for everything, including professional training, marketing drives your success!
3. **Qualifying applicants**. Although you may imagine that you are going to attract only the perfect crowd of loving, sensible, sex-positive, cooperative professionals to your SAR, you are in for a shock! When people are pushed to confront their most intimate parts of self and when their most private values are challenged, especially in the company of peers, they may become lions, not sheep; act out; or cause a furor in the SAR room. We recommend with a red pen that you devise a screening tool with your four or five top questions to screen in the best applicants and to prevent trouble. We also advocate that you ask for a realistic financial deposit along with

the application in order for a participant to secure a seat in order to gain professional commitment to participate in your SAR. That is never a guarantee they will show up at your SAR, no matter how much they may have invested. Use a reliable method to assure that applicants match your type of SAR, whether you are leading a Basic, Advanced, Specialty, or Designer SAR. Most of all, make sure that your applicants are there for the right reasons, such as to fulfill a professional requirement, to learn and grow, or to find community. You want to prevent applicants who are seeking a sex dating opportunity, a local meet-up for potential lovers,[3] or as a rival or enemy to steal or ruin your SAR. Here is an example of our screening tool, aside from contact information, and other demographics that include credit card payment information or a link to your payment site.

Using these or similar targeted assessment questions will help you to weed out the bad seeds before they plant themselves in your SAR garden.

4. **Averting media disasters**. Setting up and relying on media equipment can be a delicate balancing act. You will need to have the right equipment in working order, know how to access WiFi, set up Power Point presentation access for your guests' computers, change wiring for downloads on DVDs or from online sources, plan for blocked access to outlets, and more. First, make a list of what you will need and arrange for that to be on site or bring it with you. Next, test and get all of your necessary equipment in order. Your media must be in the proper format like on a DVD (or BluRay disc) or from a streaming site with ample WiFi access in the SAR room that permits enough bandwidth for letting it download in good working condition and speed. You may need to have on hand a variety of back-up means, such as flash drives, a portable external hard drive, or even extra computers. Make sure the room has a screen or projector or a large blank white wall on which to project images. Think about using a large, flat screen smart TV with audio, as we do. We bring our $1,000 smart TV unit and $200 BluRay player to the site with us if it is local; and often spend hours with our host facility to assure proper equipment is on site long ahead of opening remarks. You will want that, too. Make sure if you are in a hotel with WiFi set up that you also have requested audio hook up. Have proper illumination in the room, such as for wall projection, and windows that let in light that can be covered with dark blankets or shades. The last thing you want is to begin your media montage when no one can see the imagery due to glare (too much light flooding the screen) or hear it because there's not enough volume to reach across the room. (More about media in Element # 10.)
5. **Handling the money**. From the very start, you will need to have a dedicated business bank account or other means for managing monies in and

out. Doing business by the numbers is what we teach our own staff and students. Costs will include paying speakers, hotel fees, lunches for staff, materials, or transportation. SAR income will derive mostly from your participant tuition fees, unless you are fortunate enough to be sponsored by an organization that pays you a fee rather than your generating a full business for your SAR. Adding in funding from sponsorships or exhibitors will garner both positive attention at your event and income from their presence. It is always best to separate bank accounts for business and personal use; these accounts will incur fees, as will other payment mechanisms, such as credit cards, PayPal, or Stripe. We pay our speakers with checks out of the same business account that also receives the payments. You will need to have cash ready to pay speakers on site; we pay costs for gas for each trans speaker on our panel and we pay a fee by check to the organizer. Other incidental costs may crop up, including tips to helpful hotel staff, your own parking fees, cash gifts for your volunteers, a surprise order of afternoon pastries, or buying yourself a *latte grande* or a double martini after the first day's staff meeting is over. Keep a log of all expenses and income on a spreadsheet, such as an Excel workbook. Be aware of hidden fees, such as bank transfers, PayPal fees, and currency conversions if you take in foreign money, and keep careful track of income, expenses, profit, and loss, if this is your own business. Otherwise, just document expenses for future reimbursement of agreed-upon expenses that you incur as a hired SAR leader.

6. **Prepping a store on site.** One of the added benefits of leading your own SAR (and being an entrepreneur) is the option to provide an on-site store. Because Britton is the *Doctor on Duty* and host of many couples' sexual enhancement DVDs for the Alexander Institute housed at Lovingsex.com, selected DVDs are ordered and shipped in advance, then made available for sale at every SAR. Dunlap's two sexological documentaries[4] are also on sale at heavily discounted rates. Look for DVDs, CDs, sex toys, or books that are relevant to the SAR experience made by you as leaders or offered by any of your staff. Your store is also an opportunity to gain sponsors or a table for networking, takeaways, and flyers or business cards for services that relate to the group. This aspect of the SAR set-up has always been a favorite among our participants, knowing that they can cross-promote their own services or products and buy educational materials conveniently at the SAR.
7. **Staffing your SAR**. Your staff will vary depending on the length and size of your SAR. First, you will want to identify and then secure your roster of small group facilitators. All of your speakers should be booked at least 2 months in advance. You will want to lock in volunteers and/or an on-site assistant to help you with set-up and take-down, packing, unpacking, and then the fun of cleanup if you are not in a commercial public space for

your SAR. We lovingly refer to this valuable person as the *SAR Gopher*. Treat them well.

8. **Assuring creature comforts**. Here are some ideas to consider as you choose your facility and prepare for your SAR. Be sure you have access to temperature controls in the SAR room or know how to reach appropriate hotel staff; if not, this can cause serious problems when the time comes to lead the program, as we discussed happened during the Woodhull SAR in Chapter 4. Find ways to provide ride sharing for field trips or back and forth from shared lodging to the training site. Locate lodging options in advance, such as less expensive hotels or home rentals in the local area that are posted online. Create the possibility of email blasts to promote shared rooming for participants traveling from afar. If you host your own SAR, find chairs, sofas, tables, or other types of seating arrangements that make it a comfortable experience for your group. Arrange for low-cost parking and inform participants with special dietary restrictions well in advance about the lunch options, local eateries nearby, transportation, and lodging so they have time to prepare and economize. We tend to send out a few email blasts to our group before the SAR and always make it a priority to support their finding the best and easiest means to facilitate their being able to attend the SAR within their budgets. You will face that too. Most participants are not going to have a sky-is-the-limit approach to spending for SAR.
9. **Preparing your marketing, advertising, and websites campaign**. Once you have made a good reputation as a SAR leader, you will have earned traction to garner sign-ups. Until then you must do some calculated marketing. That often requires time, access to relevant venues for promotion, and money. Even seasoned SAR providers need to advertise, host a website for promotion of their next SAR, or find a way to, as marketers say, "Put butts in seats!" You can do this, too.

ACTIVITY 3: *These are types of marketing that you can do to promote your SAR. Use a pen or highlighter and circle the types of marketing that suit your skill level, budget, and time allocations:*

- Website promotion from your generic site
- A unique URL just for your SAR, i.e. Expandinprague2017.com
- Flyers (1-page electronic or printed)
- Brochures that you can print on demand
- Be a guest on friends' or colleagues' podcasts or on your own
- Guest appearances on live television, radio, Internet radio, or televised broadcast shows
- Email campaigns and blasts to your subscriber lists
- Social media ongoing promotion—in particular, Twitter, Facebook, LinkedIn
- Buying ad space at relevant conferences for the final printed programs
- Google ad placement for a unique landing page (one-page website) about your SAR
- Exhibitor space at relevant conferences
- Handouts or special cards for any speaking engagements you do, such as live networking events (Example: Britton is a member of LACAMFT and we are given 25 seconds at each monthly meeting to announce upcoming events as an audio commercial)
- Attending relevant conferences and talking about your SAR as a presentation or casually, such as CatalystCon, Woodhull Sexual Freedom Summit, National Sex Ed Conference, SSSS, AASECT, Psychotherapy Networkers, SASH, and passing out business cards or special postcards about your SAR
- Word of mouth; people who have attended your past SARs may send others to your programs in the future; offer incentives for referrals
- Becoming an approved AASECT CE Individual or Institutional provider and being listed on the roster of online CE events; submitting an application for a 1-time event
- Offering incentives such as bonuses or discounts for group sign-ups
- Asking your speakers to promote the SAR

Current Language for SAR on Our Websites

This is what we promulgate on our websites (SAR, 2016).

This unique "Sexual Attitude Reassessment and Restructuring" program or "SAR" is designed and led by two seasoned sexologists: Dr. Patti Britton and Dr. Robert Dunlap, who have created a highly effective weekend intensive to achieve the goals of traditional and contemporary SAR.

"Sexual Attitude Reassessment and Restructuring" or "SAR" is a highly provocative, experiential, cognitive and affective experience, which is designed to push comfort levels, elicit feelings and confront attitudes, beliefs and values about sexuality. Presentations encompass media, (including contemporary film, television and art), along with presentations and panels of live speakers/demonstrations showing the potential range of human sexual expression today. Topics will be revealed at the training itself; the element of surprise and the psychological state of non-expectation form part of the basis for this course. [No nudity or touch is ever required of participants.]

Small group process drives the understanding and impact of the elements of the presentations in this course. SAR is not a clinical training in sex therapy nor is it traditional sex education; rather it enables the participant to move emotionally, intellectually, spiritually and psychologically into a zone of greater knowing, acceptance, and tolerance of human sexuality in all of its possible dimensions.

ACTIVITY 4: *Here is a checklist of tasks and procedures that you will need to have in order pre-SAR. Check off each one as you get it done!*

Pre-SAR Checklist

A. ___Defined your role
B. ___Named your SAR
C. ___Application and screening tool ready
D. ___Media equipment in place
E. ___Money handled
F. ___Store ready
G. ___Staffing secured
H. ___Speakers lined up
I. ___Creature comforts addressed
J. ___Marketing campaign ready to go
K. ___Website up and running for enrollments to begin

Element 4: Budgets and Income Projections

Making Your SAR Profitable while Being of Service to Others

Budgets governing income and expense projections are key to being a success. A SAR is an income-generating event, not a social service. Think like a business-person and go for profitability while feeling like you are providing a valuable contribution. Both are true. If you are hired to run someone else's SAR or if, for your own SAR, you are using a Host Coordinator to make all arrangements, prepare all materials, set up the venue, help with promotion, and manage the SAR for you, think ahead as to how you will calculate the split of net profits. You will want to be working with a set budget, and not permit exceeding agreed-upon spending limits. You will need to set pricing together that accommodates the locale and economy of the region. You may want to each develop separate websites as SAR producers, especially if you are working in dual languages. The Host Coordinator will expect a fair portion of all leftover proceeds; if you have someone else be your sponsor or host your SAR, they do all the head, arm, and legwork. You just bring the SAR (yourself, staff, and the media) to the location and voila! You are the talent who appears in the theatrical production.

You will want to do some short calculations first:

- Imagine the cost of your SAR to include these sample Cost Items:

- **Typical expenses.** 1. Venue rental; 2. Speaker fees; 3. Snacks, coffee/tea service, lunches on site and tips for hotel staffing; 4. Notebook or folder for handout materials and other paperwork, such as color print certificates on card stock; 5. CE approval fees if applicable; 6. Gifts for closure activity; 7. Art activity materials; 8. Purchase or rental of media equipment; 9. Media acquisition costs; 10. Small group facilitator stipends; 11. SAR assistant fee; 12. Parking for you and staff; 13. Field trip entry fee; 14. Newsprint or giant Post-It notes for scribbling notes in front of group and perhaps a portable easel; 15. Miscellaneous.

- **Income per participant.** A. Student rate of $425; B. Professional rate of $650. C. Couple rate of $1000. In less well-off areas, reduced fees may apply, such as in Eastern Europe where our SAR tuition for professionals is $300–$400 per person, including two lunches and materials. You also can offer discounted rates or freebies in exchange for volunteering or as a scholarship, but charge for your hard costs such as the cost of the SAR notebook, handouts, food, and parking. You may want to negotiate to bring people to a venue where there are purchases they can make (such as a sex toy shop) to earn a commission on sales.

Let's practice here!

Calculation example: *2-day SAR at a hotel; lunches provided; 20 participants; three staff (SAR leader or yourself); one small group facilitator; SAR assistant who handles all paperwork and assists staff with any needs); one volunteer (to assist with small group details, missing materials, other duties such as chasing down hotel staff for lunch deliveries on time)*

- **Calculation of income:**

10 student participants × $425 per tuition = $4250
10 professional participants × $650 = $6500
Total income = $10,750. (Looking good so far?)
Formula: # of anticipated participants × tuition fees per category = Income

- **Calculation of expenses:**

(Note that this follows our SAR model and you will want to explore variables in this sample budget to find areas where you can cut costs, such as owning your own equipment, not offering a closure gift, showing only free media, and having only volunteers as speakers. If you host your own SAR in your office or conference room, of course you cut out the highest costs for hotel accommodations and meals.)

- Venue rental of hotel (2 days @ $500 per day) = $1,000
- Speaker fees (three panels @$150 each) = $450
- Snacks, coffee/tea service (2 days × 24 including staff/volunteers @ $10 each) = $480
- Hotel lunches on site (2 days × 24 @ $25 each) = $1200
- Tips for hotel staffing = $30
- Notebook or folder with handout materials (copies) and other paperwork, such as b/w or color print certificates on card stock × 24 including staff/volunteers @ $15 each = $360
- CE approval fees if applicable = $150
- Gifts for closure activity × 24 @ $5 each = $120
- Art activity supplies and one giant Post-It note pad with markers = $75
- Purchase[5] or rental of media equipment for 2 days = $500
- Media acquisition costs (varies; estimate only to purchase DVDs) = $150
- Small group facilitator stipends; assume for this size of group only two are needed and the SAR leader facilitates one of the small groups; 1@ $500
- SAR assistant fee = $300
- Parking for you and staff × 2 days @ $30/day = $240

- Field trip entry fee × 18 (estimate that not all participants or staff will attend); @ $20 each = $360
- Miscellaneous costs: $150

Total Expenses: $6065
Income of $10,750 less expenses of $6065 = $4685 net profit for this SAR
Formula: Income less expenses = Net profit

ACTIVITY 5: *Now, assemble your own budget here:*

Projected Income:

Projected Expenses:

Anticipated Net Profit:

If you are working solo and not for someone else, then your net profit may be well worth your time and investments, as you can replicate it easily with the same media, your own equipment, and in your own no-cost location if you have one. If you are splitting proceeds with an entity or organization or person, that's a less profitable business, isn't it? If so, let's pretend it's a 50/50 split; for all of your hard work, you earn $2342.50 for yourself. That covers all of your time to prepare, deliver, and do the necessary follow up for a great SAR! It doesn't even cover the costs for your travel, lodging, food, or lost income from being away from your income-generating source such as your clinical practice. Be wise to negotiate being compensated for those additional costs by someone else if you bring a SAR to them. Increasing the size of your SAR group, limiting lower tuition rates, saving on small group facilitators by using volunteers, hosting your own SAR event in your own office suite, or designing your SAR so that costs are reduced without an art activity, gifts, or other perks will save you dollars. Be mindful of the old saying, "Don't step over a dollar to pick up a dime." Cutting add-ons and niceties may cost you on the loss of added value you can provide, affecting your reputation to draw in future business. SAR can be profitable and rewarding if you plan your finances well.

Element 5: Logistics for Venue Selection

Venue and Ambience Can Dictate Success or Failure

Rooms for your SAR venue may include a variety of options, such as a commercial hotel, charming inn, bed and breakfast (B&B), office suite, a person's spacious home, an apartment on Airbnb, or retreat center. Whatever public space you choose, it works well if it offers lodging, meals, and at least one sizeable conference room large enough to hold your group comfortably and in privacy. Often, if you give enough lead time and are pleasant to work with, you can convince hotel or other lodging staff to discount rooms for participant and/or staff lodging, allowing for a cheaper fare than on their usual rate card and a lowered conference room rental rate if the hotel/inn knows it will fill sleeping rooms. Usually you can book a hotel package where you are assigned a certain number or block of rooms for lodging as part of your rental of a conference room; adding on meals will enhance your chances of getting a better deal from a hotel.

As criteria for selection of a hotel or other similar public venue in which you are renting a conference room and breakout room(s), here are some suggestions for what you will need:

- **Main room for presentations**. Provide a schematic for room set-up, which most hotels have available for you to select, such as theatre style, in the round, number of horizontal rows. Tell the staff your choice for the front of your room. Decide where the media equipment will be situated on tables and if other tables are needed. You may want to provide tables for writing, but we are adamant that a SAR is not a cognitive experience, and therefore no tables are allowed in the main SAR room except for display or media at the edge of the room. From their chairs participants can also easily write in their journals on their laps. Placing chairs in a semi-circle toward the front of the room, where the media equipment is placed and from where the speakers present, will enhance the participants' feeling of unity in the group and promote willingness to share comments with the whole group. Often our final group process involves moving all participants' chairs into a circle. The form of the circle creates a vortex of energy that promotes a sense of communion and community. Alternatively, Mitelman uses a half moon arrangement, with chairs at four to six tables placed around the room. The set-up allows the small group to sit together for processing the speakers and sharing their responses.

- **Breakout room or space divided with soundproofing**. Breakout rooms are the locations for your small group meetings. We include two days' lunches during small group times; so, if you follow our model, you will need to be sure that tables are available in the small rooms or, if not, laps will have to suffice.
- **Lunches available within the hotel or easily brought in, given time constraints**. Order your menus in advance. Select the least messy options, especially if the hotel staff cannot provide a private lunch setting for your small groups, which fortunately we are able to obtain at most venues. We suggest, if you have permission from the venue, buying box lunches or even deli platters from your favorite sandwich restaurant. Many hotels charge a hefty price for a coffee/tea service for your morning arrival times. Decide in advance if your budget permits that luxury. Usually we see our participants bringing in their own take-out coffees. You will want to create a safe space ruling that prohibits outside food and beverages in the SAR room, as they can be a huge distraction and cover up emotional upheavals.
- **Privacy at all times**. This is an essential and non-negotiable item.
- **Quiet surrounding the conference room at all times**. Minimize intrusive sounds that may surround the SAR room, including outside noises, such as moving vehicles, screaming children in the park below the windows, loud speaking or musical events going on in another part of the hotel, staff using your stairway as access to enter another hotel space, or anything that compromises the integrity or sanctity of your event. Be strong and take action by reporting staff or complaining to management if this occurs in the moment.
- **Waiting area for your speakers that won't cause tension or distraction**. The last thing you want is for your speakers to arrive and sit in a lobby only to be embarrassed or harassed, then leave before they speak on your SAR

stage. Ensure that comfort, respect, and an open environment are provided for speakers waiting their turn to enter the SAR room.

- **A registration area outside of the main room, such as an attached foyer or an outside hallway**. We find that having a registration table at the entrance to your SAR room may be enough. However, often the registration area is also where early arrivals congregate over coffee, shop in your on-site store, or complete late paperwork. Go for the ideal of a separate space for your sign-in/sign-out table and store.
- **Cooperative hotel staff**. You will have apprised hotel staff beforehand of your content to avert disaster if someone walks into your media montages. This is crucial for the emotional safety of everyone, especially your staff.
- **Ample toilets and one for gender neutral, with signs posted**. In today's more sensitive climate, posting signs for Gender Neutral bathrooms is accepted in most locales. At times we stand guard for women to use the men's bathroom. (Does that sound familiar to you?)
- **Clean up area and trash containers for on-site drinks, snacks, and lunches**. If you have food and drinks as a part of your SAR, you will need this to be handled.
- **Daily staff duties to include clean up and refreshment of drinking water daily**. You do not want your participants to become dehydrated or feel lacking of creature comforts as mentioned earlier in this chapter. Assign your *SAR Gopher* to manage the water and clean up, including alerting hotel staff if it's time to remove dirty dishes from lunch, add clean glasses and fresh pitchers of water, or empty overflowing trash receptacles.
- **Baked or other surprises**. At times we have made a generous spur-of-the-moment decision to place an order for piping hot chocolate chip cookies to be delivered to the SAR room on the final afternoon as a treat. Think on your feet about what your staff may be feeling about the group and what may contribute just the right additive to your event. By the way, cookies can cost you $5 apiece, so this is an ad hoc *lagniappe* that is prudent only if you can afford such a generous demonstration of appreciation.
- **AC/heat controls or highly responsive hotel maintenance staff**. You read about our horrific experience at the Woodhull Summit in Chapter 4. Don't get caught in the trap of having to cope with heat/cold issues, a disgruntled crowd not able to get their bodies into a comfort zone, or your own stress about temperature or ambience challenges. Fix it quickly. Keep focused on delivery of a great SAR. Transparency about what you can and cannot do for the group goes a long way toward smoothing ruffled feathers.
- **Handicap accessibility**. Laws dictate that handicap or disability access must be available, such as a working elevator and wheel chair accessibility. Be aware of other disabilities, such as hearing impairment, blindness, or speech difficulties, and special needs that the venue may need to address

with you. Serve your participants well by being prepared and proactive in your venue selection.

- **Easy parking**. You may have the luxury of a free parking area attached to the hotel or apartment, a paid garage, valet parking for a fee, or even no parking at all. Honor the needs of local participants who drive to your SAR by doing all you can to arrange for good parking options.
- **Affordable room rates or other feasible lodging nearby**. Despite the lovely attraction of a well-heeled hotel for your SAR, you may need to seek out a local hotel for participant lodging that has low rates and is not on the fancy end of the scale. We recommend one in Los Angeles, that is not walkable to the SAR hotel, but it is a safe, lovely, Spartan, good lodging option. Most of our international and out of town students stay there if they do not find a suitable Airbnb location, as the boutique hotel we tend to use for SAR is pricey.
- **Located near a major airport, bus terminal, or train hub**. It is critical to be centrally located for your SAR. Even though the temptation may arise to host a SAR at a darling inn in the woods outside of town, or at a sacred healing retreat miles from any public transportation options, access for participants to find and get to your SAR is a must-have.

ACTIVITY 6: *Review the list above and make your determinations based on how to maximize your venue for the best SAR possible. Get out your high-lighter pen. Does your venue meet most of them? If so, it's a go!*

You may recall in Chapter 4 we talked about our small hotel in Prague that featured a private dining room for our lunch breakouts and breakfast gatherings. In Berlin, we rented an entire apartment with generous space for SAR in the beautiful dining room, and we lowered costs by renting out two of the three bedrooms for paying guests. In Los Angeles, we obtained a penthouse suite in a Ramada Inn, not of the highest caliber but conveniently located and very spacious. The apartment included a full kitchen for meals, snacks, and coffee preparation, along with lodging consisting of three bedrooms that generated extra SAR income. In Amsterdam, we stayed at the private home and B&B of Xaviera Hollander. Getting creative about your SAR site will bring you intrigued attendees and may produce more income for you. We are firm believers in having fun at what you do, including the many moving pieces of designing, leading, and managing a SAR!

Element 6: Field Trips and Erotic Venue Options

Experience Trumps Knowledge Every Time

An outside evening or daytime field trip to a sexual/erotic venue for an experiential learning opportunity is a part of SAR that often brings us the most positive and powerful feedback. Field trips can have a lasting impact on participants' shifting to a more open and tolerant, if not sexually alive, state. The next day in the morning check-in (a staple of all of our 2- or 3-day events), we elicit comments from those in attendance at the field trip, which contributes to lively and engaging discussions. Examples include going to places such as a local strip club (male, female, or trans), sexual art display, trans or gay bar, pole dancing class, BDSM club or dungeon, sex toy boutique, tantra temple, sex expo, or private swingers' party. The list is endless and depends on local availability and affordability. You must decide prior to the event if you are paying their entrance fees or not. Many venues will negotiate a bargain rate to have the pleasure of your company. Make sure you provide or can refer to affordable transportation back and forth from your SAR venue. If you provide transportation to and from the field trip location by yourself, that becomes another expense to be accounted for, such as for gas, insurance for an additional driver, car wash, and other forms of maintenance.

Be sure to TCOY[6] at all times; maybe you'll want to offer rides in your own vehicle as we do with the caveat for a one-way trip only, as you will probably not stay as long at the event as your students. Or perhaps you can post a carpool sign-up sheet on the wall of the SAR room that afternoon. Then, again, you may just want to post the address and telephone number of the venue and advise the group to download the app for ride services, such as Uber or Lyft, to let them arrange for transport on their own. Vetting the venue and the hosts before you book it will save you plenty of headaches later on if the space is filthy, unsafe, or unethical behaviors take place in public view, as we have seen in one venue where we did not listen to our own counsel and trusted the hosts without a careful pre-screen site visit (sigh). Have a solid agreement with your own group about the etiquette expectations of each venue (most will have this posted and printed out for signature at the door), and tell your group that most venues have policing policies in place to assure safe behaviors. Assure your group that this is not your site and that the control depends on the venue owners. It's important to acknowledge that you do not bear any liability for the venue and what happens there. Element #19 talks more about liability issues and how to protect yourself at all times.

ACTIVITY 7: *What options for field trips exist where you will conduct your SAR?*

Write down some ideas here:

1.

2.

3.

4.

5.

Element 7: Curriculum Design: Content and Structure

An Elegant Design Is an Art Form

An effective SAR process is fundamentally experiential, not intellectual or clinical. It is not didactic; it is an immersion into the range of human sexual expression being illustrated, shown, or demonstrated. It also contains the Lived Experience of persons who share their stories, insights, and personal journeys.

You may remember the origins of SAR in Chapter 2, when Rev. Sutton talked about the IASHS method of immersion in the *Fuckorama*, created for its shocking effect; they then blended the experience into a cascade of sexual pattern films to normalize the range of potential human sexual expression; eventually, they brought their group to a conclusion with a gentle ending to prepare students for reentry into the real world. You can mimic this pattern, such as by adding in some moving passages, and finally bring the group back down to earth with a soft feathery landing for your finale. Here's how that might work: Day 1: Set the container and introduce each other; show a range of explicit sexual expression as media montage; live BDSM speaker panels; escalate with extreme BDSM media montage; discussion in preparation for the pinnacle of the evening field trip, often at a BDSM dungeon; Day 2: Introduce new topics to push buttons; personal awareness activity; transgender panel to generate emotional response; spirituality media montage and activity or other topic; discussions; closure.

Think of your design as though you are a composer of a great symphony. First you begin gently, bringing them into the themes and flavor of your SAR. Then you escalate with more intense passages, leading up to a full crescendo in the middle. Another analogy is to imagine the design as the sexual response cycle: begin with gentle foreplay, intensify arousal, peak at the climax, then gently descend into resolution, followed by a pleasant afterglow. The pattern first goes up in intensity, then dives deeply down and lands into neutrality. Elegant design is like music. Feel it first; then create it for your own vision of your SAR. Another way to frame your role as a SAR designer is from Thrasher, who advises, "Use the same recipe in creating your SAR, but sometimes you have to add two cups of sugar and change it to one cup of flour to make the design for your SAR. You can use a structured approach to SAR, but always be flexible to modify it" (2016).

Mitelman has a beautiful metaphor for how to conceptualize your SAR, as she states, "To deliver a SAR is to create a well-oiled machine. One must look at the functional perspective and there must be flow. Allow ample time for discussion and process time in small group." Ultimately, you are the designer and controller of your SAR.

One day SAR model/10 hours:

We are highly opposed to the one-day SAR model (or even the 10-hours approach) for SAR. We suggest that the minimum for SAR should be at least

16 hours. Our SAR programs vary depending on the venue. One model offers a minimum of 16 CEs that include 18 hours of actual time during SAR:

- 3 hours on a Friday night (optional at some venues)
- 7.5 to 8 hours Sat and Sun each with lunch that includes required small group process time and short breaks
- An additional optional 3- to 5-hour evening field trip on Sat evening
- In our view and vast experience, the one-day SAR model does not allow for ample time to process or to undergo the percolation effect of the SAR on participants. The overnight allows for personal private time and an opportunity to absorb the experience.

2-day SAR/16 hours model:

As mentioned earlier, the template we rely on and highly promote is this format:

- At least 40% of a SAR should be live speakers/panels.
- At least 40% should be media exposure.
- At least 20% held in small group process and/or dyads for sharing with others at SAR.
- Experiential activities may include: Brainstorming activities, such as eliciting values about different topics within the whole group while writing them on newsprint, before showing any media or hosting speakers; creating lists on newsprint of sexual fantasies; writing assignments; dyads or threesomes sharing; whole group discussions; art activity; spirit card activity; small group work. Some SAR leaders spend a large amount of SAR time outside of the 3-part framework of media, speakers, and small group process. Providing index cards on which participants can write down thoughts, feelings, or delicate questions is a common strategy used widely in sex education, known as the *Anonymous Question Box*. You may ask the whole group to reflect on their own sexual history and tease out issues that may affect their VABs. We have presented a values-clarification exercise called "Taking A Stand," in which we ask the group to literally stand in the room indicating *agree* or *disagree* about a values statement then discuss why they took that stand. Two examples are "Gay marriage is unnatural" or "Old people in long term care facilities should be allowed to have sex in the privacy of their own rooms." Our own art activity engages the whole person in a non-cognitive, non-verbal, self-reflection mode.
- We recommend that small group process occur a minimum of one time per day (if more than one day) and a minimum of two times per day (if a one-day SAR) for at least 20% of the time during SAR; a limit of 8–10 participants per small group that is led by a trained and competent facilitator with documented experience of having attended at least two prior SARs and with SAR small group facilitation training.

- Field trip (optional)
- Live demos during the SAR with active audience participation (no nudity or explicit SEXUAL behaviors): examples include the BDSM speakers showing their equipment and inviting participants to be volunteers for demonstrations, or a sex toy expert passing around an array of devices and lubes for testing on hands. You may discover other appropriate activities to anchor participants into their values, attitudes, and beliefs toward expanded awareness of self and others.

The art activity was a surprise addition to our agenda. It evolved at our second SAR in Warsaw, Poland, for a point in our agenda where no speaker could be found to fill the second day morning slot. In our eleventh-hour planning meeting, instead, we came up with the idea to create an art activity that asked students to design a portrait of their Ideal Sexual Self. Here is how it works: They illustrate their images in multi-media, using pictures or words from a pile of magazines, glue sticks, crayons, pastels, watercolor paints, brushes, felt-tip markers, colored card stock paper, sparkles, ribbons, feathers, stickers, and glittery pens. In a true artful gallery display, the whole group stands in a circle, and one by one each describes the meaning of their own art piece, often with tears flowing or in jubilant self discovery. The art activity has been received with such popularity and created such a potent impact that we have kept it in the program ever since. Dunlap snaps a group photo of the art as a colorful and inspiring collage placed on the SAR room floor, then sends it out to the group post-SAR as a memento.

Steps to Your Design

First you must choose the structure for your SAR: Is it for 1 or 2 days, and what number of hours are you going to allocate for topics to be covered? Pick your topics. Decide if you want a speaker or panel or to use media (or both) for each topic. Look over your budget to assess how much you can spend on speakers before you book them. Then sketch out your agenda of how the SAR outline will flow. Be sure not to overload too many topics within a short timeframe. Usually you want an hour minimally for each topic; for speakers, you will want to allow more time for a Q&A at the conclusion of their talk and/or demos. Allow ample time for breaks (bathrooms, lunches, stretch or breathing exercises in between heavy topics) and for small or large group process time.

Here is an example of how we plan for our standard domestic SAR:

Sample AGENDA for 2 days SAR

SAT. DAYTIME
AM: Overview and introductions
Explicit Sexual Expression—Media Montage
Disability & Sexuality—Speaker or Media Montage

Lunch in small group process

PM: BDSM speaker panel/demos
Adult/BDSM/Fetish—Media Montage
Small group process

SAT. EVENING: [Optional}
Sex worker/bodyworker or other topical speaker panel
Field trip to outside venue or film festival on site

SUN. DAYTIME
AM: Whole group check in
Body Art & Fetish Practices—Media Montage
Art Activity

Lunch in small group process

PM: Trans speakers/panel
Spirituality & Sexuality—Activity
Whole group process
Conclusions and closure

In Element #20 you will be able to exercise these muscles and design your own SAR.

Element 8: SAR Learning Objectives

Know What You Want to Achieve Before You Begin

1. A Learning Objective is an outcome that your student or participant can show as a product of their learning or from experiencing your SAR. In our college days, we were influenced by Mager's Behavioral Objectives (Mager's Guideline, 2016) and Learning Objectives are currently expected to be used in most training, educational, or academic programs today.

2. Next, here are some tips for writing Learning Objectives: Start with a key phrase, such as "Participants will be able to: . . ." then fill in the blank. Keep them as simple and short as possible. Make them measurable, if you can. For example, say, "Students will be able to cite at least three ways that modern sex therapy has influenced current options for the treatment of erectile dysfunction . . ." (You will notice that our SAR Learning Objectives are more vague, as we tend to rely on narrative, adult reflection essays as a qualitative research approach.) Use active verbs to begin your phrase, such as *discuss*, *define*, *show*, *enumerate*, *demonstrate*, *state*, *assess*, *identify*, *express* . . . etc. This is not a program or training evaluation; it is focused on the learner, not what you are providing in your SAR. It's about them and their takeaways.
3. Once you have your entire agenda and outline design for your SAR, and the number of hours of SAR, you can craft your full list of Learning Objectives for yourself.
4. If you are an AASECT or other organizational provider, creating effective Learning Objectives will be expected of you. AASECT requires that your Learning Objectives conform to their model and correlate with AASECT Core Knowledge Areas (AASECT, 2016), cited below.
5. Writing your own Learning Objectives will take some time and skill. First you need to know your outline for your SAR design, what you will be presenting, what topics will you cover, what outcomes you expect. Assume one Learning Objective for each hour of your SAR training.

ACTIVITY 8: *Jot down some ideas here.*

Participants will be able to (list 5 examples):

1.

2.

3.

4.

5.

SAMPLE Learning Objectives, Correlated with AASECT CKAs[7]

Participants will be able to:

1. Discuss their values, attitudes, and beliefs about a wide range of sexual expression and behaviors. A;O
2. Describe aspects of human sexual behavior and/or sexual expression that represent areas for further professional exploration. A;O
3. Distinguish between one's own values, attitudes, and beliefs and those of others. A;O
4. Utilize effectively the exposure to new or different aspects of human sexual expression in their clinical and/or sexuality educational work. A;O
5. Define specific sexual behaviors or sexual expression that represent areas that would not be relevant for working with clients or students. A;O
6. Describe elements of sexual expression or sexual behavior that are appealing for personal exploration. A;O
7. Define specific sexual behaviors or sexual expression that are not within their comfort zone. A;O
8. Discuss variants of sexual behaviors demonstrated among heterosexual, homosexual, and bisexual performers in the media, and the impact those have on the participant's attitudes and values. A;C;F;M;O
9. Evaluate and discuss the life experiences and presentations from a spectrum of trans persons, and the impact those have on the participant's attitudes and values. A;C;D;O
10. Discuss factors within the area of sexuality and disability, and the impact they have on the participant's attitudes and values. A;C;H;O
11. Define and discuss elements within the media showing adult/porn imagery and sexual behaviors (including sexual assault/rape/drug usage and polyamory) and the impact they have on the participant's attitudes and values. A;C;J;M;O
12. Describe their responses to the media showing a wide range of BDSM/kink/fetish behaviors, and the impact it has on the participant's attitudes and values. A;C;F;O
13. Define and discuss elements within the media showing extreme body modification and fetish practices, and the impact they have on the participant's attitudes and values. A;C;F;O
14. Recognize their responses to self-disclosure through an art activity, and the impact it has on the participant's attitudes and values about their own sexuality. A;C;D;O
15. Define and discuss aspects of sexuality and spirituality, especially through a self-awareness activity, and the impact it has on the participant's attitudes and values. A;C;D;O
16. Identify elements that inform your ideal sexual self. O[8]

AASECT Core Knowledge Areas, as Noted for the 16-hour SAR Example

List of AASECT Core Knowledge Areas

To ensure the coursework meets AASECT Certification requirements for sexuality educators, counselors, and therapists, indicate one or more core knowledge areas for which the event will provide applicable knowledge:

AASECT recently updated the Core Knowledge Areas (CKA) required for certification and certification renewal of all Sexuality Educators, Sexuality Counselors, and Sex Therapists. All candidates for certification must have knowledge of the following as they relate to sexual health and pleasure.

1. Ethics and ethical behavior.
2. Developmental sexuality from a bio-psycho-social perspective across the life course.
3. Socio-cultural, familial factors (e.g., ethnicity, culture, religion, spirituality, socioeconomic status, family values) in relation to sexual values and behaviors.
4. Issues related to Sexual Orientation and/or Gender Identity: heterosexuality; issues and themes impacting lesbian, gay, bisexual, pansexual, asexual people; gender identity and expression.
5. Intimacy skills (e.g., social, emotional, sexual), intimate relationships, interpersonal relationships and family dynamics.
6. Diversities in sexual expression and lifestyles, including, but not limited to polyamory, swinging, BDSM, tantra.
7. Sexual and reproductive anatomy/physiology.
8. Health/medical factors that may influence sexuality including, but not limited to illness, disability, drugs, mental health, conception, pregnancy, childbirth, pregnancy termination, contraception, fertility, HIV/AIDS, sexually transmitted infection, other infections, sexual trauma, injury, and safer sex practices.
9. Range of sexual functioning and behavior, from optimal to problematic, including but not limited to common issues such as: desire discrepancy, lack of desire, difficulty achieving or maintaining arousal, sexual pain and penetration problems, difficulty with orgasm.
10. Sexual exploitation, including sexual abuse, sexual harassment, and sexual assault.
11. Cyber sexuality and social media.
12. Substance use/abuse and sexuality.
13. Pleasure enhancement skills.
14. Learning theory and its application.
15. Professional communication and personal reflection skills.

16. History of the discipline of sex research, theory, education, counseling, and therapy.
17. Principles of sexuality research and research methods.

Element 9: Topic Selection

Defining the Bones of Your SAR

First you will select the range of your topics, all calibrated according to the time allotted for content versus group process. Next you will move onto the task of deciding if you want to show media and/or hire a live speaker or panel for that topic area. Sometimes you will elect to show media with live speakers.

The goal for curating your explicit media is the construction of immersive and diverse media montages or an array of short clips that you wish to show the group. In our view (with few exceptions), no single film or DVD or program should be shown in full length in this modern era. Those exceptions may include an International SAR where live speakers are not available and a documentary is your only option, such as presenting *Trans the Movie*; this may also apply to shorter programs, such as a program in which a couple disrobes from bodysuits, which lasts about 20 minutes in its full length and is worth every minute. This recommendation applies to full-length commercial porn, Hollywood films, television episodes, or other 1–2 hour selections that tell a story about the topic you are featuring. Select content that elicits lively small group discussion!

We recommend that SAR content should cover the topic areas[9] featured in the box (at least six of them). Review this list of suggested topics, then choose which six or more you would like to feature in your SAR. Of course, the number and scope of topics covered also has to do with the availability of speakers and/or media and time allotted for your entire SAR program. Feel it out. If a topic strikes you as highly significant or evokes your passion, choose it!

ACTIVITY 9: *Go over the list below and then circle the topics of your choice.*

Adult/XXX/porn/erotica (visual)—showing a variety of types of adult entertainment or adult baby play/diaper fetish
Aging and sexual expression
Asexuality
BDSM experience and expression
Bestiality/zoophilia expression
Bi or pansexual expression
Cybersex
Disability experience and sexual expression
Drugs for sexual enhancement (prescription and natural/alternatives)
Ecosexology
Fantasies
Female Genital Mutilation
Fetish play (other objects of fetish attraction, i.e., leather, latex, feet . . .)
Furries
Gay male sexual expression
GLBQQIAS and/or "Queer" or "fluid" sexual expression
Group sexual expression
Heterosexual expression
HIV/AIDS
Legal issues in sexology
Lesbian female sexual expression
Male Circumcision
Masturbation
Monogamous/long term monogamous/monogamish relationships
Objectum Sexualis
Paraphilias (unusual sex practices)
Politics of sex or sexual expression
Polyamory experience and expression
Sacred/spirituality and sexual expression, e.g., Neotantra, Ray Stubbs, sexual shaman
Serious health issues related to sexuality
Sex toys for sexual expression
Sex trafficking
Sexological or other erotic bodywork
Sexting
Sexual abuse, rape, and sex crimes
Sexual art/crafts
Swinging lifestyle
Trans expression and experience

As discussed in Chapter 5, you may choose to include some of the *taboo topics*.

Element 10: Media: Selection, Editing, and Legalities

Media Are a Gateway to Visceral Response

Media selection is a very important part of any SAR, as we recommend it to occupy 40% of all content in the ideal structure for a SAR. Pawloski parallels our view in noting that few participants have not seen Sexually Explicit Materials (SEM), advising SAR leaders to choose their media with an educational intent. To select videotaped or other forms of recorded media, it is important not to duplicate the Lived Experience of your speakers. For example, if you have a transgender panel there is no need to show any video or other media that replicates the content for the topic. Another example is if you have a BDSM panel, you do not need to show media such as Dunlap's now-famous documentary on BDSM/kink/fetish, *Beyond Vanilla*. Our SAR is based on the careful selection of various types of footage that represents the spectrum of LGBTIQ sexual activities and identities as much as possible. Our media reflects the full potential range of sexual expressions, such as gay male, gender queer, sex and aging, bisexual, lesbian, polyamorous, trans, sensual play, spiritual sex, and kink. Participants are confronted with the *immersion experience* of a montage of media. Part of the challenge for our participants in this experience may be just the act of viewing explicit sexual depictions or behaviors within a group of peers, and later discussing their own responses to the media in small group process.

International SARs have certain media selections that will not work in that context even though they are highly successful in the United States. (See Chapter 7 for more about that.) The content may appear to be *too American*. A good example is Marty Klein's documentary based on his book, *America's War on Sex* (2006). Although footage about the negative political climate for sexuality in the United States from this important film was popular for American audiences, few International SAR events would be well served by using this documentary. Another good example of media to avoid internationally might include comedy shows, such as the satirical political commentary of Bill Maher,[10] clips from the hit HBO Series *Entourage*,[11] or more crass comical affronts to attacks on sexual freedom in the United States.

The length of video clips is important. We use the *media montage* presentation method for our SARs. This allows 8 to 15 minutes per segment of a variety of sexual expressions. Media is derived from Hollywood films, television episodes, classical adult entertainment, commercial porn, sexual pattern films, explicit sex educational programs, and documentaries that we curate consistently. Our media has proven to be effective, based on verbal and written evaluations, and we are always seeking to update or alter media content. Always on the lookout for better media, we replace older, outdated media with newer media on an ongoing basis. Technology demands that you deliver media that reflects quality. For example, VCRs and videotapes have now been replaced with DVD or BluRay players and DVDs. Video monitors and televisions have migrated to Smart TVs and projection equipment for home use. Analog sound is now digital sound with speakers that project a home theater auditory environment. Television has evolved from standard (4 × 3 520 lines) to HD (16 × 9 1080P) format, and is moving to full digital 4K theatrical quality at a rapid pace. We have replaced almost all of our media over the past 40-plus SARs with newer formatted content to DVD. Even our classical videos that we show have been enhanced digitally for quality of presentation through the hands-on conversion of analog standard video to digital DVD.

We create the media montage for each topical area in the SAR. Once you have found and selected media for your SAR, it is highly advised to place your selected clips onto a single DVD as we do. This requires editing of the media. Facing a stack of selected DVDs that require loading and unloading just does not work as a smooth platform through which you will show your SAR media. You will have to find what we call the *ins and outs* of clips. How will you cue those up? Will you have the luxury of seeing the time code as you play it through your machine in real time? Imagine that you are scrounging around to find that in-out time code in your notes on the SAR leader table, as you speak to the group for the introduction to the media, watch the group for any questions or disruptions, line up your media presentation in its proper sequence, and in the back of your mind wonder if your next speaker or the lunch break is going to be on time. Do you see that this is a demanding role? Be as prepared as you can be ahead of time, have all of your media labeled, organized, and prepared well in advance. Make it easy on yourself. We recommend that unless (like Dunlap) you are an accomplished filmmaker with editing skills and equipment, you will need to hire a professional to assist you with the conversion or upgrading of your media, montage or not.

One of the best single sources for SAR media is SexSmartFilms. Its founder Schoen says, "Films as media are tools used to facilitate a response." As a filmmaker of world-recognized contributions to sexology, such as *Trans the Movie*, *Belly Buttons Are Navels*, *Becoming Orgasmic*, and many other couples' sexual enrichment programs at Sinclair Institute, Schoen is an expert on media and its potential impact on understanding about human sexual desires and behaviors. His own mentor, Derek Calderwood of New York University's graduate programs in Human Sexuality, identified four steps (known as the 4 Ps) that apply to using media in adult education, particularly relevant to SAR: 1) *P*review: Watch the media as the SAR presenter to be sure that you know its content thoroughly and to ensure that it will elicit the response you want to prompt; 2) *P*repare: Set the groundwork and place the media in a context before showing it, such as describing why this film is being shown in a particular topic area; 3) *P*roject: Show the film or other media to the group while remaining in the presence of the group and noting responses in real time; 4) *P*rocess: This is the most important part of showing any media, which is the process discussion of how the media affected viewers and their shared results. The process can be accomplished by inviting journal writing or sharing in dyads, in small group, or in whole group discussion.

Schoen also remarks that over time in the field of sexological study, luminaries such as Kinsey, Masters and Johnson, Calderwood, Money, and IASHS faculty have used SEM for teaching adults about human sexuality. Without being able to locate the best media for their purposes, they often found it useful to create media of their own. At SexSmartFilms, Schoen himself has curated and amassed over 500 films and a large collection of internationally televised commercials, all showing the potential range of human sexual expression. These media reflect a broad span of cultural, social, and political attitudes about seminal topics such as condom usage, nudity, and comfort with sexuality in general. In addition, his site (which requires a small subscription fee per annum) regularly adds new content, much of which would serve you well as a SAR leader for obtaining instantly streaming content among a huge variety of sexually related media. One of the most significant contributions of Schoen is having produced a series of contemporary *sexual realism* films,[12] showing the process of sensate focus with real-life couples who are males, females, gays, lesbians and/or heterosexuals. Now a part of SexSmartFilms, these valuable media provide an opportunity to stream content for your SAR, some of which we ourselves show in a montage of sexual expression across a broad spectrum. You will want to assure a good Internet connection to enable your streaming media in real time without hiccups or stalling of the transmission to your SAR room.

We have stayed away from using the Internet during SAR. Having to be connected via WiFi in a public venue, such as at a hotel conference room, can be very risky, daunting, and complicated. This process requires using a *smart TV*, flat screen with proper portals for wiring in the necessary equipment, or a computer with reliable and steady WiFi transmission, and it can be unreliable at best. Avoid complications by planning well ahead and being totally aligned with your media up front.

One common question we are asked is about the legality of fair use of copyrighted materials for an educational event. Here is what the University of Texas says:

Educational multimedia projects *created under these guidelines incorporate students' or educators' original material, such as course notes or commentary, together with various copyrighted media formats including but not limited to, motion media, music, text material, graphics, illustrations, photographs and digital software which are combined into an integrated presentation . . . Educators may incorporate portions of lawfully acquired*[13] *copyrighted works when producing their own educational multimedia programs for their own teaching tools in support of curriculum-based instructional activities at educational institutions (University of Texas, 2007).*

An interesting insight shed light on the element of music in SAR media. Rev. McIlvenna commented that often it was the soundtrack music that determined if someone liked or disliked a film during SAR. Ravi Shankar's sitar music was Rev. Sutton's favorite, as opposed to an opera aria for McIlvenna's taste. Consider the type of music you play at a SAR or if you are creating a media montage with a score. What mood do you want to provoke?

See Activity #10 for a potpourri of media genres that we have used in the past. All are from either DVDs, streaming sources, videotaped converted to digital, or taped live lectures at our own SARs. As you have read in Chapter 5 about the SilverSAR™, we ourselves show a modified clip from a classical film about a couple engaging in sexual play in their seventh decade. "A Ripple in Time" is derived from the original collection of IASHS *sexual inema verite*. You may want to access that collection for your own use.

ACTIVITY 10: *What can you curate for your SAR? Be creative and don't get caught in the trap of finding new media just because yours is old. Old can be gold. Highlight those you can find and use.*

Media types and sources: * Hollywood films *foreign films *sexual pattern films *sensate focus films *explicit sex educational films *couples' sexual enhancement entertainment *commercial porn/adult XXX *female-friendly erotica *documentaries[14] *self made media *premium television cable specials *international television programs * Internet series *news segments

Element 11: Speaker Selection: Revealing the Soul of SAR

Speakers/Lived Experience (Recommended for at Least 40% of SAR)

Before you book a speaker, be sure you have vetted them properly. We once hired a SAR speaker who gave out inaccurate information, appeared harried and disheveled, and spoke sarcastically about the medical professions to a group in which we had two physicians. She created a huge controversy that stole hours of staff consultation time in addressing the negative reactions she prompted. Assure that your speaker will serve your audience well. Use your skills in engaging that person well in advance about what you expect; time allocations; financial compensation due if any; and the purpose, tone, or content for their talk. Discuss your expectations in a personal email and with a phone conversation or, better yet, on a cyber video platform. Exceptions include qualified referrals from trusted colleagues, such as our transgender panels from the Los Angeles Gender Center for every Los Angeles-based SAR, or regular speakers from a bureau, such as when we work with the Los Angeles Center for Positive Sexuality staff, who thoroughly prepare their speaker volunteers to present on their Lived Experience within BDSM/kink/fetish (LAGC, 2016). Even then you can be burned if you have someone who has a particular axe to grind or is just plain expressing a nasty edge to their day. SAR is meant to push buttons, but never because your speaker irritates the group!

When we invite speakers who identify as sex workers, or Surrogate Partner Therapists, or sexological bodyworkers, depending on the legal status where the SAR is being held, they may be disclosing activities that are considered to be illegal. We salute these speakers who are courageous and generous enough to share their stories with our group. One beautiful female escort remarked, "I break the law every day and I love my work. I consider myself a true healer and so do my clients." The speakers reveal details about decriminalization or legalization of prostitution, along with the grey areas that may be unclear in terms of the laws concerning working in sexually explicit dynamics with clients. This is always a favorite part of SAR, creating a powerful emotional impact and usually shifting attitudes toward greater acceptance and compassion.

We recommend that speakers comprise at least 40% of your SAR in which they present their Lived Experience. The range of possible speakers is truly endless, similar to your media; some of the most commonly sought-after speaker genres include, but are not limited to:

1. Sex workers, such as prostitutes, escorts, madams, brothel owners
2. Trans persons of varying identities
3. Polyamorous or *swingers* or *lifestyle* persons
4. BDSM/kink/fetish practitioners[15]

5. Asexual persons
6. Disabled persons
7. Sacred sexual masters
8. Sexological or sexually oriented bodyworkers
9. Sexual artists or performers, such as from the adult industry, or crafts persons with unusual products
10. Famous authors or speakers on a rare or significant topic in sexuality, such as on pedophilia, zoophilia, or fetish practices
11. Experts on a topic, such as trans therapists, filmmakers, attorneys, advocates on sex trafficking, sex offender laws, or prostitution cases
12. Sex toy experts

ACTIVITY 11: *Make your own list of types or genres of speakers here.*

1.

2.

3.

4.

Now go back and start to plug in beside each type the tentative sources to find the speakers of your dreams.

Element 12: Materials and Supplies

Preparation Is a Key for Success

Put your paperwork in order before you open the doors to your live SAR. These are some of the materials we recommend that you have ready to go:

- Sign-in/sign-out sheets for Continuing Education Credits or CEs. If you offer CEs (and even if you don't), keep track of who has attended, with their name, signature, license number if applicable, which CEs they are seeking to earn from your SAR (according to what you offer), and their times of arrival and departure. You want to assure that you are providing them CEs with integrity and covering your obligations as a CE Provider to document everything required.
- MOUs: Memorandum Of Understanding is part of self-protection for your SAR container and its intellectual property, and MOUs assist in creating a safe space for participants. Before each participant signs in and receives their notebook, folder, and other enrollment materials, they must sign the MOU with the SAR assistant acting as receptionist. No one is allowed into the SAR room without having signed that document, which is retained along with other paperwork for at least 5 years. We take a hard-line approach to this safety precaution.

Take a peek at our sample MOU in the box.

ACTIVITY 12: *What's in yours? (Practice writing your version here)*

Your MOU includes the following:

SAR (SEXUAL ATTITUDES REASSESSMENT & RESTRUCTURING)

(MOU) MEMORANDUM OF UNDERSTANDING

Re: Confidentiality and Non-Disclosure Agreement on SAR program

I ________________ (printed full SAR Student name) agree to honor this agreement to keep confidentiality and non-disclosure for the SAR as follows:

I will not disclose the content, format, structure, discussions, personal or any other private information shared at this SAR program. That includes identifying the media, panel presenters, other speakers, names of attendees, and/or the specific outline of topics, other than to meet Certification requirements for the content topic areas.

It is my understanding that SAR is a privately offered training, whether for CEs or not, and that the intellectual property fully belongs to the SAR CE provider, Dr. Patti Britton.

Signature of SAR Student: ________________________________

Date: ________________

Location: ____

- **Written evaluations for Learning Objectives (and CKAs if you use AASECT criteria)**. You may replicate other SAR leaders in posting a pre-assessment online, such as at surveymonkey.com or qualtrics.com. Post-SAR assessments mimic the pre-test and can be required for online completion prior to issuing the final certificate of attendance. Evaluation forms are contained in the student enrollment packet, along with these other documents: Simple (one-page) Agenda, Safety Rules/Guidelines; contact information for SAR Leaders and other staff; topic-driven information sheets, including the popular and helpful conceptual model of the Trans Genderbread (2016), BDSM definitions, disability and sexuality factsheets, or anything else that pertains to your selection of topics. Remind yourself, SAR is not a didactic teaching modality; it is experiential. Just enough information to take home may reinforce the learning that does take place in the SAR room. This is also a chance for you to promote your SAR speakers and their programs, services, and additional opportunities for personal or professional expansion. We also include an updated factsheet on local eateries, a map of local landmarks (such as the former Selznick Studios where *Gone with the Wind* was filmed or SONY Pictures headquarters and MGM Studios), suggested nightlife nearby, or other pertinent updates, such as directions to the field trip venue. Our standard method is to circulate an email sign up list so that permission is given to share names, emails, and phone numbers after SAR. Similarly, we use newsprint on the walls to list ride shares, SAR buddy assignments to create safety and bonding, and other ad hoc postings that may arise. We also sometimes include a SASE[16] for testimonials to be sent in after the SAR afterglow period has faded and for those aversive to sharing comments via email. Be sure to get all printing or copying done well in advance, depending on the number that have signed up; and always leave room to print and prepare extras as you may have last-minute arrivals. A hot tip is to assemble your packets and folders the day before and not on the day of your SAR. Leave room for hiccups and for your own energy to be conserved. Procrastination and holding back in your prep work will bite you down the road.
- **Purchases required**: You are going to want to review your budget before you go madly shopping for fun treats or slick marketing tactics to add into your participant materials, such as expensive pre-printed gold stickers sporting your logo or fancy lanyards for name tags. However, prepare for these:

  - Newsprint pads or giant Post-Its with a pack of thick markers
  - Each participant will need to be given a multi-pocket folder, which we select in two colors to differentiate each of two small groups. In it you may put all of their handouts and information sheets, promotional materials, a list of local cafes, and anything else you deem relevant. You

can also buy a plastic envelope, which sometimes go on sale at your local discount office supply mart, and reflect value to the attendees as a recyclable gift. You also may ask for recyclables to be returned as a statement of your *green* philosophy, as it is becoming more prevalent today, to recapture folders, plastic nametag holders, and other reusable items.

- Student journal or a blank notebook to keep track of their thoughts, feelings, and responses
- Reasonable snacks (such as apples, nuts, or candies in the late afternoon); this is optional and in some hotels forbidden unless you purchase directly at high costs from the hotel catering menu
- A nametag for each day with names written to show personality in colors and styles
- Pens or pencils (yes, there are still pencils being made to use today!) for writing in the notebook; we do not allow computers in the SAR room, as it can easily become a distraction for checking emails, social media, or just checking out of the moment. These expectations are also stated in our Guidelines for SAR.
- Colored markers for writing their names on nametags for easy visibility
- Art activity supplies, such as tablets of white card stock, colored paper, glue, glitter sticks, stickers, ribbon, fur, feathers, paint, crayons, pencils, paint, and brushes, as mentioned in Element #7
- Whatever else you think is necessary; make a list and keep it tightly managed.

If you mirror our approach, you too will opt to close the last day with a circle ritual of some kind. Often we provide a beautiful gold plastic tray on which we lay an array of objects, each symbolizing an aspect of SAR and our goals for their re-entry back to their norm. We have purchased small polished stones, wrapped chocolates, red-and-gold-embossed envelopes that we buy each year from a Chinese market, and silver coins that we gather from our international travels. We work metaphorically and symbolically in this process. You may choose to go another route, such as a thank you card for each person or nothing at all. Find your unique characteristic style and go with that. Our symbols guide the ritual part of our closing circle, showing appreciation for the SAR experience. While we all stand in a circle, we ask for each person to pick their chosen objects from the tray while saying their one-word takeaway. Sometimes that one word is a paragraph! Symbols include tiny red Chinese envelopes for gratitude, coins for prosperity, stones for spirituality, and candies or small balloons for happiness. We end the circle by sending up our hands in unison and chanting words like "Peace," "Love," "Abundance," "Sex" while shouting out for love and sexual healing to happen everywhere! It is a magical and powerful ending to our SAR that never disappoints.

ACTIVITY 13: *Build your own shopping list here.*

1.

2.

3.

4.

5.

6.

7.

etc.

Element 13: Student Journals or Notebooks

Self-Reflection Is a Journey to Healing the Self

We have printed a Student Journal in the past, listing all process questions that follow along with the detailed outline. Look at the process questions for Element #15 for an example of how you can structure and print a working notebook for handing out to your participants as their journal. Often we print the Student Journal cover in color on card stock, showing a funny, erotic, or artful image[17] to promote discussion, an aura of celebration, and themes about sex. This special product may be time-intensive and costly to produce. Often just a plain lined bound notebook is enough to provide a written documentation of the SAR journey and the feelings, thoughts, attitudes, beliefs, takeaways, and other personal expression that participants will want to write down and capture for themselves. So choose what works within your resources of budget and time availability. Don't go overboard on handouts if you are tight on cash. Look for back-to-school sales at big box retailers or office supply stores to stock up on heavily discounted student notebooks, if that is going to be your preference. Occasionally, we will have a SAR attendee who is a right-brain person, habituated to making doodles or drawings. Once a student kept a 55-page notebook filled with beautiful scribbles and images in pen-and-ink that spoke to his entire experience.

Element 14: SAR Leaders

Who You Are and How You Need to Be

SAR leadership is a privilege, not a right. It takes a seasoned, experienced, and strong leader to conduct a SAR. As Mitelman advises, "Don't assume that anyone can facilitate a SAR well!! It takes training and having attended at least one other SAR. Most people will forget what is said but will never forget the energy or trust fostered in the room." She notes that the ability to create trust in the room falls on the facilitators, whether SAR leaders or SGFs. She adds, "Before ever asking others to share their most intimate truth, they must be experienced and have looked at themselves first. A facilitator has to be able to avoid becoming triggered. We all are at risk of that possibility" (2016).

Think of your SAR leadership like the head, heart, and the blood of SAR. You are its conceptual designer, the feeler or senser who guides what should go where, and the energy that drives the engine to make sure that your SAR is delivered adroitly and with the sensitive on-the-spot management that is part of the hallmark of SAR. You are the steward of an oftentimes frail river raft ride in choppy waters, in which your passengers have given you their trust; it takes skill to guide the delicate journey to its final destination. Many of us take it for granted that we can design, lead, and claim SAR successes. That sense of confidence did not evolve out of a vacuum. We tested and retested new methods, we failed at parts of the process, picked ourselves up again and walked forward each time, SAR after SAR. Even today we find that parts of our design may need tweaking or we get excited at the thought of shifting around the format or changing the media selections ad hoc with careful forethought.

As Wayne Palowski says, "A SAR must reflect thoughtful intentionality." We agree. We have engaged in a team effort with allied staff and volunteers, discovering our own strengths and weaknesses along the way. For example, Dunlap curates and edits our media montages, Britton is the resident wordsmith, and both are the energy readers of the group. Both are empathic and compassionate as role models, leaders, and small group facilitators. Neither knows it all and both know some of what it takes to create, lead, and sustain the container known as a SAR. Your team must be comprised of compatible parts to make the whole SAR sizzle and for your most positive attributes to shine. If you are about to dive into your new role as a SAR leader, here are some criteria you need to know about yourself for you to achieve success.

Criteria and Qualities of a SAR Leader (or Provider)

Our recommended Provider or Leader Criteria include the following: The SAR Leader should have attended at least 30 hours total of SAR with at least two different providers of SAR. The only exception is having attended an IASHS 6- or 8-day SAR, plus one other weekend format SAR. This person also is expected to show documentation of having been a trained SAR small group facilitator at least one time, and show proof of having led at least one small group at a minimum of one SAR event.

Here is our sample introductory outline description and sample script for how we open a SAR. You can modify it to match how you will do the same.

Outline description: (75 minutes) We begin with a SAR overview of what to expect, what is going to happen, and how to enter into the SAR experience. Starting with introductions of the SAR staff with a short presentation of each of our backgrounds, we create a container of who is going to hold the frame for the entire SAR process. It is always an upbeat, positive, and joyful part of our opening words. In particular we emphasize that we are caretakers for everyone. We point out who's who on staff, and encourage finding those persons one may need for certain components of the process, such as completing paperwork, special dietary concerns for lunches, AASECT requirements for certifications, locating the nearest pharmacy, buying gluten-free snacks, or finding a good massage therapist in the hotel.

Next we go over business. Payments first must be cleared with the SAR assistant. Materials are discussed, including what should be in each packet or folder and Continuing Education paperwork requirements. We present the value of the Student Journal and assure that all necessary paperwork, such as MOUs and sign-in/sign-out sheets, are signed, and that all are wearing nametags. We present housekeeping details, such as when breaks or lunches will occur approximately, note the location of the restrooms, and talk about creature comforts, such as inviting input for temperature control. We strongly speak about being on time and present. We also point to the location of our on-site store and when that is open for business.

Next we share as a team the important discussion about SAR expectations. We review how SAR works and why they are there.

Here is a sample script we use that you may model for your own SAR:

Hi, and good morning, everyone! We are so thrilled that you are here with us today. First, let's take a Mindfulness Moment[18]*: Get settled, sit comfortably, let your mind clear by focusing on your breathing; breathe slowly; focus on your breath. (Allow 2–3 minutes.) Now, slowly open your eyes, and use your eyes as fresh eyes to see in this SAR as if for the very first time.*

Let's go over some of the basics, before we begin. This SAR is based on the classical model that we learned firsthand at the Institute in San Francisco. We present it to you with a modern twist and a contemporary spin of media and some of the most compelling sexological expression we could find today. You're about to witness human sexuality in its many dimensions of expression. In today's world of short attention spans and 140-character communiqués—yes, tweets—people can't sit still for a long time focusing on only one thing. That is one reason why we do not show anything in full length. Instead, we have put together media montages, designed to push you on what you like, don't like, comfort and discomfort. So don't judge! Don't judge yourself, the media, the speakers, or others. Let yourself be a sponge. Inhale and exhale as you go. Take the ride with us! Let yourself float in and out, like riding the waves, some gentle, some rough. It is a sensitivity training, not a clinical or practical skills training. SAR is created to show you your limits and stretch your boundaries of acceptance, tolerance, and expansion of yourself. Now we want to give you a hint. SAR can be a very bumpy and emotional ride. We may take you to places that you've never even thought of! So, take care of yourself along the way, and take care of each other.

You have a small group for support and us as your SAR leaders. If you need to get some support or process something outside of the small group process, please find someone to talk to. You do have a SAR Buddy assigned to you, and that's a good person to get to know. Use your SAR Buddy as an accountability partner and friend during this weekend. Please make sure you are on time. After the SAR you may require personal care, as you may experience what we like to call the trickle-down effect. You may be standing in a grocery store or watching the evening news and "boom!" It hits you. Something you saw or heard in the SAR smacks you into a new awareness. You get it. You were affected after you left the room, maybe days, weeks, or months later. Let it happen and honor the process of the SAR afterglow period.

SAR is something that not anyone can lead. It requires vast experience and training as a SAR leader or small group facilitator, clinical and educational skills, and awareness of the infinite spectrum of human sexual expression. Leading a SAR takes mastery skills to create and hold safe space, along with noticing what is needed in the moment. We are always monitoring you and the process. Never worry that we have checked out. We're here 100% for you. We, as your SAR team, are like a fish tank filter, always clearing the space energetically for your greatest healing and highest good. If we look tired, or distracted, focus back on yourself. We are working 24/7 for you during a SAR.

Our content includes media montages, as you will see shortly on the simple agenda in your packet, along with live speaker panels that you are going to love. We ask our BDSM speakers if possible to bring their toys and show you demos of what they know, so be open to trying out new things. Tonight we offer a fun field trip to an outside venue. (Cite which venue it is.) Take advantage of that. Going outside of this room to a new environment, seeing people express themselves in a dungeon, or being shown the new generation of sex toys at the shop may affect your life deeply. Stay open to busting your own boundaries and expanding your horizons for yourself.

SAR is for you, not your clients. Wear your personal persona, not your work identity in the SAR. That will stretch and enrich you to be a better educator or clinician or whatever it is you do in sexuality. The focus on this weekend is to look inside of yourself and let yourself be present to expand and delight in knowing who you are. You should have a notebook or Student Journal in your materials, and that's a good place for you to document your experience. Use it to write down any thoughts, feelings, and experiences that come up for you in the SAR, as this is a process, not an event. Turning inward is the essence of SAR, as you explore outside of yourself in the company of peers. Each day we will meet in small groups. That's your sanctuary and support group in which to process the experience. We'll meet in small groups twice today and at both days' lunches, and close with a whole group discussion tomorrow. There should be plenty of time to share your experience with the small and large groups.

You have a simple outline of events and topics. Each morning you must fill out your lunch order. Lunches will be served in small groups in this room and in the foyer. We'll let you know which group meets where, and your group is designated by the color of your folder. (We tell them which color goes with which group). If you need to change your group for any reason, please let your small group leader know that by end of Saturday lunch meeting.

Next, let's quickly review our Guidelines in your folder. You should have signed an MOU when you arrived. If not, raise your hand. That's one way that we protect confidentiality and emphasize that this SAR is our intellectual property. Our Guidelines cover safety, confidentiality, honesty, participation, "I feel" statements, being on time and present. We do not allow any electronic devices during SAR. We follow the IASHS rule, if you are found using a smart phone, tablet, or any other device, we impose an immediate $10,000 fine. Get it? NO devices! Devices take you out of being present in the room. We expect your full cooperation and participation. Any questions? Finally, no outside food or drinks are permitted in the SAR room. That's another distraction to keep you from being present and the hotel won't allow it. Please honor those rules. (We review the list of Guidelines here and invite heads to nod yes in acceptance at the end).

Finally, it's that time! We want to know who you are, why you are here and get to know each other for the first dive. Ready? So, let's go around the room. Everybody is going to take a turn, say your name, where you are from, what professional role you play in sexuality, and (pause) your hottest sexual fantasy or a sexual secret about yourself you have never shared. We know you can do it! Let's start here. Usually this icebreaker creates the opening into safe space and laughter abounds for 30–40 minutes, and it is followed by a 15-minute break.

As Mitelman guides, "Act as the controlling timekeeper to assure that your speakers end on time, clear the room in a timely manner, and that you usher participants quickly to their small group for processing the prior speaker panel. This is not a good time for breaks." Being vigilant as the primary timekeeper and guardian of the agenda for your SAR will assure its flow.

Here are some of the qualities you will need for yourself to be a SAR Leader.

ACTIVITY 14: *Put a checkmark beside the qualities that you (or your hired SAR leader) meets before you begin your SAR. Your SAR Leader exhibits:*

- Public speaking skills and poise under duress
- Counseling acumen
- Group process facilitation, development, and trouble spotting
- Troubleshooting skills with difficult participants
- Ability to think on your feet; examples: speaker does not show; lunches are late
- Flexibility
- Authenticity
- Familiarity with the scope of human sexual expression
- Well-tested expertise leading groups of an experiential nature
- Dynamism as a speaker
- Role modeling for participants in how you handle confusion, emotional triggers, and conflict
- Creative thinking, planning, and organizing (easily can move the agenda when needed)
- Highly honed observation skills
- Good listening ability
- Excellence at time allocations and redirecting time usage in the moment
- Response and responsibility to the needs of the group; other-directed
- Ability to express deep emotions of your own / willing to self-disclose for benefit of others
- Great tolerance
- Sense of humor
- Keen intellect
- High Emotional Intelligence
- Empathy and kindness, yet is firm and bold
- Knows how to create and maintain 'safe space'
- Role models Extreme Self Care (ESC)

Element 15: Small Group Facilitators

Building Your Dream Team

Small group facilitators (SGFs) will evolve their own facilitation style. Dunlap runs his group in a militaristic fashion. He sits his group in a circle and insists that each member of the group answers specific process questions one by one, in order, no matter what. Britton uses a more flowing technique of asking who would like to comment, allowing for group interaction to be less authoritative and more organic. Both are effective strategies for moving the conversation around the group. Neither lets group members sit silently, but will come back if an emotional disruption occurs or someone is stuck on a distraction that removes them from the moment, such as a family emergency or illness during the SAR. You will want to notice behaviors such as heads down, no eye contact being made, sullen expressions, hushed sobbing, or manic laughing as signals that you need to focus in on that person and elicit a response as to what may be going on inside of them. As SGFs we push the sharing to utilize the "I feel," not "I think," approach, correcting and shifting speaking patterns on the spot. You will find your own style as a SGF (assuming that you act as both SAR leader and SGF). Train your staff in the systematic methods you prefer as you hone your skills.

Our friend and SAR leader Pawloski (2016) recommends the following as he prepares his SGFs: "Your role as the SGF is to facilitate not lead. You are expected to encourage dialogue, circulate the group conversation, and enhance flow among participants. It is never about you." Sometimes we open our small group with an authentic disclosure statement about our own emotional condition, for the good of the group not us. As an example, after just viewing "The Sessions" film montage before the lunch break, it is not uncommon for Britton to be flooded with emotions and a few tears, even after viewing it 20 times. She might acknowledge her state by saying, "Right now I am feeling a deep level of sadness and compassion from seeing that media. Give me a moment to center myself, will you? Perhaps we can begin to eat our lunches, then open up for sharing. OK?" Often, because we know as group facilitators how to work the *vibratory tone* of a group, we use personal disclosure to take the group energetically down into a profound feeling state, changing the dynamic out of their heads into their guts. Eating food together is by nature a bonding experience. Dunlap always asks his group, "Did you get the correct lunch? . . . Are you happy with your food?" He is consistently checking for any additional unmet physical needs as a way of showing care for his group. Emotional disclosures can be difficult while eating. Be mindful that having lunch with small group may demand a brief period for social interaction and digesting first; then invite a group sharing of deep emotional takeaways. Small group facilitation may appear to be more of an art than a skill at times. Frequently Dunlap does not eat his lunch during group process time but saves it for later when our speaker guests present. He believes in focusing exclusively on the needs of his group. Britton needs the fuel, so she eats along with the group, balancing that action with watching, eliciting, timekeeping, and speaking. All SGFs discover their own natural flow.

Been There Done That *Syndrome*

You will face a universal theme that every SAR leader we know echoes as a point of frustration for themselves. What SGFs tend most to dread is the feedback and immediate demonstration of resistance in small group, known as the *Been There, Done That* syndrome. This will happen to you, unless you offer your SAR for residents of a remote island, with no Internet, smart phones, radio, television, or access to modern media. To us *Been There, Done That* is a form of resistance and one of the greatest challenges of offering a contemporary SAR.

As you recall from Chapter 2, SAR began in the 1970s when media had to be made specifically for SAR, and when exposure to explicit sexual imagery was limited to adult theaters or relegated to the privacy of a peep show booth. Today's world is filled with explicit sexual imagery, some of it even sanctioned on mainstream broadcast television or suggested in TV commercials, such as ads with nearly naked women displaying barely visible lingerie on prime time shows. One of our sexologist peers remarked that as a young teen male his form of erotic stimulation was the women's underwear section of the Sears Catalog and the special swimsuit editions of men's sports magazines. Your SAR participants will show up having watched *porn du jour* and habituated to it perhaps over years of exposure. Here's the difference: They have watched it alone for masturbatory self-stimulation or in the intimate company of sexual partners. Instead, during SAR they are being asked to focus not on the eroticism of the media or on the familiarity of the visuals, but on the experience of viewing your media in the presence of professional peers, and they are expected to process it. As Stayton so aptly puts it, "You must contextualize SAR up front, emphasizing with your participants that SAR was created to help people to get into their feelings and attitudes and process their experience in a group context" (2016). Processing their experience of watching the porn or other explicit media *in the room* is the key for a SAR event to be effective. They may also have been an aficionado at a local BDSM play space or identify as a trans person; they may balk at having to listen to a peer because they are armoring themselves or don't want to confront their own feelings in public. Or they may just be feeling smug, in which case, bring them out to share.

Notice if your participants are staying neck up, thinking about the quality or content of the media footage, judging you for what you are showing or not showing, and reliving the experience as a repetition of their habits. Some of the most highly trained individuals, especially if they are at your SAR merely to tick off the required check list, may be the most self-protected, wearing the shell of a turtle. They intellectualize their feelings. That's not what SAR is about. Your role as the SGF is to redirect participants out of the cognitive realm into the affective realm. Being pushed to talk about what they feel—yes, we mean deliberately pushed during small group—is the name of the game. You want them to talk in the group about how it feels to be in the room with other professionals, what is feels like to get aroused in the room with strangers, and what it feels like to begin to feel embarrassment or boredom (also a signal of resistance). Don't permit them to shift to a critique of the media instead of the result from their viewing it. If a film or media selection is not perfect, don't worry. As Schoen recommends, use the imperfections as a SGF to spark dialogue; in sexuality education, we call this the *Teachable Moment*.

It can also be a comfortable escape hole for your group members to rely on the *Been There Done That* syndrome so that feelings of vulnerability never arise. Related to this syndrome is the attempt by participants who are mental health professionals (or naturally born helpers) to try to fix what may show up as an emotional reaction by a (re)-traumatized participant. We call this the "Do Not Therapize Others" rule. All of the management of the *Been There Done That* phenomenon is part of your role to facilitate a plunge into the feelings of your group and to elicit discussion. It's not an easy role. It is, however, a requirement you must fulfill in order for your SAR to work.

Translation

Like us, you may need a translator on premises during your SAR. You can determine how many will speak the primary language (English is assumed) and how many need help in listening, watching, hearing speakers, and sharing in groups. We have used simultaneous translation in many countries and at times this has become a great distraction for the rest of the group, but it remains a necessary add-on for multi-lingual SAR programs.

Small group facilitators must possess certain characteristics to be effective. These are some of those qualities, skills, and traits. Ask yourself if you and/or your small group facilitator(s) can check off those traits.

ACTIVITY 15: *Use a checkmark for all that apply. Your small group facilitator is:*

- A good listener
- Skilled at group process and facilitation
- Knowledgeable enough to read the tone of a group
- Sensitive to nuances being expressed
- Able to handle upsets, e.g., a triggered reaction to media
- Competent to assure that all voices are heard
- Skilled as a speaker, knowing when and how to ask pivotal questions and to restate what someone has said
- A person with a sense of humor
- Understanding of the stated purpose of the SAR and the learning objectives
- A team player; knows when to ask for help from the SAR leaders; shares with team
- Willing to disclose about personal issues within the group for the good of the group and/or to facilitate group sharing as a role model
- Courageous
- Engaged to assure that everyone is heard without being militaristic as a group leader
- Capable of spotting and stopping problems before they escalate
- In possession of good intuitive ability and counseling or coaching skills
- Good time management skills
- Sensitive to over-talking; quickly and efficiently manages group
- Nurturing
- Approachable
- Wise and mature (does not get reactive to upsets in the group)
- Knowledgeable about when to ask a participant to seek help and/or leave the group due to disruptive behaviors being exhibited
- Is familiar with the SAR outline, has previewed all of the media, is aware of who will be speaking, and has cleared him/her/oneself about any potential triggers that may surface in facilitating based on the content

Element 16: Creating "Safe Space" (and other Demands)

The Secret Sauce of SAR

If you have been trained in healing or shamanic techniques or if you intuitively know about clearing negative energies, you will find this element as easy as breathing. We as individuals rely on both left and right brain intelligence for managing the energy flow in our groups. Both of us were born empathic, having been gifted with natural abilities to observe, feel, and shift energies in ourselves, in the environment, and in others. We literally can feel or read what may be happening in a space or within a person in the moment as part of qualities that we bring to SAR. As author Grout writes, we are made up of energy fields and can read others' fields. "Energy is a . . . nebulous thing. You can't see it, scratch it, take it out to dinner. But you can (and do everyday) influence how it flows through you" (2014). Einstein's relativity theory is only a part of the story. To us, sending, receiving, reading, and redirecting the energies in the SAR room is a huge part of our SAR stewardship.

Advanced training in Feng Shui also assists us in managing and understanding the presence of energies in spatial settings. Britton has also studied esoteric methodologies and has been trained as a Reiki healer, offering shamanic processes such as setting sacred space, ritual work, and energy clearing. Shamanic clearing techniques can include the use of sage, raven feathers, sacred beads, incense, chants, candles, music, and intentional energy transformation. Both are graduates of famous personal empowerment intensives.[19] Dunlap pulls from his vast experience as a well-trained professional Hollywood actor to embody what others are feeling or doing, and he can fully be present in the moment. Without any effort, his stage skills and directorial acumen as a filmmaker become evident in SAR leadership.

Having explicit agreements with your group about safety guidelines and the use of MOUs help to establish boundaried space and behaviors. You can always institute and emphasize our #1 Groundrule, the "Las Vegas Rule," which states that what goes on in the room stays in the room. We routinely burn the smoke of sacred sage or aromatherapy candles to clear the negative energies from the SAR room wherever we go, before any other person arrives as we set up.

We have found a pattern of rituals for powering up ourselves help to create an inner safe space. We also sometimes use sea salt baths, sacred crystals, feathers, music, or other means to clear ourselves back in our hotel room when we are *off duty*. Occasionally, we also will obtain a therapeutic massage the night before a SAR to relax our physical bodies or eat a lovely meal at a restaurant instead of at home on the night before SAR to prepare ourselves for the intensive activities to follow.

We also are so fortunate to have each other, which becomes a process container of its own. We monitor each other 24/7 when it's SAR time, by nurturing, caring for and assuring that our human engines are operating at full tilt and energizing each other when our batteries appear to be wearing down. We open our SAR early on day one with a group circle of staff, holding hands, setting our positive intentions, and envisioning success. Staff meetings, when needed, also help to create an internal *safe space* among us as a team, allowing for time to blow off negativity, combine observations for clearing out difficult participant issues, and hold each other in group hugs as a regular feature of our time together.

Finally, to maintain the role of SAR steward, we highly recommend that you get plenty of rest and eat well so that you can run and manage the energy of the group each day. Do not push yourself beyond your own limits. Take breaks when you need them, privately, to reboot. Ask for what you need. Practice conscious breathing to anchor back into your own safe space of your body when you feel triggered or when the tension of upsets are surrounding you. Safe space shepherding and nurturing of the group require intensity of your own stores of energy and centeredness for effective SAR leadership.

ACTIVITY 16: *Write down three gifts that you possess that will help you to create and maintain safe space:*

1.

2.

3.

Element 17: Small Group Process and Takeaways

Excelling at Group Flow

The role of the small group facilitator (SGF) can make or break your SAR. Some SARs do not use small group facilitators at all and instead give assignments to the self-managed groups to talk about their reactions to the topics and presentations. We strongly encourage you to use a small group facilitator for the groups to stay on track, be managed well, and to assure a safe and appropriate container is maintained for all. Everyone in the small group deserves airtime, so always assure that a fair share of attention is spent on each person. Be sure that your SGFs are well trained and polished in their ability to create a safe group setting and hold that space. They will need to meet the traits and characteristics that we outlined above in Element #14. Our formula for small group size is a maximum of 10 participants, with an ideal average of 8.

Our colleague Thrasher has some strong views about the role of SGF and offers these helpful tips:

1. While the whole group watches the media or listens to the speakers together, the real work takes place in the context of the smaller group.
2. SGFs must be well trained to understand group dynamics; there will always be difficult participants, such as the group blocker, the over-sharing dominant, or the person with unfulfilled special needs (such as being triggered by old sexual traumas), all of which can upset the container of the small group.
3. If your SAR averages 20–30 attendees, attempt to provide small groups of ideally only four to six participants.[20] With only 45–60 minutes for sharing in small group at a time, having a larger group eliminates ample talking time for everyone.
4. Try to customize who is in each small group according to the personality fit of your SGF; you may also want to arrange your small group to incorporate a mix of race, ethnicity, sexual orientation, experience, and any other attribute for a diverse conversation to occur.
5. For the *Been There, Done That* resister who tends to disrupt the flow of the small group process, address them separately. Sometimes this is a seasoned sex therapist of many years who has to tick off the SAR requirement for certification. Help them to see how their participation of resistance affects the outcome for the group. Pull them aside and say, "We're in this together. Think about the effects this is having on the group. Let's make this a good experience for everyone, can we?"

The process itself is an opportunity for your participants to feel safe within a smaller portion of the larger group. Being a part of a group smaller than the original size creates a feeling of intimacy and improves capacity for sharing innermost thoughts and feelings among group members. The goal of the small group is to elicit feelings and to help members share their authentic expression. We deliberately split up couples or co-workers into separate small groups to promote privacy. Often the small group process evokes conversations about what they have just learned, what has triggered responses, what buttons were pushed positively or negatively, what memories may have surfaced, what shifts they are undergoing, or what their current VABs are showing them to themselves and to their peers in the small group setting. Eliciting responses from each member of the small group is a critical component of SAR, providing a sense of intimate disclosure, provoking fresh ideas and beliefs, and allowing for a shared bond of trust and awareness of the similarities and/or differences group members possess.

Small group process constitutes one of the key elements that distinguish a SAR from other sex education programs. We recommend that at a minimum your small groups meet two times the first day of a 2-day SAR and once more the second day. Some SAR small groups meet after *each* topic is presented, deconstructing their experience one topic at a time. Our format is calculated to create four unique group process experiences.

Small Group Facilitator's Guidelines, based on a sample SAR outline, are provided above in Element #15. Use this as a sample guide to process your small group during SAR. Note that these process questions often form the basis for the Student Journal.

First Meeting Suggestions

As a SGF, create a safe container for everyone, based on your small group leadership training. Get the group going immediately. Go around the group to introduce one another and capture any urgent unprocessed emotional reactions. Talk about the value of the small group process. Emphasize the importance and value of writing in the Student Journal or notebook. Invite the group to take in all that happens in the SAR, saying something like, "This is a process. Use fresh eyes. Let it affect you, focusing on feeling over thinking, and being present for whatever comes up for you or others." Be sure to emphasize the importance of utilizing a SAR buddy for support, processing thoughts/feelings/attitudes, and accountability.

Start all discussions with "What did you feel . . .? Or what do you feel about . . .?" No thinking, all feeling. Make sure all voices are heard. If group members are quiet, go around the table or room to engage all participants. Focus their sharing on the topics that were just presented before each group meeting and to capture any brewing issues. Don't let the group intellectualize their experience! At your final small group meeting, acknowledge the sharing and bonding that has occurred and thank them for this special time together. Let them say good-bye to each other as small group members.

Here are three sample excerpts from our own SGF guide (and tips for the final whole group process activity).

Topic 1: Hetero, Gay, Lesbian, Bisexual Expression Media Montage

Process Questions

- *Think about the range of sexual expression, from the authenticity of the heterosexuals to gays or lesbians or bi scenes to aging from "Ripple in Time."*
- *What was your response to seeing naked people sucking, fucking, humping during sex? Same sex? Bi? Old folks?*
- *What about the sexual pattern film, "Ripple in Time," on aging and authentic sexual expression? How did it make you feel to see very old naked people engaged in intimacy and sex?*
- *Did any feelings arise for you in watching the media montage?*
- *What was your favorite part of this montage and why?*
- *What do you wish had been different and why?*
- *What touches you the most from this montage?*
- *How can this media let you be a better therapist or sex coach?*
- *What else?*

Topic 2: BDSM/Speaker(s) and Demonstrations

Process Questions

- *What was your favorite part of this discussion and depiction of BDSM and why?*
- *What were the uncomfortable parts of this topic for you (if any)?*
- *What buttons were pushed and why?*
- *What impact did this all have on your possible work with clients or for yourself?*
- *Do you feel ready and competent to work with the BDSM client?*
- *How much more do you need to learn to feel okay about that?*
- *What feelings come up when you think about BDSM activities, seeing demos of rope bondage, Dominance & Submission, painful torture, flogging, fetish worship, electric knife play, and more?*

Topic 3: Trans(gender) Panel of Speakers

Process Questions

- *What was the overall impression you got from watching and listening to these real-life stories of life as a trans person?*

- *What emotions came up for you? Any judgments?*
- *How did you feel seeing a trans man tell his story? What about a trans woman? What about the family of a trans person and their experience affected you the most?*
- *What had the most powerful impact on you by being present to learn about the life of a trans person from him/herself?*
- *Write about any feelings, new awarenesses, or conflicts this section sparked.*
- *Could you work with this population? If not, why not?*
- *What else?*

Whole Group Final Process Activity

After the afternoon segments are complete, and it's time for the last group sharing activity, as a SGF, help to facilitate the whole group toward takeaways, while emphasizing a focus on the positives.

Process Questions

- *What thoughts, feelings, attitudes, beliefs of yours were challenged by this SAR course?*
- *What touches you the most from this experience?*
- *How have your values been shifted?*
- *How has SAR affected you as a person?*
- *How has SAR affected you as a therapist, educator, and/or counselor?*
- *What is your biggest takeaway from this whole experience?*

ACTIVITY 17: *Write yourself notes here about how you want to use process questions for your SGFs. Will you create a guide for them to follow? Will you ask them to work more organically and in the moment? What questions will you want the small group to process overall? How will you know this is enough?*

Element 18: SAR Evaluations

Making Sure You've Hit the Mark

It is crucial to evaluate the effectiveness of your SAR. As you know by now, the effects may not be present for days, weeks, even months because of the trickle-down effect. Also, research findings vary (as discussed in Chapter 2) as to how to properly evaluate a SAR. Evaluation can be conducted in several formats:

1. **Pre-post tests, online or on site, at the beginning and end of your SAR**. You can develop a set of values-clarification statements or questions for your participants to self-assess before and after SAR. You may choose to use an online survey mechanism, such as Qualtrics.com, to mount your survey and obtain ready results. Use a 5-point Likert-type scale, such as 1–5 with 1 = disagree and 5 = agree. Test before and after SAR to determine if any shifts may have occurred in values, attitudes, or beliefs. Examples of values-laden assessment statements may include: *BDSM is a healthy aspect of human sexual expression. *Watching porn always has harmful results. *Furry or plushy fetishes are within the spectrum of normal sexual behaviors. *Prostitution should be decriminalized and legal everywhere. We have not used a pre-post test format.
2. **Quantitative approach to the content of SAR by topics**. Use a Likert-type 5-point scale using 1–5, with 1 = least and 5 = most, for each topic or component of the SAR outline. This may yield skewed results, as often a student will respond to whether or not they liked/disliked a segment, not whether they appreciated the segment for its significant impact on them. For example, when we feature the topic of disability without a speaker, instead relying on a media montage, we include footage of Dwarf Porn. These clips are explicit, rough, edgy, and produce a rash of negative comments for many who watch it. (On the other hand, it also evokes compassionate understanding among many when they learn of the impetus for this particular media selection.) Be aware of the results you are attempting to measure and think well about a quantitative approach for a mostly qualitative experience.
3. **Qualitative or narrative style at conclusion of SAR itself**. We use a narrative qualitative approach in garnering feedback as indicated in the sample Evaluation Form below. You can create your own or use the process questions that you will include in their Student Journal.
4. **Reflection essay one-week post-SAR due by email or snail mail**. This requirement allows the student to have time to feel their response to the entire SAR process and to articulate that response one week after the close of SAR. Most students send this to us in a one-page electronic document. Mitelman, who also follows this approach, shares, "Most participants meet

this expectation, as they are treated as adults and each is committed to their own learning process" (2016).

5. **The post-SAR essays are often the most telling expressions of the profound impact the SAR has had on participants**. Not everyone can discuss the effect of an experience in the moment. We find mostly positive and some negative reflections in their essays. For some persons, the essay shows that they have more work to do on their own, in confronting biases, triggers, or perhaps within specific topic areas. For others, it is their metaphoric dumping ground for letting out the sludge that has built up from the triggering effect of being in a SAR. Regularly, a negative SAR evaluation or comment is a signal of something that has been evoked, not of the design or leadership of the SAR itself. If everyone complains about a part of your SAR, listen seriously to that feedback. If it's one or two persons and the rest are glowing, interpret the complaint as opinion or personal projection. Be mindful that SAR can be a draining and difficult training for its leaders, as we have hinted throughout our book. That's true in part because of its intensity and due to the harsh critique that can be expressed when someone is piqued due to being exposed to some of the SAR content, not just the process.
6. **Journal**. The Student Journal is for each student to generate a personal recording of their process and any effects from attending the SAR. You should emphasize the importance of self-tracking via a notebook or journal. You also can inform the group that you will collect each person's Student Journal at the end of the SAR and return it to them with comments. They may choose to send it to you right after the close of SAR in an electronic format, as most students today avoid paper and pen and instead use their laptops, tablets, or smart phones to document their studies. Requiring submission of the Student Journal also reinforces the value of the journal for processing their SAR journey. At IASHS, every student was graded on the basis of their journal. Often these journals filled more than one notebook or up to 100 pages. We each have kept our original SAR journals as keepsakes from that precious contribution to our own sexological growth.
7. **Other means**: Rev. Sutton remarked that in the original SAR days, relying on a *gut feeling* served well to guide whether or not SAR was working. Pawloski commented that his evaluative technique is based on how deep the small group goes; Dunlap finds that it is when a dramatic emotional breakthrough occurs in his small group that he knows the process of SAR is working. Britton feels the energy of the group as alive and present, or a deeply felt emotional catharsis takes place that indicates the depth of experience that SAR intentionally provokes.

Here is a sample evaluation based on three topics from the sample design in Element 5.

SAR EVALUATION FORM

Location for SAR/ USA or International
Dates for SAR

Name: ______________________________________

Gender: Male__ Female___ Other___

The primary objectives for participants in SAR trainings are included in your handout for Learning Objectives and Core Knowledge Areas as required by AASECT. That serves as your formal quantitative evaluation. This evaluation is qualitative.

Write your comments below to reflect and express how this SAR affected you personally and professionally; express how your values, attitudes, and beliefs may have been challenged, changed, or validated.

[Below are three samples according to topic.]

Topic 1: Explicit Sexual Expression

What affected you the most about this section?
Favorite or least favorite parts?

Topic 2: BDSM speaker/demos

What affected you the most about this section?
Favorite or least favorite parts?

Topic 3: Trans speakers/panel

What affected you the most about this section?
Favorite or least favorite parts?

Overall

Please rate the facility for this SAR: On a 1–5 scale, with 5 being highest value

SCALE: 1 = poor 2 = fairly good 3 = good 4 = very good 5 = excellent

Comments:

Please rate the SAR Leader (Name:)

SCALE: 1 = poor 2 = fairly good 3 = good 4 = very good 5 = excellent

Comments:

Please rate the Small Group Facilitator, A (Name:)

SCALE: 1 = poor 2 = fairly good 3 = good 4 = very good 5 = excellent

Comments:

Please rate the Small Group Facilitator, B (Name:)

SCALE: 1 = poor 2 = fairly good 3 = good 4 = very good 5 = excellent

Comments

What was your most favorite part of the SAR overall and why?

What was your least favorite part of the SAR overall and why?

Please add any suggestions, comments and insights you would like to share for future SARs. (Other side may be used).

CALL TO ACTION!! If you would like to write a *testimonial*[21] on the value and power of this SAR, please add it in your own words with your name (if you wish it used) and attribution.

Thank you so much for being a part of this experience . . . Your SAR Team!!!!

ACTIVITY 18: *Once you have your agenda of topics in order, go over each part of it and craft a simple evaluation form. Use the technique(s) that best serve your style, your learning outcomes, and measurements for a successful SAR. Ask yourself if you want to use a pre- and post-test or quantitative or sheer narrative reflection approach to your evaluation or a combination of all of the above. Write your thoughts here:*

Element 19: Damage Control: Preventing SAR Fallout

Protect Yourself!

Brendan Burchard, one of our business gurus, admonishes that if you are going to run an event in a public setting like a hotel, obtain event protection insurance. All you need is for one person to get food poisoning or slip on the wet ladies' room floor; even though the hotel has protection, you can also be sued. Avoid that risk at all costs. You may also be liable for emotional damage, such as re-triggering trauma. Using a disclosure MOU up front, where they release you from such potential damages, is one layer of protection only. Anyone can sue you for anything. Get a good lawyer's advice for any legal issues that plague you as a SAR leader before you do any SARs.

One example is an MD who attended a SAR with his partner. When he saw the extreme body modification of tattoos and piercings, he winced. He reacted from his professional training to *Do No Harm* and could only view this as unsafe health practices, rather than erotic preferences. SAR helped him to reframe that.

Here are some helpful tips. (Where to find more information is listed in the Resources at the end of this chapter.)

- Cover yourself and your business with professional liability insurance for your services as a clinician, coach, or whatever professional standards you work under. As a SAR leader or group facilitator, you are still performing duties within your profession. This is sometimes referred to as malpractice insurance or, in our field of sex coaching, it is known as Health and Fitness Coaching.
- Obtain liability insurance for your office space, which is often referred to as premises coverage; or carry a type of add-on to your own renter's insurance for your rented space, known as umbrella coverage. Having a supplemental umbrella policy may protect you if someone slips on the carpet entering your own space or leaving down the steps to your parking lot.
- Secure a rider for yourself if you want extra protection against hosting an event in a hotel or other commercial location. Event insurance is a one-time cost and can be useful in providing ample coverage in case of an accidental injury.
- Talk to your own attorney about prevention of theft of your Intellectual Property beyond the MOU agreement. We highly support having legal counsel available at all times. One of our favorite resources is The Rodgers Collective, which offers a program for small businesses that includes downloadable documents and sound legal advice. However, even with a pre-paid program for legal resources, you should always have the contact information for an attorney to sort out any real legal quandaries or emergency occurrences.
- If a SAR participant becomes angry or upset at you or the SAR itself, or walks out of your SAR, you should have a refund and/or grievance policy

in place (as noted in Chapter 5). Be sure your terms and conditions or policies are thoroughly stated on your website or other promotional materials. You may also want to include a printed version of your policies and any disclaimers in your handout materials for each student.

Occupational Hazards

- **Professional**. To become visible in our profession as a sex expert or a SAR leader at someone else's SAR may prove threatening to you. If you want a pure SAR experience, the best way is to attend anonymously or incognito, as your identity can come back to haunt you. Pawloski tells the story of attending a SAR in which the leader outed him for who he was and for his expertise. Imagine how he felt when asked to share in small group? That dampening effect ruined any chances for him to experience a safe container, which then may also have contaminated the entire group process. Find safe sources to attend someone's SAR, inform them of your preference for privacy and anonymity, and make sure they use a careful screening device for your and their protection.
- **Personal**. For you as a SAR leader or SGF to also come out as a person of Lived Experience can produce another layer of risk for you. For example, Britton used to be a speaker, humbly disclosing the life journey of her daughter, who lived with HIV/AIDS for 20 years until her death in 2004, despite the cultural shift toward HIV as a lifelong manageable disease with proper medications. The talk came as a shocking surprise to the group. It was scheduled near the end of the second morning and set up as a ritualized memorial to her daughter with candles, somber jazz music, pictures on storyboards on a table with her daughter's photo in front of it. Britton reveals, "It ripped out my guts every time. I wept and fought back the inability to form words, reading from my writings about her dying, the horrors of the disease, and the courage it took to fight the medical system to get her to the peaceful landing place in the hospice where she passed away." That reading took weeks of emotional and mental preparation to garner the strength to revisit such pain for both of us. Although evaluations showed it to be one of the single most powerful sources of personal transformation in our SARs, it became too wearing on us as leaders to continue to offer our HIV/AIDS talk. Taking care of yourself is paramount to taking care of the needs of your group; don't let yourself become a martyr for the cause when it is not 100% essential.

Dos and Don'ts!

- **Don't** schedule a venue without visiting it first or having someone on your team visit it to assure it will work.

- **Don't** show media that you have not carefully screened and shown to your SGFs. All media should be in alignment with your intended outcomes for your SAR.
- **Don't** exceed your own boundaries for personal or professional safety; for example, don't agree to be the volunteer to be flogged topless in front of your group or being tied up in Shibari rope or testing out the violet wand for erotic electrical pulsation, if you feel afraid of crossing that boundary.
- **Don't** ever compromise your own values about anything.
- **Do** dress for success! Showing up in career attire, rather than going for a casual look, will go a long way in establishing your professionalism and authority.
- **Don't** fight back in temptation to quell upsets or resistance. If someone pushes your buttons, don't defend; instead, say something like, "What wonderful material this is for you to work through." You may remind them of their mean-spirited Aunt Tessie or their ex-husband and it's really not about you but about them. If it escalates, you can always say, "Look, I'm not here to fight with you; I'm here to facilitate."
- **Do** listen to your gut, that is your intuition, in making any SAR decisions. If something doesn't feel right, honor that feeling and take appropriate action. When in doubt, leave it out!
- **Don't** be guilty of what Britton likes to call the *Humpty Dumpty Effect*. If someone falls apart during a SAR, you or one of your staff must be equipped to handle that in the moment. Never open up what you are not prepared to help put back together again.
- **Don't** ever deny what your own body is telling you. Monitor, monitor, monitor the room, the tone of the group, what you feel, and what is running through your energy systems. Then take actions needed.
- **Do** set your own personal boundaries for what you will and will not tolerate in response to the SAR process from staff, participants, or guests. If someone is violating guidelines or boundaries, it's okay to ask them to leave. Don't shy away from offering a full or partial refund and saying, "This is not a good fit." Don't settle.
- **Do** be a role model for Extreme Self Care (ESC) as we discussed in the checklist for Element #14; take a break when you feel depleted; fulfill your own needs for quiet time or a hug when you are not leading the group or a small group; find ways to acknowledge yourself and what you need in body/mind/spirit at all times. Be a clear vessel for what is important for you and show that transparently to your group. Think about what is good for them, not you, while you model healthy self-care and positive self-regard.

ACTIVITY 19: *Write honest answers to these self-referential questions.*

1. What are my worst fears about leading a SAR?

2. How can I self soothe when the going gets rough for me?

3. What have others taught or shown me as *hot buttons* to watch out for?

4. What are my methods for extreme self care?

5. How will I know I have succeeded?

Element 20: Your Ideal SAR

Getting to the Gold Medal Zone

Now it's your turn to apply all that you have learned and create the template you're going to use for your SAR. Remember, this is based on number of days, number of hours/CEs, number of topics, and availability of both media and speakers. Go to work!

ACTIVITY 20:

SAR AGENDA TEMPLATES (TWO VERSIONS)
Location for SAR (name your location):
Dates for SAR (set your dates)
Hours for SAR/CEs: 10 or 16 hours/CEs

[VERSION A]
Sample for 10 hours, 1-day SAR
DAY 1 DAYTIME
AM: Overview and introductions (1 hour)
TOPIC 1: Media Montage or experiential activity (1 hour)
TOPIC 2: Speaker panel/media (1.5 hours)
Lunch in small group process (1 hours)
PM: TOPIC 3: Speaker panel/media (1.5 hours)
TOPIC 4: Media Montage or experiential activity (1 hour)
Small group process (1 hour)
Total = 8 hours
DAY 1 EVENING: (Required)
TOPIC 5: Speaker panel/media (1 hour)
Whole group process/closure (1 hour)
Total = 10 hours
(Optional)
Experiential: Field trip to outside venue (1–4 hours)

[VERSION B: ADDING ONTO VERSION A]
Sample for 16 hours, 2-day SAR
With no required evening prior/only optional field trip and/or speakers
DAY 2 DAYTIME
AM: Whole group check in (.5 hour)
TOPIC 6: Media Montage or experiential activity (1 hour)
TOPIC 7: Speaker panel/media (1.5 hours)
Lunch in small group process (1 hours)
PM: TOPIC 8: Speaker panel/media (1.5 hours)
TOPIC 9: Media montage or experiential activity (1 hour)
Whole group process (1 hour)
Conclusions and closure (.5 hour)
Total = 8 hours
Total for 2-day = 16 hours total

Element 21: SAR Readiness Checklist

This is your final activity and handy planning tool. Think of it as the roadmap to your ultimate destination. These are the steps and components that we recommend for you to design and lead a successful SAR. Check them off as you accomplish each step along the way.

ACTIVITY 21: *SAR from A to Z*

PREPARATION: Use this as your handy checklist to make sure you are on track.

___SAR Leaders trained
___Small group facilitators trained
___Venue identified, site visit completed, venue selected
___Host Coordinator Contract signed, if applicable
___Meals booked with venue, if applicable
___Dates and # of hours/days set
___Curriculum elements designed
___Learning objectives written
___Paperwork submitted for CEs
___Fees and budget set
___Website and other marketing done
___Field trip option(s) selected and booked
___Speakers identified and booked
___Media selected, edited, and ready for playing
___Group facilitators secured
___Materials for handouts prepared (including final circle gifts)
___Equipment secured and tested on site
___Evaluations prepared (pre-post tests; qualitative)
___Participant applications reviewed
___Pre-SAR instructions sent to approved participants (e.g., emails)

ON-SITE SAR DELIVERY

___SAR conducted
___SAR evaluations collected
___Distribution of CEs and/or certificates of completion
___Payments made to staff/speakers and bookkeeping completed for SAR

POST-SAR FOLLOW UP

___Post-SAR debriefing completed
___Post-SAR thank-yous sent by email (e.g., to speakers, participants, venue)
___Post-SAR evaluations review completed
___Budget/income reviewed and net profits assessment completed
___Distribution of profits completed, if applicable

Notes to self:

SUMMARY

Congratulations! You have completed the SAR Leader's Tool Kit and are now ready to run a successful SAR. In the next chapter, we will be looking backward at the evolution of SAR until now, reflecting on our own journey of SAR, and highlighting treasured memories. You will also read pearls of wisdom from selected luminaries who have led the way for SAR for so many decades, including SAR originals McIlvenna and Sutton.

NOTES

1. Samples are shown from Britton, 2016, position paper.
2. We label our domestic SAR "The Amazing SAR Experience!", our international SAR "The Ultimate SAR Experience!", and our SAR for Grown-Ups as ASPEX.
3. Although if that happens organically, good for them, as these are consenting adults attending your SAR!
4. *Beyond Vanilla*, *Xaviera Hollander: Portrait of a Sexual Revolutionary*.
5. If you purchase equipment and media, the costs will be amortized over a year's worth of trainings.
6. Take Care of Yourself.
7. Britton is an approved AASECT Individual CE Provider and these are the actual learning objectives and CKAs for our SAR programs.
8. From Britton, 2016 website (drpattibritton.com).
9. In alphabetical order, not order of priority or importance.
10. Host of HBO *Real Time with Bill Maher*.
11. We often show a clip montage about furries from this comedic but insightful show.
12. "Guide to Sexual Pleasure" series is available at SexSmartFilms.com.
13. Materials "are *lawfully acquired* if obtained by the institution or individual through lawful means such as purchase, gift or license agreement but not pirated copies" (University of Texas, 2007).
14. Clips from *Beyond Vanilla* on BDSM, *Trans the Movie* on trans, and *Xaviera Hollander: Portrait of a Sexual Revolutionary* on prostitution are our most commonly shown documentary sources.
15. The BDSM speaker(s) should present an array of implements used in power play and offer live demonstrations to the SAR audience; anyone who makes products should bring products to demonstrate or show.
16. Self Addressed Stamped Envelope.
17. Examples may include XXX DVD covers, erotica book covers, silly photos, pictures of sex toys, photos of popular media sex symbols or celebrities, and other sources that connote sexuality or eroticism.
18. Open each SAR day with the *Mindfulness Moment* to clear the space for focusing on the present.
19. EST, Crossroads and Insight Transformational Seminars.
20. This is a much smaller size than we offer and than you might be able to accommodate.
21. This is good promotion for marketing your future SARs.

References

AASECT. (2016). Core knowledge areas. Retrieved August 1, 2016, from https://www.aasect.org/print/certification/core-knowledge-areas

Dr. Patti Britton. (n.d.). SAR—Sexual Attitude Reassessment and Restructuring (October 22–23, 2016). Retrieved August 15, 2016, from http://drpattibritton.com/event/sar-la-oct2016/

Grout, P. (2014). *E²: Nine do-it-yourself energy experiments that prove your thoughts create your reality* (pp. 57–81). Carlsbad, CA: Hay House Insights.

Klein, M. (2006). *America's war on sex: The attack on law, lust and liberty*. Westport, CT: Praeger. [1st edition is basis of documentary].

Klein & Associates [Producers]. (2014). *Talking to your kids about sex* [DVD]. Web.

Mager's guideline [Module item]. (n.d.). Retrieved August 17, 2016, from https://weber.instructure.com/courses/307280/pages/magers-guideline?module_item_id=2379272

McIlvenna, T. (2016). Personal conversation. July 25, 2016.

Miletski, H. (2016). Personal conversation. August 24, 2016.

Mitelman, S. (2016). Personal conversation. September 14, 2016.

Pawloski, W. (2016). Personal conversation. August 4, 2016.

Schoen, M. (2016). Personal conversation. August 22, 2016.

Stayton, W. (2016). Personal conversation. August 31, 2016.

Sutton, L. (2016). Personal conversation. July 20, 2016.

Thrasher, C. (2016). Personal conversation. September 2, 2016.

University of Texas. (2007). Copyright crash course. Retrieved August 16, 2016, from https://copyright.lib.utexas.edu/ccmcguid.html

WAS 2017. (2016). WAS: 23rd Congress of the World Association for Sexual Health, Prague, Czech Republic, May 28–31, 2017. Retrieved August 16, 2016, from http://was2017.org/

Wiener, L. (2016). *SAR Online Survey 2016* [Scholarly project]. Survey respondent.

Zientara, G. (2016). Personal conversation. July 26, 2016.

Here Are Some Recommended Resources for You to Explore for Your SAR

URLs that feature possible SAR content include:

AVN.com—for adult video news and commentary on porn industry
Candidaroyalle.com—women and couples' erotica
Dodsonandross.com—general information on sexuality with explicit teaching videos
DrMaryLou.com—on sexuality/disability
DrMitchellTepper.com—on sexuality/disability
Fandango.com—about all movies
Fetlife.com—for people engaged in or interested in BDSM
Imdb.com—information on all movies, tv shows, and celebrities
Lovingsex.com—couples' sexual enhancement DVDs and streaming programs
Netflix.com—source for movies and tv shows
Pornhub.com—explicit porn source

SARfilms.com—original SAR sexual pattern films
Sexsmartfilms.com—resource for sex education films, commercials, and other media
Toppornsites.com—source for porn sites
Vimeo.com—media source similar to YouTube
Xbiz.com—on adult industry especially on products such as sexual enhancement toys
YouTube—for topical videos (nothing explicit)
Search for sexually related films, such as: *Transamerica; Crying Game; Boys Don't Cry; Brokeback Mountain; The Kids Are All Right; The Girl with the Dragon Tattoo; Shame; Don Jon; Secretary; Vicki Cristina Barcelona; The Sessions; Coming Home; Klute; Private Sessions*; and many more
Recommended television shows: *Transparent; Masters of Sex*; episodes of *Entourage*; cable networks that show explicit sexual content

Key Sexological Organizations

AASECT.org: American Association of Sexuality Educators, Counselors and Therapists; national credentialing organization in sexology
CatalystCon.com: sex positive conferences in the United States
Cosrt.org.uk: College of Sex and Relationship Therapists
Sexedconference.com: National Sex Ed Conference; for sexuality educators
SexScience.org: Society for the Scientific Study of Sexuality/SSSS; national sexual science organization
Sstarnet.org: Society for Sex Therapy and Research/SSTAR
Woodhullfoundation.org: Woodhull Sexual Freedom Summit; sex positive advocacy organization with annual conference in the United States
Worldsexology.org: World Association of Sexual Health; bi-annual international conference

Authors' Websites

DrPattiBritton.com—Personal home site
Drrobertdunlap.com—Personal home site
Expandinprague.2017—Register for ASPEX 2017
SexCoachU.com—Online training for Sex Coaches worldwide
SexologyU.com—Online training in Clinical Sexology worldwide
WorldAssociationofSexCoaches.org—Sex Coach certification

Part Three

Reflections

Looking Back, Looking Forward

7

Looking Back

Lessons Learned

"The only unnatural sex act is the one that cannot be performed."

—Alfred Kinsey

Looking back on our own journey, we are amazed at how rich and intense the ride has been! The road was not necessarily paved with gold in money earned, but in the wealth of experiences we have had for ourselves and provoked for almost one thousand individuals. We are grateful to have met so many dedicated professionals (and a few brave consumers) who sat in the SAR rooms with us. We are stunned by the diversity among participants (from sex escorts to imams), speakers (from MTFs to electric-knife-wielding duos), and media we have curated (think German fetish play, Brazilian HIV+ trans workers, Scandinavian zoophilia documentary, and an American television special on disability and sex). We are humbled by the ripple effect from our SAR attendees who serve as ambassadors for SAR to continue and expand wherever possible.

Reflecting on our lessons learned, here are highlights.

THE SHEER POWER OF SAR TO TRANSFORM LIVES

SAR can make a difference in a person's life. At the conclusion of SAR, we ask participants to write a testimonial. Examples that speak to the impact a SAR can have on personal sexual evolution include the testimonials in the box.

> *"I remember you, saying that the power and the change that SAR gives you can come to you months after. I participated in the last SAR in Warsaw. Since then my life has changed, completely. One day I woke up and I realized that I had so much to explore, I started to perceive sex shops as a place for my fantasy, as so many possibilities, I started to buy toys, I met a very nice guy and my relationship has a brand new quality. I didn't like sex, it was quite boring after few times but now I love myself, I love expressing myself*

in bed and it is not only a pleasure but also the emotional perspective. I feel that I am alive. Thank you. You showed me that I have passion, I just need to feel free and enjoy the way I am. Thank you, I'll never forget this." Barbara P, Participant, Warsaw, Poland

"The Ultimate SAR is truly a transformative personal experience—no matter where you are in your journey—the SAR is an experience you owe to your professional and personal development. It is a process—if you open yourself up to the possibility of what can happen in terms of shifts—you will see shifts happen during the SAR and continue after you re-enter into your regular life. Dr. Patti and Dr. Robert talk about energy a lot in their practice. During a SAR experience with them, you get to experience that energetic approach in real life. By immersing yourself into it, you get to see what is possible for your clients. Personally, I can say that this was a deeply powerful, personally transformative experience. The connections made with fellow participants are invaluable." Bradley W, Canadian Sex Coach U student

"I am feeling very grounded after the SAR. I feel stronger as a sex therapy coach and a therapist. I attribute to being in this emotional and spiritual place because of your unconditional regard and support, as well as the experience of the SAR. Thank you, Thank you, Thank you!" Gina L, California LMFT LPCC

"Dr. Patti's SAR was an utterly enlightening weekend! The experiential aspect of the course was stimulating, engaging, and opened up new ways of approaching sexuality, both personally and professionally. Dr. Patti and Robert's years of expertise are obvious in the seamless organization of a weekend that delivers what it promises, full of growth, fun, and sexiness!" Zoe S, California MFT

CONTRARIAN VOICES

Not every review of SAR is positive. Often the evaluations are a dumping ground for complaints or unspoken truths that were too delicate to pose in public within the small or large group or reflect an upset about a component of the SAR content, as we have discussed in Chapter 6. Group alignment with the SAR leadership can create a wall that may exist between honesty and submission to the group norm of what is being expressed. One incident occurred where there were many sex coaches and sex educators at a particular SAR and a few therapists seeking their desired credential for certification. One such therapist became triggered in small group and never found her voice to articulate how she felt increasingly ostracized from the group. It was only after the week had passed and she submitted her SAR reflection paper that she admitted that it felt like a bias was prevalent toward the non-therapists, and that her safety was compromised by our not keeping her free from the unwanted discomfort she felt both in the SAR room and at the BDSM field trip venue. It's critical to honor the divergent and often opposing tone of the unique populations that may converge together in the crucible of a SAR environment. Some will come for the required credit only, others for real professional growth, others to push their own sexual boundaries, others to find community.

Then, again, you may have someone who sits with their arms folded across their chest, with a judging demeanor, who metaphorically is looking for ammunition to fire at you as the SAR leader. That's one of the armoring postures that we see occasionally. If that person complains about a single media clip, which group you assigned to them, or how you processed one person's comment in small group, they may use that complaint to stonewall against anything as being acceptable to them and generalize it for the entire SAR. Be wary of those!

In this case, we were reminded that a SAR is not a One Size Fits All event. There will be pushback and blaming on the part of participants, accusing the SAR leaders of ignoring their needs. They may resent you for placing people in sticky situations, for causing potential retriggering of trauma, or for just making them feel ordinary anxiety when confronted with the challenges of a SAR. Beyond apologies, post-SAR aftercare through repeated emails or phone calls, and attempting to find local support to process retriggered trauma with a qualified supervisor in your attendee's region, the lesson is this: You can do what you can do to prevent this from ever happening. But it will. When it does, breathe, be in full compassion and service to your participants, reach out, find them whatever help they seem to need from you or your referral network, then move on. The truth is that each participant is an adult learner who is expected to meet the SAR guideline for Take Care of Yourself and be able to sustain the SAR experience start to finish. It's really up to the learner, not the facilitator, if your SAR is designed and managed well, to own their own stuff! (You can breathe now.)

USING "THE SAR APPROACH" AS A MODEL FOR TEACHING AND TRAINING

As we mentioned in Chapter 4, from 2007 to 2009 we offered several courses at CGI/TCS as 11 units toward a California certification, using SAR as the theme and approach that drove the conceptualization and implementation of this program of seven unique courses. Taiwanese college educator and doctoral candidate Yi-Li Lin is exploring SAR for dissertation work at the School of Human Sexuality, Shu-te University, which is the first educational institution to implement SAR as a formal program in Asia for the past 13 years.

Lin has this to say about SAR as a teaching technique: "Our SAR program is similar to the original SAR, but the only difference is we extend the length to a formal semester program, which runs two hour-long classes per week for 16 weeks, plus a one-day (8-hour) intensive workshop. The benefit of the extended hours is the ability to offer more learning activities, such as historical content, principles, and methods of SAR, case studies or case debate of sexual diversity/behaviors, and group oral presentation of sexual topics" (2016). She adds that SAR helps the students who are coming from different sexuality backgrounds to "improve their sexual comfort, positive sexual attitudes, and understand how to apply theories and practices of SAR into their profession." In her university, they offer SAR not as an event but as "a course based on attitude change theories and constructivist approach. Therefore, at our SAR course, we usually survey students' background, (for example their professional, age, learning preferences, sexual knowledge, attitudes, etc.) before it starts; and we adjust the SAR curriculum to adapt to the students' needs. After the course is ended, we evaluate the effectiveness of the SAR course by questionnaire and reflective writing" (2016). You, too, can design a college or graduate level course using SAR as your method to make a huge impact on your student population.

CROSS-CULTURAL PERSPECTIVES AND TREND-SPOTTING

We have noted almost unlimited perspectives that show up in the SAR room or in the location in which we lead a SAR. Whether it's religiosity, snubbery or snobbery, or terror of the unknown, nuances must be observed for you to keep safe and on track. Like us, find the inner means and outward behaviors for yourself that indicate respect for cultural, religious, ethnic, social, and geographical customs wherever you go. Imagine that in the Deep South of the United States, ultra-conservative religious norms stop participants from sharing their real names; one imam in Southern California could not watch any explicit media, even of two gay males' gentle and non-genital caresses of one another's naked bodies; speakers have come out as illegal sex workers, much to the shock and surprise of our less open group members; long-term monogamous attendees had to swallow hard to listen to the swingers and polyamory speakers; in Poland, rage erupted at the repressive nature of how transgender care is handled by medical professionals. And the stories go on and on.

Here are some prime examples of culture clashes and infringements on the SAR process that could also occur for you:

- At one SAR, a Chinese attendee felt entitled to snap photos and even record social conversations among our group during a break. Her behaviors resulted in a lack of group safety and required intervening to ask that she stop at once.

- Prospective SAR leaders have sent emissaries to our SARs to learn the ropes and replicate our SAR for their own purposes, despite the MOU disclosure that prohibits purloining our intellectual property. An MOU is essential but does not prevent a stealth strike against your hard-earned content.
- BDSM professionals must emphasize in heavy red underline that erotic power play rests on consent, not non-consensual violence. We have no tolerance for violence. Often it takes repeating the message about consensual domination or submission, for example, and including a segment on defining *consent* before any power play demonstrations take place.
- Field trips and Advanced SARs that allow clothing optional may offer a chance to be nude, promoting a different atmosphere than a clothed SAR. Check with your group far ahead of time to ensure that this is well understood and acceptable. Make sure that the clothing-optional policy is posted throughout any promotion. In Germany, for example, nudity is natural, and a group sauna or spa dip does not even demand a conversation. As you read in Chapter 5, nudity is not necessarily sexual. But it can easily be abused if not explicitly dealt with.
- Humor is a big part of any training that we lead. We are both funny people, and Dunlap has built an entire career in comedy. Britton, too, always imbues her work with a gigglish twist when appropriate. Humor is a social lubricant, and allows nervous energy to dissipate. If you are in a foreign culture, your brand of humor may be an insult to your group. Check carefully to assure that you can prevent such social faux pas that may emerge.
- As sexuality educators, we always make a statement about the use of Safer Sex whenever possible. Your adult media may not show condom use or safer behaviors, so note this in the group if you are being challenged for promoting unsafe activities.
- You may be in favor of premarital sex, polyamory, monogamish relationships, spiritual pathways for sexual expression, sensual bodywork with clients, or other behaviors that are within your values and beliefs. However, your audience may be much more conservative in their values; be mindful of the values your group brings, especially if you are hired to produce a SAR for a conservative type of organization.

Finally, as Certified Erotologists, in our travels around developed nations we produce, collect, and then curate photographs and videotaped images of our explorations of sexual/erotic expression. Over the years (as noted in Chapter 4), we have visited world-class museums, small fine art galleries, grand halls, and tiny steps leading down to sacred private chambers that are a reflection of global cross-cultural values and attitudes about sexuality. We have discovered four dominant themes that seem to be universal and in effect everywhere we go; our findings formed the basis for a documentary "Erotic Art Around the World," which is shown at various sexological conferences:

1. **Art as sexual empowerment:** Female sexual empowerment in China and Hong Kong was indicated by some of the street art that we found, such as commercial wall art for trendy OPI nail polish. The famed Prague Mucha Museum was designed to illustrate Mucha's obsession with and reverence toward female empowerment and feminine sensuality, through his depictions of popular female performers on theater playbills, on the paper currency, and on Czech postal stamps.
2. **Art as an outlet for repression/suppression of political, cultural, religious, emotional values:** The prevalent theme from visiting the Prague Sex Machine Museum was in their expression of *the hidden*, including rarely found implements of torture (as discussed in Chapter 4). These included gas masks, leather dog or pig faces, a body bag hanging in suspension on the ceiling, the *Peep Show Box* where visitors could watch sexual acts, priests' robes on walls with holes for penile penetration, and other artifacts of the pain/pleasure continuum. At the Brugges, Belgium, Dali art gallery, we found 200-plus paintings, sculptures, and multi-media installations that showed Dali's intended backlash against social norms, with outrageous quotations and a exhibition of imagery of bestiality/zoophilia, GLB, pan-sexuality, BDSM, fetish, body modification/Dysmorphia, and pictorial plates from banned materials.
3. **Art as revealing cultural/historical values, norms, and messages:** At the Sino-American Sexological Conference in China in 2013 where we were keynote speakers, we received a treasured art book from the delegation. This hardbound art book showed sexual/erotic imagery from ancient artifacts to the present time, revealing Chinese cultural heritage and spiritual values. At the IASHS is a remarkable collection of valuable porn posters from the mid-20th century, showing the marriage of fine art, sexology, and adult entertainment. One single poster of 100 smaller porn poster images is now a collector's item that informs the breadth and depth of sexual/erotic expression possible from among adult films of the past era.
4. **Art as spirituality:** Perhaps most memorable was our visit to the Warsaw Tantra Temple, housed underground in the heart of the old city. The Temple is a former Tibetan shop and atom bomb shelter, and it contains a teaching space for tantra devotees, along with a large main room for ceremonial rituals known as the *Womb Room*. This heart of the temple is decorated in red velvets and silks, with red cushions on the floor facing the dancing Shiva and Shakti statues as candles sparkle all around the holy space. This unique venue and the videotaped interviews of the owners gave us a taste of what a truly sacred space for honoring sexuality should be.

As you can tell, our passion for collecting images and depictions of the power of human erotic nature is a part of our SAR experiences that we cherish!

THE LUMINARIES SPEAK OUT!

Finally, a few words from the SAR originals lends credence to what we have been talking about so far in this book. Read through the wisdom from McIlvenna and Zientara from their vast pinnacles of expertise and vision.

Rev. McIlvenna Reflects: SAR Leaders must be the "switch," taking on the tough role of the *adult guarantor*, the person about whom participants can say, "I can trust that person." As for small group facilitators, McIlvenna says, "Nobody cares how smart you are about sex. They want a better sex life (for themselves and for their clients)." Personal disclosure[1] of the SAR leader's own sexual stories is essential for SAR to work (McIlvenna, 2016).

- A SAR leader and even SAR itself by its essential nature is permission-giving. Just like the P in the PLISSIT model (Annon, 1976), which to this day serves as a foundation for sex education, counseling, and therapy for how a client is taken through the therapeutic process over time, Permission is the key for sexual freedom to be realized. SAR is an exquisite vehicle for that permission. (McIlvenna, 2016)

Looking Back by Dr. Zientara: The elements that define a SAR include: speaker panels that may comprise two-thirds of the lecture or didactic components; media, such as the original sexual pattern films or other curated content, which can occupy as little as 10% of the curriculum; the *Fuckorama* as discussed in Chapter 3; a day's outing to participate in the San Francisco Gay Pride Parade; an expanding collapsible agenda that can be altered for a 5-, 6-, or 8-day span; presentations on the social-sexual response cycle, masturbation, safer sex, and all topics covered in the *SARguide* (described in Chapter 2). As he says, "Content and methods have changed over time and are culturally dependent, due to new social/sexual norms or trends, new media, availability of speaker panels and number of students in attendance. Always the small group dialogue forms a critical part of SAR process to this day." Furthermore, the transition back to return to a normal life is a key component of SAR. Zientara compares SAR to being away at a summer camp, where reentry is important for SAR-goers to ingest, digest, and reintegrate for return to their old life.

- Teaching SAR has always been a team effort. Often leaders and small group facilitators derive from the roster of competent sexologists who are graduates of IASHS. As he warns, "If you are going to lead a SAR, do not attempt without a thorough background in sexology." These graduates are happy to return to spend time in SAR and experience the freedom for participants (and themselves) that is normally a universal outcome in the safe container of SAR.
- Students continue to self-assess through the daily journal writing process. There is no formal evaluation form, as IASHS is structured and based on adult learning principles that use the self-reflection method, as many of us as SAR leaders also rely on today.
- Some of the greatest challenges that the IASHS team has faced in contemporary times include lack of adequate budget for a lengthy SAR, such as materials, speaker fees, outings, and staff salaries. The climate for recruitment of free speakers has shifted, as well, so that many trans or BDSM speakers of the past no longer are readily available to present on a weekday for low or no compensation, and fewer are living in the area who may have been favorites on speaker panels. The lack of community recognition for IASHS—and SAR itself—also are contributing factors, as the social landscape for IASHS has morphed into a new cultural norm for San Francisco and environs. Now viewed by many as the *new Silicon Valley,* where many artists and activists have been driven out of the area for less expensive living conditions, the San Francisco Bay Area is no longer the sexual mecca it once was.

SUMMARY

Our final chapter, Chapter 8, will bring you into the greatest minds of past SAR leaders and illustrate our own predictions for the future of SAR. Be prepared as we tease you into imagining cyber SARs, SAR in a Box, no SAR at all, and some surprises. Ready?

NOTE

1. As you know, this is a point of contention among SAR leaders. You'll evolve to what works best for you.

References and Resources

Annon, J. S. (1976). The PLISSIT model: A proposed conceptual scheme for the behavioral treatment of sexual problems. *Journal of Sex Education and Therapy*, *2*(1), 1–15.

Lin, Y. (2016, August 13). Interview for SAR book [E-mail to the author].

McIlvenna, T. (2016). Personal conversation. July 25, 2016.

Zientara, G. (2016). Personal conversation. July 26, 2016.

8

Looking Forward

Future SAR Delivery Options

"I'm a trisexual; I'll try anything at least once."

—*Xaviera Hollander*

Let's take out the periscope and view the landscape for imminent sea changes before we leave you. SAR is here to stay, as long as dedicated and wise sexologists like those we have cited in this book will push for its continuation. And, we ask you to join the call. So, what's the future of SAR? What do SAR luminaries have to say? What's our prediction?

SELF-CURATED

We have spoken with forward-thinking, cutting-edge university faculty who are suggesting that their undergraduate students select the media for their SAR experience. On their own, these students would browse media at their fingertips, choose sexually related films, videos, photographs, or whatever form the media takes; they then share the location of the media with their peers to review or to present for discussion in the classroom. For example, the subjects might encompass a short video about a trans stage performer, or a Pro-Dom mistress in her dungeon showing off her skills with a willing submissive, or extreme fetishistic or paraphilic behaviors. As SAR is aimed primarily at professionals who work with sexuality in their career functions, and as the media used in SAR is carefully chosen by experts, this is a new direction. But in truth, SAR can be for anyone.

At first, we buckled, then we softened. Maybe allowing students to search feverishly across the broad spectrum of media for self-curated exposure to a wide range of sexual expression is impactful on their sexual values, attitudes, and beliefs, which after all is the purpose of SAR. Many young people today indulge in the universe of free accessible visual programming for their personal education and connectivity with their peers for social and other reasons. Perhaps it makes sense to encourage them to peruse the Internet for porn sites, free hosting sites (such as Vimeo, Wistia, or the ubiquitous YouTube, which purportedly does not allow anything explicit), or anywhere else that user-friendly SEM or non-explicit sexual/erotic content can be found. We believe, as do our seasoned peers, that this method may be effective as long as in-person dialogue within the container of group process is a component of this radically different SAR approach.

SAR in a Box

We have been asked by some of our international SCU students to excuse them from our in-person SAR requirement to enable them to earn their certification. Financial constraints and travel restrictions have prevented some of our adult learners from attending a live SAR event from Egpyt, Australia, Brazil, Russia, and elsewhere. We have constructed what we consider to be a minimal *SAR Replacement*, which includes watching key media assignments (originally to be sent as a box of DVDs, hence *SAR in a Box*), reading specifically charged materials, and interviewing select members of sexually relevant populations in their local region or by video platforms. It is not the same as being in the room with peers. We know that (sigh).

VIRTUAL SAR

To date we do not have the ability to actually transport ourselves into the room by watching a screen; but we are closer than ever to being with others via distance learning and virtual technological advances. If medical doctors can perform intricate surgeries under a makeshift tent in an undeveloped rural area clinic, while being guided by operating room staff from thousands of miles away in an urban hospital hub, a virtual SAR is not that far away!

We can envision having participants gather for the SAR welcome and opening remarks, seeing each other on their cameras that log everyone's faces and expressions, along with the environment from which they attend; they will watch the media on their home or office computer being shown on the shared screens in real time; they will view the panels of speakers presenting live to them from their own locations, including showing demonstrations of their practices perhaps even in the sanctuary of a BDSM dungeon, or tantra festival puja; they then will separate into in-real-time video chat rooms led by competent facilitators to process their VABs before they return to share one by one in the full group virtual room experience. Using action recording devices from your smart phone, or on your special glasses, or mounted on your headgear, we can then follow you to the erotic venue of your choice to record your actual journey of exploration in the flesh (pun intended). This experience can take place over days or even weekly. A virtual form of SAR is one step away from the three-dimensional experience of the physical presence of things that occupy space, adding in the aspects of time and energies present, such as in a hotel or training conference room. But it's close. Our world is indeed shrinking to become more inclusive of diversity in all of its forms as it also is growing more cyber-driven every day. We sense we may see you in one of those virtual platforms one day in the not too distant future.

IMAGINE THIS!

ASPEX-like intensives may well form the future of where SAR takes us. Going beyond the listening and watching of films and talkers, to the doing, is what a *SARs For Grown Ups* provides. In our ASPEX trainings, we create a journey to the core of the sexual self; that may include experimenting with areas of personal sexual/erotic or psychological growth that include physical wall-busting. Some sexuality educational trends today are engaging the learner in the actual experience of (rather than intellectual learning about) certain sexual behaviors, such as fisting, erotic genital piercings, cuddle party play, and furrie conventions. Remotely controlled sexual pleasure devices and cyber-controlled sexual acts exist today through technology; more will emerge for consumers as the pleasure products industry thinks up new twists on the pleasure game. Intimate group sexual encounters abound that allow their attendees to break boundaries and that let sexual/erotic explorers (or their avatars) navigate to wherever their fantasies can take them. SAR is a pathway for all of this, at advanced levels. We can even imagine ideal SAR residential communities that offer a lifestyle of 24/7 activities with classes, discussion groups, shared housing, and multiple partners in conscious community, similar to the story of Eye, whom we described in Chapter 4 and who lived a SAR life.

Despite all of the potential for human and professional growth in sexology, we also must acknowledge that more and better research is needed (Wollert, 1978) to show that SAR is effective and that its effects go beyond the weekend intensive glimmer effect. Finally we must be mindful of the explosion of porn-dependency and the misunderstood realm of erotic fantasies. Too often our clients are suffering from their reliance on external forms of erotic stimulation and are haunted by their starvation and loneliness for human touch, intimacy, and real skin-to-skin, heart-to-heart, soul-to-soul contact. SAR is a way to help helping professionals to know how to address these wounds and to be voices of acceptance for infinite pleasures without judging or pathologizing. SAR is a leveling ground for healing to occur for those healers who rarely get to touch that place in themselves to become and to stay whole.

SAR EXPERTS REVEAL THEIR FORECASTS

Our friends and colleagues have looked into their own crystal balls, reflecting on what has worked and not worked in their own SAR leadership history. The wisdom they share about the future of SAR is compelling. Here are some of their observations.

FROM TED McILVENNA~

- Things that lead to greater intimacy, even emphasis on the art of romance, should be part of SAR; every sexologist should prepare their unique "Game Kit" showing the aspects of sexual fun and expression that relates to them to share with others.
- A take-home kit that contains media and a workbook, then a live group experience of 1–2 days is required; although distance learning can be the new norm, the personal engagement in a group of people is a necessary ingredient.
- Scream out loud: "Sex is the most important spiritual movement of our times."

FROM LAIRD SUTTON~

- In today's world, we need more touch and more contact. SAR is a relevant counterpart to the technological society of today.

FROM BILL STAYTON~

- Most of the media today is not seen in the context of talking about themselves and their reactions, either alone or with a partner, and not in a group context. That's what is so important and invaluable in producing effects of a SAR.
- We are always dealing with the whole area of sexual value systems (SVS), asking people to look at sources of their sexual values. Everything in a SAR is measured against their own and others' SVS, to get them to evaluate where they come from and assessing sources of one's SVS. They then get to integrate who they are and all the pieces of the sexual self.
- The act of peacemaking with self is one of the goals of SAR. I love doing it and seeing the change in people.

FROM GERRY ZIENTARA~

- SAR requires live, trained organizers to run it, as it is an event led by a team of experts. SAR is all about personal transmission, like a shaman or priest or guru in the room. You must be in the room to experience it.

- Media is not real; SAR is about the real thing for real people. Human contact is essential for SAR to work. The human heart is where inspiration comes from.
- SAR is a hands-on tradition. Although cyber technology may make it possible for a group to be together by a virtual means, the essence of what SAR is about will be lost.
- To completely abandon SAR for future training of sexologists, "In a word that's a crazy notion that can only lead to unhappiness!"

FROM HANI MILETSKI~

- I recently wrote a book chapter on training professionals who work with Wounded Warriors, emphasizing that watching media on your own is not the same as watching it with others. The key is the processing of it and being able to talk about it openly. When you are with others, you process on a different level; speaking about your thoughts/feelings about sexuality has a much more profound effect; SAR is absolutely needed today.

FROM STEPHANIE BUEHLER~

- Participants should take the SAR early on in their journey of a career in sex therapy, counseling, or education. Later in the journey—when it is a tick off on a box of requirements—SAR leaders must throw more questions at them to have to dig deeper into their own experiences and share, to the extent that they are able, how this may feel to a client.
- Therapists tend to lean on intellectualization. Even though as a SAR leader you are an expert, be mindful not to be the *answer box* for people who want your knowledge. Instead put it back on them.

FROM MARK SCHOEN~

- Technology has changed the world. Children have access to porn on the Internet (adult films can be seen by 11-year-olds). For some that is their only sex ed and it's doing them a disservice. We need better sex education for our children and with an impact that lasts into adulthood. SAR may be the only contained sexuality education.

- The important thing is audiovisuals today. The United States is a society of attitudes reflected in our media; for example, we don't broadcast condom ads, but in other countries they are ubiquitous. Our rates of HIV and teen pregnancy are horrific when compared to other developed nations. Media is a cultural message.

FROM CHRIS THRASHER~

- Yes, of course, we still will need SAR. It is a unique experience in our field. I believe we need to require a *SAR renewal* for all working professionals in the field of human sexuality. We in sexology can become complacent. SAR opens us up again to a fresh view of our own attitudes, values, and beliefs. We must affirm the importance of SAR as a requirement for our field.
- Short of SAR, there is no experience in education or counseling that will push the learner as far, if done right! We all must get into ourselves, understand ourselves, and challenge ourselves.
- Certain things about SAR require human interactions, what it means to be a human being. For example, viewing media or a live stream discussion in front of a screen is totally different than sitting in a room with other live humans. We need to ask people to sit face to face to engage in an experience together. That's part of what makes SAR so effective. Every SAR is unique, so we should not be hearing complaints about going to more than one SAR, as there are no two alike, because of who is there as a group of participants and who leads the SAR.

FROM STEPHANIE MITELMAN~

- SAR is needed more than ever today. There is more access to porn today and it is so much more prevalent than in past generations; furthermore, porn is accessible at earlier ages, with more kinds of porn readily available among youth. Practitioners will have clients or students involved in activities that they have been exposed to or want to do and have no idea what those are; that lack of awareness causes discomfort among practitioners. SAR is created to address that discomfort. An explicit example of seeing or hearing about intimate behaviors is important: If we were to learn how to fix a broken sink, we would look at that demonstration; if we were to learn how to fix a broken bone, we would have seen that demonstration; to see sexual expression gives meaning, knowledge, and a firsthand view, leading to greater understanding, compassion, and expertise to better serve our clients.

- The concept of a virtual SAR is frightening, as the human in-person experience is what makes SAR a SAR. It's not an intellectual exercise. Even though much is being converted to online learning, and anyone can pick up a textbook or watch something on a computer screen, it is not emotional understanding as happens in the live experience of the SAR room. For example, it may be difficult to watch people being flogged rather than reading about it or watching a short video. Without in-person SAR, people will miss out on the realness and authenticity of the purpose of SAR.
- We are the experts who have been offering SAR for the long term; to have a self-curated SAR smacks of having participants say "I know better (than the experts)!" That sense of over-democratization can negatively impact how SAR in constructed. SAR has been a necessary and required live event for a reason.

HOPEFUL SUGGESTIONS FOR A MORE SEXUALLY POSITIVE AND HEALTHY WORLD

SAR may take on virtual or cyber or semi-live formats, but the fully human experience will (gulp, hopefully) never be replaced. Neuroscience, mindfulness, sociology, and psychology are all on board to echo that sentiment. Being present with oneself and others cannot occur while sitting at the dining room table and squinting at a tiny electronic screen in your palm, while you simultaneously check your social media feeds and listen to the nightly news broadcasting from your smart TV in surround sound. Nor will the aspect of community and feeling the emotional tsunamis possible in a shared intimate enclosed space be moved aside for the webinar of the future—not even if the avatar on your flat screen television seems human enough. Technology is creating more and more real-like figures or depictions that represent the human self. Yet human life is not going to go away anytime soon. People and their innermost feelings and energies are the heart blood of SAR. May cyberlife never eclipse the authentic human skin-on-bones experience. Now, "What are you taking away?" We hope it is a fire in your belly to design and lead successful SARs!

References and Resources

Buehler, S. (2016, August 7). SAR [E-mail to the author].
McIlvenna, T. (2016). Personal conversation. July 25, 2016.
Miletski, H. (2016). Personal conversation. August 24, 2016.
Mitelman, S. (2016). Personal conversation. September 14, 2016.
Schoen, M. (2016). Personal conversation. August 22, 2016.
Stayton, W. (2016). Personal conversation. August 31, 2016.
Sutton, L. (2016). Personal conversation. July 20, 2016.
Thrasher, C. (2016). Personal conversation. September 2, 2016.
Three-dimensional. (n.d.). Retrieved September 20, 2016, from http://www.mathsisfun.com/definitions/three-dimensional.html
Wollert, R. W. (1978). A survey of sexual attitude reassessment and restructuring seminars. *The Journal of Sex Research*, *14*(4), 250–259. doi:10.1080/00224497809550987
Zientara, G. (2016). Personal conversation. July 26, 2016.

Index

adult-child sex 86–7
adult learning styles 3–4
adult sex shops 34
Advanced SAR Model 76–7
Advanced Sexological Personal Exploration Xperience (ASPEX) 14, 79–83
advertising and marketing 100–1
Affordable Care Act (ACA) 44
agenda sample 119, 168
American Association of Sexuality Educators, Counselors and Therapists (AASECT): core knowledge areas 123–4; guidelines from 75; introduction 5; learning objectives and 120, 122
America's War on Sex (Klein) 126
Amsterdam, Holland SAR event 45–9
Angel, Buck 68
anonymous question box 117
anxiety-triggering factors 25–6

Barratt, Barnaby 26
Basic SAR Model 75–6
Been There, Done That syndrome 147–8
Berlin, German SAR events 56–60
Berlin Sex Shop 59
bestiality 83–5
Beyond Vanilla (documentary) 35, 36, 126
binary, end of 10
bisexual advocate experiences 33
bodily-kinesthetic intelligence 3
body dysmorphic disorder 82
Bondage and Discipline, Dominance and Submission, Sadism and Masochism (BDSM): consent and 181; in curriculum design 116; demonstrations 65; dungeon meeting space 70, 186; first exposure to 33; focus on 23; introduction 11; positive mental health aspects of 42; process questions 155; speakers for 69
brain-based learning theories 4
breakout room 109
Brecher, Edward 17
budgets for SAR 104–8
Buehler, Stephanie 189

Calderwood, Derek 26, 128
California certification 179
California Graduate Institute 9
California State Certificate Program 8
Cannabis Liberation Day 46
Catholicism 12
Center of Excellence for Sexual Health 77
centrality of location 111
Certified Erotologists 87, 181
child pornography 86–7
Chilgren, Rick 21
CIS-gendered 43
Clinical Sexology Skills 9
clitoral stimulation 32
clothing-optional policy 181
cock-and-ball-torture (CBT) 60
Cole, Ted and Sandra 22
Coleman, Eli xiii
consensual dominance 57
consensual non-monogamy (CNM) 9
consensual submission 57, 59
content and structure 116–18
Continuing Education (CE) credits 87, 134, 140
cross-cultural perspective on SAR 180–3
curriculum design 116–18

damage control 163–6
The Danish Girl (film) 44
Dark Tantra 65
Designer Relationships: A Guide to Happy Monogamy, Positive Polyamory,

and Optimistic Open Relationships (Michaels, Johnson) 9
Designer SAR 77–9
disabled veteran experiences 33
diversity and SAR 12–13
dominatrix experiences 33
dungeon meeting space 70

educational multimedia projects 129
empowerment rituals 150
English-language SAR 64
erotic boundaries 57
Erotic Museum 59
erotic art and SAR 182
erotic venue options 113–15
event management 97–8
experiential activities 117
experiential learning theories 4, 94
Extreme Self Care (ESC) 165

Facebook 11
female submissive 48
female to male (FTM or F2M) 43
Feng Shui 150
fetish, defined 66
field trips at SAR events: clothing-optional policy 181; example events 44–5, 47–9, 50–1, 55–6, 59–60, 67; planning for 113–15
finances for SAR 63–4
First Amendment rights 86
floggers 70
Free Love Movement 17
free speech 12
Fuckorama event 34, 37, 116

gay male activist experiences 33
Gay Men's Health Crisis 33, 78
Gay Pride Parade 33, 37
gay sex 32
gender fluid (GF) 43
gender neutral bathroom facilities 110
gender queer (GQ) 43
gender-reaffirming surgeries 44
Glide Foundation 32
Green, Cheryl Cohen 36
group resistance 147–8

Haberman, Hardy 69
handicap accessibility 110–11
Happy Hooker (Xaviera Hollander) 35
Hartley, Nina 69
heterosexual expression 155
Hippie Era (1960s) 17
HIV/AIDS epidemic 32–4
HIV/AIDS Prevention Teacher Training Project for ETR Associates 33
Hollander, Xaviera (Happy Hooker) 35, 45–8
humor in training 181
Humpty Dumpty Effect 165

Ideal Sexual Self 118
immersion experience and media 126
implosion techniques 27
inaugural SAR 39–40
inclusivity and SAR 12–13
income projections 104–8
Institute for Advanced Study of Human Sexuality (IASHS) 6, 17–18, 32–3, 35, 39
Internet access 11
interpersonal intelligence 3
intrapersonal intelligence 4
-isms 12–13

Jagiellonian University 64–5
Jenner, Caitlyn 10
Jeremy, Ron 50
journals 137, 139, 159
Joy, Petra 58

Kinsey, Alfred 83–4
Klein, Marty 126

leadership role 97
Leader's Tool Kit: agenda templates 168; budgets and income projections 104–8; creating safe spaces 150–2; curriculum design 116–18; damage control 163–6; field trips 113–15; group resistance 147–8; how SAR works 94; instructions for success 93–4; leadership criteria 139–45; learning objectives 119–24; materials

and supplies 134; media and 126–9; planning and preparation 97–104; purpose of SAR 94–5; readiness checklist 169–70; sample agenda 119; SAR evaluations 158–62; small group facilitators 146–7, 149, 153–4; small group processes/takeaways 153–7; speaker selection 131–3; student journals and notebooks 139; topic selection 124–6; translators 148; venue selection 108–13; whole group process activity 156–7
learning objectives 119–24
LGBT issues 77, 126, 155–6
Likert-type 5-point scale 158
linguistic intelligence 3
live demonstrations 118
live nude models 81
logical-mathematical intelligence 3
Los Angeles Gender Center 43
lunch rooms 109

Mager's Behavioral Objectives 119
Maher, Bill 126
main presentation room 108–9
male to female (MTF) 40, 43
Marcus, Bat Sheva 88
marketing and advertising 100–1
Marriage and Family Therapists (MFTs) 8, 9
Martin, Betty 82
masturbation 32, 78
materials and supplies 134
McIlvenna, Ted 17–19, 129, 183, 188
MEBES© model 80
media and SAR 126–9
media disasters 98
Memorandum Of Understanding (MOUs) 134–5, 141, 143
mental health care deficit 8–9
Miletski, Hani 78, 83, 189
Mindfulness Moment 141
Mirror Activity 82
Mitelman, Stephanie 78, 139, 144, 190–1
money matters 98–9
Morehouse School of Medicine 77
multiple intelligences 3–4
musical intelligence 3

naming your SAR 97
narrative qualitative approach 158
National Sex Forum (NSF) 17–18
naturalistic intelligence 4
Nazi Germany paraphernalia 56
negative evaluations 178–9
Nelson, Jim 21
nude SAR 79

Obamacare *see* Affordable Care Act
obstetricians, gynecologists (GYNs) 8
One Size Fits All event 179
on-site store 99
on-the-spot management 139

Palowski, Wayne 77, 140
parking access 111
participants in SAR: example SARs 41–2, 46, 49–50, 52–4, 57–8, 64–5, 70–1; income per 104–8; qualifying applicants 96–8; values of 181
peep show venues 34
personal empowerment intensives 150
Planned Parenthood 31, 85
planning and preparation 97–104
polyamory 9–10, 51, 65, 69, 70
pornography 7, 86–7
post-SAR essays 159
Prague, Czech Republic SAR event 51–6
preparation for SAR: Advanced SAR Model 76–7; Basic SAR Model 75–6; Designer SAR 77–9; grievance policy and procedure 88–9; introduction 75; liability protection 89; nude SAR 79; online surveys 89–90; planning and preparation 97–104; SAR for Grown-Ups 79–83; taboo topics 83–8
pre-post tests 158
pre-SAR checklist 103
pre-screen site visit 114, 164
Prevention Teacher Training project for ETR Associates 33
privacy concerns 109
professional medical training 8

profitability of SAR 104–8
purchases required for SAR 136–8
purpose of SAR 94–5

qualifying applicants 96–8
Qualtrics.com 89
questioning queer (QQ) 43
quiet concerns 109

racial justice 12–13
readiness checklist 169–70
Red Light District (RLD) 48–9
reflection essay 158–9
reflective learning theories 4
registration area 110
Reiki healing 150
religious conservatism 12
Religious Right 12
Rhoades, Chuck 26
room rates 111
Royalle, Candida 58

safe sex 181
safe spaces 150–2
sample agenda 119
sample purpose statement 94–5
Sanger, Margaret 59
SAR gopher 99–100
SARguide for a Better Sex Life: A Self-Help Program for Personal Sexual Enrichment/Education (National Sex Forum) 23–4
SARs For Grown Ups 187
Satcher, David 77
saturation methods 27
Schoen, Mark 26, 128, 189–90
self-curated exposure 185–6
self-reflection and healing 139
sensitivity training 4, 6
Sensorium experience 37
setting intentions for SAR 94
Sex Coach University (SCU) 5–6, 49
Sex Knowledge and Attitude Test (SKAT) 27
Sex Machines Museum 5, 56
Sex Museum Amsterdam 49
sexological bodyworkers 131, 131
sexological worldview 27–8
Sexology University 5–6
Sex Positive Institute (SPI) 62
The Sex Researchers (Brecher) 17
SexSmartFilms 26, 127–8
Sexual Attitudes Reassessment and Restructuring (SAR): adult learning styles 3–4; binary, end of 10; classical *vs.* contemporary 14; cross-cultural perspective 180–3; defined 5–6; distinctions within 13–14; evaluations 158–2; first SARs 31–8; future of 187–91; -isms and 12–13; mental health care deficit 8–9; mission of 13; negative evaluations 178–9; overview 4–5; polyamory 9–10; pornography and 7; professional medical training and 8; religious conservatism 12; self-curated exposure 185–6; significance of 6–7; summary 15; teaching and training with 179–80; technology impact 11; transformational power of 177–8; virtual SAR 186–7
Sexual Attitudes Reassessment and Restructuring (SAR), experiences: Amsterdam, Holland 45–9; Berlin, German 56–60; field trips 44–5, 47–9, 50–1, 55–6, 59–60, 67; finances 63–4; inaugural SAR 39–40; Los Angeles, California 40–1, 44–5; participants in 41–2, 46, 49–50, 52–4, 57–8, 64–5, 70–1; Prague, Czech Republic 51–6; small group process 40, 46–7; speakers at 47, 51, 54–5, 58–9, 65–9; Vancouver, British Columbia 49–51; venues for 45–6, 49, 52, 56–7, 61–3, 67–8; Warsaw, Poland 61–7; Woodhull Sexual Freedom Summit 67–9
Sexual Attitudes Reassessment and Restructuring (SAR), historical perspectives: early days 21–2; guidebook for 23–4; overview 17–21; prior research on 24–7; sexological worldview 27–8; summary 28; topic-specific models 22–3

Sexuality & Aging Consortium (SAC) 78
Sexuality Information and Education Council of the United States (SIECUS) 32
sexually explicit films (SEFs) 25
sexually explicit materials (SEM) 24, 28, 126, 185
sexual magic 65, 70
sexual pattern films 32
sexual realism films 128
sexual terms 24
sex with vegetables 85
sex workers 131–2
shamanic practices 70, 150
Shibari demonstration 55
Siefkes, Jim 21
SilverSAR™ 77–8
Sinclair Institute 128
Sino-American Sexological Conference in China (2013) 182
sissy boy male 66
slasher films 86
Slut Walk 67
small group facilitators (SGFs) 146–7, 149, 153–4
small group processes 40, 46–7, 117, 153–7
snuff films 85–6
social justice 12–13
Society for the Scientific Study of Sexuality (SSSS) workshop 69–70
spanking experiences 58–9
spatial intelligence 3
speakers at SAR events 47, 51, 54–5, 58–9, 65–9, 131–3
staffing concerns 99–100, 110
Stayton, Bill 25–6, 76, 87, 188
stripper experiences 33
student journals 137, 139, 159
success in SAR 93–4
supplies and materials 134
Surrogate Partner Therapy 39, 131
Sutton, Laird 17, 19–20, 32, 116, 188

taboo topics 83–8
Take Care of Yourself guidelines 179
teachable moments 148
teaching and training with SAR 179–80
temperature control of environment 110
Thrasher, Chris 77, 190
topic-specific SAR models 22–3
transformational power of SAR 4, 177–8
transsexuality: lack of support for 66; process questions 155–6; transitioning 66–7; trans movement 36–7
Trans the Movie (film) 10
Turen, Elise 36, 43

Uhse, Beate 59
Universal Sexual Rights 76
US First Amendment 12

values, attitudes, and beliefs (VABs) 5, 94, 181, 186
Vancouver, British Columbia SAR events 49–51
venues for SAR: erotic venue options 113–15; example SARs 45–6, 49, 52, 56–7, 61–3, 67–8; logistics of selection 108–13; pre-screen site visit 114, 164; rental costs 104
violence films 85–6
virtual SAR 186–7

waiting areas 109–10
Walter Reed Military Medical Center 78
Warsaw, Poland SAR event 61–7
Warsaw Sex Positive Institute 61
website campaigns 100–2
Wheel of Consent 82
whole group process activity 156–7
Woodhull Sexual Freedom Summit 67–9, 78
Working Group for Sexual Health and Intimacy for Wounded Warriors 78
World Association of Sexual Health (WAS) 60, 76
WPATH (World Professional Association for Transgender Health) 44
written evaluations for learning objectives 136

Zientara, Gerald 18, 20–1, 183–4, 188–9
zoophilia 83–5